"Donald Sheehan combined his cultured erudition and literary gifts with deep and all-embracing faith. As this volume attests, he had an uncanny ability to traverse the expanses of the biblical, patristic, and literary worlds and to present them to others with the insight and meekness of his Orthodox Christian heart. Reading him provides nourishment for the mind and a balm for the soul."

—Alexis Torrance, associate professor of Byzantine theology,
University of Notre Dame

"Greeks of the Orthodox tradition speak of a man like Donald Sheehan as a κοσμοκαλόγερος—a monk in the world. Through a life of noetic prayer, he stands solidly in the world while apprehending the invisible reality of God's nearness. Such persons become the intimate friends of God. You might say that they *become* prayer. With this book, Sheehan and his beloved Xenia show us how such lives occur, how far such lives reach."

—Scott Cairns, author of *Slow Pilgrim*

"*In the House of My Pilgrimage* is so rich that to categorize it would inevitably be reductive, for it contains Donald Sheehan's own poems, brilliant and utterly original readings of others' poetry, autobiographical reflections, and preeminently, meditations on his own spiritual journey. The book is radically eclectic, yet also truly coherent by way of the enlightened and enlightening spirit that informs it. That spirit will be familiar to generations of colleagues and students, and welcomed by new acquaintances."

—Sydney Lea, Vermont poet laureate (2011–15)

"One man's journey to Christ from a life of street fighting and estrangement, animated with a lifetime search for God, Donald Sheehan's work tells a moving story of overcoming violence and confusion with love and faith. Courageous and spiritual, this book conveys both the capriciousness of human life and the awesome permanence of God."

—Lasha Tchantouridze, Davis Center associate, Harvard University

In the House of My Pilgrimage

"The Gift of Light." Portrait of Donald Sheehan at The Frost Place,
by Fr. George Davis, monk of St. Tikhon's Monastery, 2023.
Commissioned by the Sheehan family.

Dear Donald,

As the sun's last languid, golden rays linger,
bathing everything in radiance before making its celestial journey
from our Pocono horizon and deep into the invisible,
I find myself alone but not lonely in a field carpeted with tall hay-grass
amidst buzzing flies and a deer too skittish to run.
My thoughts turn to you, who enlightened the world with the light of your words.
You now take your place among the eternal, glistening stars.

Love, Fr. George

In the House of My Pilgrimage

—— *Violence, Noetic Healing, and Personhood* ——

Donald Sheehan

COMPILED AND EDITED BY
Xenia Sheehan

FOREWORD BY
Stephen Freeman

RESOURCE *Publications* · Eugene, Oregon

IN THE HOUSE OF MY PILGRIMAGE
Violence, Noetic Healing, and Personhood

Resource Publications
An Imprint of Wipf and Stock Publishers
199 W. 8th Ave., Suite 3
Eugene, OR 97401

www.wipfandstock.com

PAPERBACK ISBN: 978-1-6667-7539-6
HARDCOVER ISBN: 978-1-6667-7540-2
EBOOK ISBN: 978-1-6667-7541-9

09/14/23

Cover: The cross atop the iconostasis at Holy Ascension Orthodox Church, Mt. Pleasant, South Carolina, was made by Andrew Gould of New World Byzantine Studios. It was presented to the church in honor of Subdeacon Donatos Sheehan at the time of his funeral. God contributed the sunbeams and Fr. John Parker captured them on camera.

Graphic: The hand-drawn graphic on the title page and chapter openings is also by Andrew Gould, used here with his permission.

This book is dedicated by his wife in grateful love

to Donald Sheehan

who learned personhood by turning "the full light of
sympathetic intelligence into the depth of hope and
terror and beauty that was—and is—true art,"

and to Gary Scrimgeour

his first Teacher, whose example he followed lifelong:

"a *living voice* . . . created to love us
by the texts he had learned to love,
and one that therefore bestowed creativity
on those who through him learned
to love the texts in return."

Memory Eternal to both these fine teachers!

Thy statutes have been my songs
In the house of my pilgrimage.

—Ps 118:54 LXX

Contents

Foreword

FR. STEPHEN FREEMAN

ONE OF THE GREAT themes of theology, often overlooked or unspoken, is the problem of *distance*. At its most profound level, distance is the problem between God and humanity. There were a variety of takes on this problem in the early fathers. St. Gregory of Nyssa famously wrote of the diastema ("spacing") between God and creation. In his work, it is a space that is never truly overcome, but filled with a perpetual movement of one towards the other. His approach did not carry the day, however. Others, such as Dionysius the Areopagite and, later, St. Maximus the Confessor, focus on union rather than distance. The "gap" between God and creation is overcome in the Incarnation, and continually in the sacraments and abiding work of divinization.

These are heady thoughts for the opening of a foreword. However, it is such thoughts that come to mind as I read Don Sheehan's various essays, and consider the loving work of his wife, Xenia, as she has continued to gather and edit his work. The fathers explored the problem of distance under the problem of language itself. What is the relationship of our words to the concepts they describe? It is a problem for the poet as much as for the theologian and philosopher. To an extent, Donald Sheehan was all three.

That "space" in which we encounter God is, interestingly, also the space in which we encounter one another. When the Scripture tells of God's relationship to creation, it begins with words: "Let there be light." However we describe that relationship, we first encounter the light itself. It is only later we discover that the light we encounter is also a word, now respoken by ourselves, becoming a thing which others encounter. It is not enough to say that words are merely human creations, sounds that signify but do not somehow bear any connection to what is signified. The poet knows better.

I first encountered Don Sheehan's words some years back as I was researching Dostoevsky. One of his articles was posted on a Dartmouth University website. It was not only an exposition of certain themes within *The Brothers Karamazov*, it was an autobiographical disclosure of a life formed in the trauma of family violence. As I read his description of dangerous moments created by the rage of his father's alcoholism, I was taken back to similar experiences in my own life. It was a familiar exercise in Sheehan's world. Courtney Cook's contribution, included in this volume, describes Don's freshman composition courses at Dartmouth, where every student is asked to "remember violence—to dredge up their memories of bullies and bullying, of beatings inflicted or experienced, of anger, of isolation, of rape," as part of an exercise to help each student discover what it means to truly be a "person." We must become persons in order to become writers.

To be a person, in my experience, is to enter a "largeness." The truly personal life is a larger life, precisely in the sense that it gathers, reconciles, encompasses, transfigures. In so doing, the person is able to meet others with the same willingness to gather, reconcile, and encompass. The larger life that is a person begets the larger life in others. Christ comes among us as the first revelation of the truly personal. Those who encounter Him are never diminished. It is sin and violence that make us smaller.

As I have made my way through this collection, my first intuition was to look for the single intellectual thread that linked everything as one. This, I think, is a mistake. Don's loving wife and editor, has given us the link in a different form: Don himself. These words, these images, these insights and stories, are an encounter with the personal. Like my own first encounter with Don's work, they are transfiguring in their effect, and enlarging.

At a time when many voices in our culture suggest that the way forward for humanity can be found in avoiding "triggers," Don's pedagogical courage is all the more striking. I have no doubt that his students had no trouble finding examples in their lives of violence: it is universal. In the Buddhist tradition, no spiritual understanding is gained until Gautama *leaves* his sheltered life and encounters pain, suffering, and death. For Christians, the way of the Cross is the way of life.

Having said that, however, is to state only the most obvious fact of our existence. It is not encountering violence that grants us salvation, that allows us to live fully as a human person: it is *transfiguring* violence that yields that fruit. St. Porphyrios of Kavsokalyvia taught: "Whoever wants to become a Christian must first become a poet."[1] He gives this explanation:

> You must suffer. You must love and suffer–suffer for the one you love. Love makes effort for the loved one. She runs all through the night; she stays awake; she stains her feet with blood in order to meet her beloved. She makes sacrifices and disregards all impediments, threats, and difficulties for the sake of the loved one. Love towards Christ is something even higher, infinitely higher.

It is love, I think, that draws Don Sheehan's work beyond the boundaries of the mundane and into a land best described by the poetic voice. Violence makes the world smaller, surrounding us with fear and diminishing the joy of our existence. Poetry and the poetic voice lead us into a larger place where the soul can find healing. Sheehan describes something of this in the encounter between the deeply troubled King Saul and the young poet and musician, David. Sheehan says that David's music had the power to "ensoul" the listener. The Scripture says that Saul was "refreshed," though its Hebrew meaning is to enter into a spacious openness.

> Saul regains his soul because David's music has this power to bring the listener up into that spacious place where one's soul can breathe freely and fully. Here, then, is what I am calling the second moment in the formation of David's mind: he actively practices the heavenly music wherein we become psychologically coherent.

This particular book, assembled from Sheehan's work and that of a few friends, is not an exposition on "how to transform violence," nor is it an analytic work on the nature of violence itself. Rather, it is something of a psalmic work that shares stories and insights from the "spacious place." As such, it represents a journey of transformation.

In a manner that is decidedly Orthodox, Sheehan eventually directs our attention towards the face of God. Violence wounds us and bids us to hide our face in shame. The shameless (those who refuse to bear the shame of their violence) run the risk of losing all proper relationship to the self. Here, we are invited to turn our face away from our own selves and the violence within that torments and fascinates. We turn to the face of God and are "overwhelmed by the splendor of His gaze." It is the self-offering of Christ, who "turned not His face from the spitting and the shame," that shows us the way towards a transformation in which our face becomes the very image of His glory.

The "poetic journeys" gathered together in this volume are the fruit of a life that lived the journey instead of merely thinking it. It is a recognition that the right words, spoken (or written) at the right time, have a creative spaciousness that is an icon of the word of God that re-creates us all.[2]

In the Greek, Ephesians 2:10 tells us that "we are God's poem." It is most often translated "workmanship," which seems largely to miss the point. In this work we can be reminded of that true meaning and discover its depths within us.

Fr. Stephen Freeman

Feast of the Holy Bodiless Powers, 2021

Preface

"I Fell Down into My Heart"

Xenia and Donald Sheehan

Peace I leave with you, my peace I give unto you:
not as the world giveth, give I unto you.
Let not your heart be troubled, neither let it be afraid.

John 14:27 KJV

I PREFACE THIS BOOK with a brief account of an event that occurred around 1990. I was quite new to the Orthodox Church, having received Holy Baptism on Lazarus Saturday 1989 and taken the name of the saint who is now my patron, Xenia of Petersburg. That summer, Don and I, with our firstborn, David, and his wife-to-be, Tara Mooney (of blessed memory!), assisted by many generous and hard-working friends, cleared the land and built the foundation and shell for our house deep in the woods of Sharon, Vermont. Come fall—the house closed in but by no means finished—we moved from our large tarp-tent into David's small wood-heated cabin along with our younger son, Rowan Benedict, age nine (who had spent the summer at camp), our cat, a couple of rambunctious kittens, and our aging dog Starlight, who at last lived up to her name as her blonde coat reflected the stars to guide us home through the forest on dark nights!

We both worked, Don teaching at Dartmouth in Hanover, New Hampshire, and managing the Frost Place in Franconia, and I editing at the University Press in Hanover or seeing therapy clients in Montpelier, Vermont. Late each afternoon, we would collect Rowan, drive home to Sharon, and navigate in all weathers our three-quarters of a mile of rough dirt road, carved out between a steep upward slope and a plunge downward to a fast-running brook. Then we'd light the gas and kerosene lamps, crank up the wood stove, get water from the spring-fed brook that ran nearby, and cook dinner on the little gas stove. It was a surprisingly delicious year for all of us.

This sweet cabin is where the event occurred. Don's brief, vivid, and very personal account has not been shared before. I include it here, first, as an offering to St. Xenia in thanks for her benign and loving presence to our family's life for so many years—a presence far greater, I suspect, than I know. And second, it offers a profound yet simple image of what is loosely the subject and arc of this book: a path of movement from violent disorder to holy peace—in a person, a life, a relationship, a family, perhaps even a community, an environment, or a world! It is a movement we must continually initiate (or choose to take hold of when it offers itself to us) and give ourselves to wholly; but the movement itself and the peace that results from it are as diverse as persons and their lives—and of God's making, not our own, "not as the world giveth." It is the sort of movement Don would at times call "downward" (referring to his academic career, for instance, as one of downward mobility—resulting from his own clear choices). It is a movement that generally involves letting oneself become smaller, with the result that we actually—NB: not seeking this!—become larger, more spacious, truly personal.

Whether the details related here are "true" in a biographical sense, I cannot say; I can only confirm what I saw and heard as witness to the event from the outside—and also from what I know of St. Xenia and of Don. You will not find most of these details in the hagiographical accounts, although, to my knowledge, Don's account does not conflict with those. The event was certainly true for him subjectively, and, always a faithful raconteur, he wrote it down shortly afterward.

Don's Account

I fell asleep that night exhausted but otherwise fine. That is, I felt merely tired, nothing else.

An hour or so later I awoke with a high fever, and a few minutes later I began shaking and couldn't stop. The air around me felt churning and menacing, as if harmful "spirits" were swirling around me. And I began to feel very badly frightened.

I woke my wife. She felt my brow, and she went to get cool water and a washcloth. I began to talk—in the spinning rhythms of my now violent trembling—about the churning menace in the air. She found my Bible and began to chant the Psalms aloud to me in Orthodox fashion, and I followed the phrases, saying them aloud ahead of her voice and spinning her clear rhythm into my broken trembling. I was "de-reading" them; and I felt thin, scattered, uncentered and terrified. She kept on chanting.

Then I had it: she needed to bless me with holy water. She put down the Psalms, took up our bottle of holy water from last Theophany and began to bless me, in the name of the Holy Trinity, on brow, eyes, nose, lips, throat, chest, hands and feet. Instantly, at the very first blessing, my trembling ceased; and as she continued to bless me, my feeling of thinness began steadily to deepen, the scattering cohered, and the terror faded into depths of great peace.

When she finished the blessing I became aware of a vivid presence in our room: the living figure of blessed St. Xenia of Petersburg.

St. Xenia of Petersburg. Icon by Fr. Andrew Tregubov, Tregubov Studios, Claremont, New Hampshire. Used by permission.

My wife's saint's name is Xenia; and three feet away from us stood her original and true icon of St. Xenia. Also, while my wife was blessing me, she had placed on my face a thin taper-candle from St. Xenia's church in what was then Leningrad, brought to her by our friend Irina, of blessed memory. When St. Xenia appeared to me, she was unmistakable. I asked her: "Tell me what happened to you.". . . She answered:

St. Xenia's Story

"All that night while my husband lay dying in bed I sat in the room downstairs, dark and alone, knowing my life was dying out. Then at the blackest hour they came, doctor and servant: 'Come see him, he is gone.' I stepped up to the bed where he lay and I looked at him now moments dead, and I could not believe the world was this way, we'd been so young and in love and beautiful, and now this cold darkness. And my mind broke into a thousand pieces, I felt it go all apart in my hands, and I fell down into my heart without my mind, I fell and fell. And at the bottom, Christ waited for me, and He caught me and stood me up, and then my legs gave way, and I sank to the floor and knew nothing.

"When I opened my eyes again I saw light streaming in the curtains of the room [where] I'd sat waiting in darkness, and then I raised up on my elbow, and the servant and doctor again were there. And again they said: 'Come.'

"I walked back upstairs with them to the room where he was, and I went up to the bed again, and—again—my mind broke apart and I fell again into my heart where Christ was. But my legs held and I kept on gazing as my mind kept on breaking and breaking, and Christ's hands on me grew stronger and solider.

"I saw my husband's coat by the bed, and I reached out and put it on, and the sleeves fell over my hands, and the hem touched my ankles: but it fit me perfectly. And I walked down the stairs and out of the house and into my heart where Christ forever lives in me."

I said to my wife: Now read aloud to me the molieben to St. Xenia.[3] And as my wife Xenia's clear voice began to chant the beautiful words, my fear and trembling were now banished wholly away and I fell deeply into most peaceful sleep.

[This ends Don's written account.]

About St. Xenia

St. Xenia lived during the eighteenth century in St. Petersburg, Russia (for a brief and terrible time Leningrad, but now restored to its original name). She was a young noblewoman married to, and much in love with, Army Colonel Andrey Fyodorovich Petrov, who is said to have spent much of his time at court as a singer. Still quite young, he died there suddenly, without either repentance or benefit of the Holy Mysteries. Thereafter, accounts vary somewhat, but, over her family's strenuous objections, Xenia Grigorievna Petrova soon gave all her property away to those who needed it and, wearing her husband's overlarge army coat, went out to live in the city's streets and places of poverty as a "Fool for Christ."[4]

It was thus she entered, clad for battle, into forty-five years of spiritual warfare. Serving the afflicted and poor where she found them, refusing clothing and shelter for herself, she is said to have prayed all night in all weathers in the Smolensk cemetery (some nights carrying bricks up the ladders to the church steeple to be ready for the bricklayers in the morning). In that cemetery she herself is now buried and her relics venerated.

For all of this and more, she came to be greatly loved and honored among people of all conditions. One may read numerous accounts of her charitable works and small, life-changing interventions in people's lives—often only a word or two spoken at the right moment. We heard one first-hand account of a miraculous contemporary healing of a child in Ousinki, Alaska, where Don and Rowan Benedict and I visited in 1994. We were told there are many such stories of both St. Xenia's and St. Herman of Alaska's healing interventions, especially at times when access to the mainland hospital was impossible for this small island community, as it often was and no doubt still is.

St. Xenia was canonized by the Russian Orthodox Church in 1988. The following year I was given her name in a small New Hampshire church high on a hill overlooking a paper mill, planted there in the nineteenth century by faithful Russian immigrant workers to watch over their difficult lives in a new land. For Don, who was received in this same church five years earlier, St. Xenia's living iconic presence came to be second only to that of the Theotokos, Mary, Mother of God, whom he deeply loved. What the encounter he describes here surely revealed to him was not only the shape and strength of her life, but something of the true shape of his own. For Don's own pilgrimage took him through violence to personhood.

A Brief Word about Don Sheehan

Raised in a family afflicted by alcoholic violence—poet at heart, teenage gang member and streetfighter, almost-soldier, student, linguist, translator, Doctor of Philosophy in Literature, lifelong teacher, Orthodox Christian, Subdeacon, loving husband and father, comic storyteller, great with a chainsaw! and best of friends—Don Sheehan delved deep to transfigure his inheritance into an ability to love: that is, to love with great care, as St. Xenia had, each person who came before him.

On his eighteenth birthday, as he tells us in the opening chapter, April 2, 1958, the image of his hand on the door of an army post library passed "straight into my heart," and he found himself called into a world of poetry that held him spellbound for an entire day. On that day, a process began in him that would change the course of his life. Twenty-five years later, in April 1983, on the day before his forty-third birthday, he would kneel by an unmarked grave in Tennessee to ask his father's forgiveness and to offer his own. Two days after that, at five in the morning, he received the Prayer of the Heart: "Lord Jesus Christ, Son of God, have mercy on me, a sinner." From his first consenting movement to join his voice with the voice of this ancient holy prayer, it *prayed him*. Waking him each morning at five, continuing throughout his days of teaching, conversing, simply living, for over most of a year it guided him step-by-step to the Orthodox Church, where he was received by Chrismation on September 8, 1984, the Feast of the Nativity of the Theotokos. In the Church, whose teachings he slowly worked into his own, he found a path of knowing and loving God, all the time growing in his ability to love and serve others through his prayer, his teaching, and his writing.

These two dear lights of my life, Don and St. Xenia—what gentler or brighter lights could I ask for? They inspire me to keep seeking to receive and honor the brightness they have long reflected toward me. It is in such a spirit of seeking and honoring (and also simply because I miss him, as I'm sure many of you do) that I have immersed myself in the writings Don left behind and here offer them to you—both the shining gems of his own understanding and something of what I have learned from gathering them all together—a luxury Don never had. A certain amount of mining may be required at times (at least I've found it so), but I promise that the reward is worth the effort. I have probably only scratched the surface.

Historically, we live in an increasingly violent moment in which almost all that *can* polarize appears to be doing so. Everything Don writes of here seems about to be put to the severest test—or perhaps by the time you read this may already have been. I pray that, whether we live or die in this testing, whether or not our minds break apart, we may answer God's call, as St. Xenia did, to fall into our hearts "where Christ forever lives."

—Feast of Pentecost, 2023

Editor's Note about Style

In honor of the late Donald Sheehan's quiet reverence for the things of God, which he might think of simply as Good Manners, and contrary to most contemporary publishing practice, this book has been styled Up. Like the small bows that an Orthodox believer makes in Church—or like C. S. Lewis when surprised by Joy—Don would use initial capital letters to recognize and honor the presence of the Holy. I have made an exception in regard to pronouns for Mary, the Mother of God, as he was not consistent in their capitalization, though he hadn't the slightest doubt of her holiness. He never overdid it, but the reader of this book will perhaps find more initial capitals than is usual in a book nowadays, and they are often contextual rather than applied by rule. The publisher has very kindly consented to this older style.

"That we may answer God's call." The Bells of Holy Ascension
Orthodox Church, Mount Pleasant, South Carolina, 2009.

Introduction

Thy Statutes Have Been My Songs

XENIA SHEEHAN

Listening
to voices not broken
by our inner accents
—to regain the whole rhythm
of motion and change—
that (had we but listened)
were deeply singing, and are.

—D. S.

I. Straight into My Heart

THE NOUS AND INWARDNESS

DON WROTE THE LINES of the above epigraph in his long poem "Rhapsody."[5] Our human capacity to *listen* in such a way—beyond and behind our given material reality and the skewings of our own inner turmoil—has long been recognized and understood within the tradition of the Eastern Orthodox Church as the function of the *nous*. I do not know the relation of this function to the imagination, which creates new psychological realities on the basis of our experience. The *Philokalia* tells us, rather, that the nous is the part of the mind "enthroned in the heart." It is given us that we may listen, beyond ourselves, to God.[6]

Here at the beginning, I point out some threads that will recur throughout the book, for the tiny poem of the epigraph has a chiastic quality (as perhaps all things do when we know how to see and listen): a shape and movement that works its way toward a unifying center from both ends of a poem, even when their meanings are opposite, as in listening and not listening. Oppositions seem to spark us into some kind of response. Here, we are *listening*— to voices beyond ourselves. This is matched by "had we but listened" we'd have heard their deep song, the opposing silence forever implied. The pair is centered in "the whole rhythm of motion and change," which Don understood to be God's statutes, embedded within us and in all of His Creation. "Thy statutes have been my songs."[7] Here we must ask: Would they have been singing if we had *not* been listening? I think the answer is, of course, but perhaps not for us if we have absented ourselves from the one who created and moves in "the whole rhythm of motion and change." For to listen and hear truly, we must deny ourselves. When we do so, as Fr. Mircea tells us in chapter 8, the enemy cannot harm us—the "enemy" that entraps us in our denial of God, that is, in our*self*—for by denying yourself "You have removed the ammunition that he can use against you."

I don't know whether Don knew when he wrote this poem, or even sought to know, what or whom he was hearing in those "voices not broken by our inner accents"; the point for him, I think, was that they were clearly *other* than his own. They sounded from beyond himself and his own pain, in which he had long felt trapped. They were a pathway out, a connection to something real, a part or sign of his movement toward healing. When the Prayer of the Heart came to him at forty-three, he did know the voice. It came immediately following—surely in response to—his profound act of forgiving his father for the years of violence that had so disfigured his family's loving. Don went on to immerse himself in St. Isaac the Syrian's teachings on *ascesis*. For that is the Orthodox way out. It is how the *self*, with all its misdirected hungers and "inner accents," is redirected to seeing and hearing more truly "the whole rhythm of motion and change" in order to become instead a *person* in and of God. Forgiveness may be the deepest ascetical act we can perform, especially when we have been deeply hurt.

For each of us, the noetic part of our mind is uniquely inspired and nurtured, growing in us (or failing to grow) as we grow, nourished (or not) by the beauty of the creation itself, by God's love reflected in and by the people around us, by beautiful music or works of art, and by good stories and poems, especially when we experience them in our early years. In

Don's case, the stories his father read aloud to his children stayed with him all his life as points of joy in a home where words, when they weren't disturbingly absent, had so often created confusion and pain. These moments of living together in stories must have become models for him of the way words can create goodness where it is missing, models even of the activity and presence of God as Word, Maker, *Poetes* of heaven and earth, who saw what He had made and pronounced it good. This was something he himself could do to bring light into the world's dark places. At the end of Dostoevsky's great novel *The Brothers Karamazov*, Don's favorite, Alyosha tells his young friends that "even if one good memory remains with us in our hearts, that alone may serve some day for our salvation."[8] Don believed this. And he took note of the importance Dostoevsky gave to memory as confirming that the noetic capacity is already within us and has no need to be acquired or taught, only remembered.

Which brings us to *inwardness*. The word will keep cropping up in the book, often with Don's very specific meaning (see the glossary). In his language, our inwardness is how we are able to "sustain communion with God." In Psalms, he says, inwardness is "the action of memory wherein God incarnates in the human mind while the human mind becomes deified." The psalmic enemy "seeks to destroy the divine inwardness of the human person at the same instant it escalates into violating the whole of creation—and thereby seeks to escalate further into assaulting the Creator Himself."[9] Our inwardness, in other words, is crucial to our humanity, allowing us to participate in Christ and thereby to re-musicalize not only our own soul, but—in fulfillment of our human calling, according to St. Maximus—all of God's creation (see section II of this chapter). Don connects our inwardness with God's statutes—His songs— which he calls "the divine patterns of our earthly souls" and of all God's Creation. Thus, we might think of the nous as the eyes and ears of our inwardness, our faculty for becoming aware of God's songs, His statutes. And then we can reach—or fall with St. Xenia—into our heart—where we will find Him who resolves all antinomies in Himself: the God-man, Christ Theanthropos. Perhaps the nous, enthroned in the heart, is itself the *where* of our inwardness.

STORIES

In Don's and my lives, stories mattered a great deal. They took us out of— Don might say *into*, in a good way—ourselves. We were both read to—Don by his father with gusto (perhaps enhanced by alcohol, though he was sober for several years), I by my mother, as she had been by hers, with a quiet but involved sobriety. We both remembered the experience with love and continued the practice in our own family. C. S. Lewis, describing his long journey of return to Christianity in *Surprised by Joy*, considers the relation of the imaginative to what I call here the noetic experience:

> I do not think the resemblance between the Christian and the merely imaginative experience is accidental. I think that all things in their way reflect heavenly truth, the imagination not least. *Reflect* is the important word; this lower life of the imagination is not* a beginning of, nor a step towards, the higher life of the spirit, merely an image. . . . But it still had, at however many removes, the shape of the reality it reflected.
>
> *That is, not necessarily and by its own nature. God can cause it to be such a beginning.[10]

There is no question in my mind that Lewis created many such images and "shapes" in his stories (I, too, am drawn to the in-forming shapes of things), and Don and I did find them to reflect heavenly truth. They opened doors in us to genuine Christian understanding. Lewis's novel *Perelandra* is a shining example, particularly in the way Tinidril, the unfallen Eve of her young world, remains close to Maleldil (Christ's name in Old Solar)—a closeness such that she seems in continual inward conversation with him.[11] During her temptation, however, He withdraws, for she must ultimately make her own choice, freely. What a blessed image of how we were created to be! And can be.

Don began listening to stories under his father's tutelage. A complex and bright man discounting the ruination wrought by drink, on the occasions when George Sheehan was flush and sober he liked to collect rather beautiful special editions that he would read aloud to his children, and he made some excellent choices. Don describes in chapter 1 his father's "rich and varied" voice intoning *The Wind in the Willows* to convey "Badger's deep, warm growl" or Toady's "imaginatively obsessive urgencies," or "Ratty's clear intelligence." In "The Piper at the Gates of Dawn," chapter 7 of that book, Rat and Mole set out by moonlight to find Little Portly Otter, who's been missing for days:[12]

> Rat, who was in the stern of the boat, while Mole sculled, sat up suddenly and listened with a passionate intentness. Mole [the pilgrim "seeker" in this story], who with gentle strokes was just keeping the boat moving while he scanned the banks with care, looked at him with curiosity.
>
> "It's gone!" sighed the Rat, sinking back in his seat again. "So beautiful and strange and new! Since it was to end so soon,

I almost wish I had never heard it. For it has roused a longing in me that is pain, and nothing seems worthwhile but just
to hear that sound once more and go on listening to it forever.
"No! There it is again! . . . Oh, Mole, the beauty of it! The merry
bubble and joy, the thin, clear, happy call of the distant piping!
Such music I never dreamed of, and the call in it is stronger than
the music is sweet! Row on, Mole, row! For the music and the
call must be for us." (Grahame, *Wind in the Willows*, chapter 7)

They come to a small island "fringed close with willow and silver. Re-
served, shy, but full of significance, it hid whatever it might hold behind a
veil, keeping it till the hour should come." After passing through "broken,
tumultuous water" to its "flowery margin," they moor their boat.

"This is the place of my song-dream, the place the music played
to me," whispered the Rat, as if in a trance. "Here, in this holy
place, here if anywhere, surely we shall find Him! Then suddenly
the Mole felt a great Awe fall upon him . . . an awe that smote
and held him and, without seeing, he knew it could only mean
that some august Presence was very, very near. . . . Trembling, in
that utter clearness of the imminent dawn, while Nature, flushed
with fullness of incredible colour, seemed to hold her breath for
the event, he looked in the very eyes of the Friend and Helper
[and] . . . saw, last of all, nestling between his very hooves, sleeping soundly in entire peace and contentment, the little, round,
podgy, childish form of the baby otter . . . and still, as he looked,
he lived and as he lived, he wondered.
     "Rat!" He found breath to whisper, shaking, "Are you
afraid?"
     "Afraid?" murmured the Rat, his eyes shining with unut-
terable love. "Afraid! Of *Him?* Oh, never, never! And yet—and
yet—Oh Mole, I am afraid!" (141–43)

All this, Don writes, would "come alive in us; and the stanzas of the *Rubaiyat*
pass straight into my heart, although at age nine I understand almost nothing of them. But I love them."

I doubt it can matter much to a Christian child, or even a sensible
parent, that the Piper in Grahame's story is the god Pan. Nor would it matter
that the *Rubaiyat* author was a Sufi astronomer. After all, so were the Wise
Men who traveled four hundred miles by camel to welcome and honor the
birth of the Christ. These stories draw the reader *beyond*—to look for God
beyond or *within* the surfaces and logics and self-interests of daily life—perhaps even within the Deep Woods where Badger lives. Yet, after all is said
and done, Grahame's adventurers, like many others, enlarged and chastened

by their wanderings and seekings, bring it all home to their modest holes in field and riverbank and go on living as before, perhaps a bit more gladly and wisely, among lifelong friends and neighbors.

One morning recently I awoke much too early and clicked on my Audible to hear Tolkien's Frodo Baggins being called to *inwardness* as he sits on the High Seat of Seeing, where he decides at last that he must serve truths that lie deeper than the world's logics and his own fears. In *The Wind in the Willows*, the call to inwardness comes from Pan, the animals' god. Grahame's characters are equally called *away!* But it's the *away!* of waking up from their everyday world—to something *inward*—not to escape their world but to *true* it. Don and I received not simply enjoyment but sound spiritual teaching from writers such as these as we raised our sons (and ourselves) on their books.

Another worthy writer for young adults is Madeleine L'Engle, who wraps up her *Wrinkle in Time* with advice from St. Paul's First Corinthians. It is delivered as a sort of talisman—by a bizarrely attired angel—to the book's gawky teenage heroine Meg, to strengthen her in her mission to rescue her brilliant little brother from being absorbed into the mind of a machine that holds an entire planet in thrall to a vast encroaching shadow that is, bit by bit, swallowing up the created universe:

> God hath chosen the foolish things of the world to confound the wise; and God hath chosen the weak things of the world to confound the things which are mighty;
>
> And base things of the world, and things which are despised, hath God chosen, yea, and things which are not, to bring to nought things that are:
>
> That no flesh should glory in his presence.
>
> But of him are ye in Christ Jesus, who of God is made unto us wisdom, and righteousness, and sanctification, and redemption:
>
> That, according as it is written, He that glorieth, let him glory in the Lord. (1 Cor 27-31, KJV)

Good things for a child to know. Meg saves Charles Wallace by loving him—the one weapon the powerful enemy does not have. One of L'Engle's gifts is her ability to make size and age, strength and status, even time, completely irrelevant. No matter how small we are, or how old or incapable, we are called equally to the work of making whole and well, by means of love, the world we are given. Complex, deep, and clear theology for children (or adults who weren't offered it in childhood).

Images and, by His grace, beginnings. For me, Tolkien (*Lord of the Rings*) and Lewis (in the *Narnia* series and the Space Trilogy), along with the medieval literature I came to love in graduate school, were my Christian background, and judging from the marginal notes I made in my book of lyric poems of the Middle Ages, my teacher had a very Orthodox mind.[13] I even began to think of myself, half-seriously, as a medieval Christian—easy, as there was no way to act on it, but a beginning.

A Teacher

In chapter 1 of this book, an autobiographical account, we learn of a seminal moment in Don's life when, wandering alone past the army base library on his eighteenth birthday, he is drawn to enter it for the first time. "I looked at my hand as it reached for the knob," he writes, "and turned it and pushed open the door: and this image of my hand at the door passed straight into my heart." Once inside, he picks up a book of Japanese poems from a table, opens it, and for the next seven or eight hours is wholly absorbed into a new world: "The 'I' of the poems," he says, "rose up out of them and claimed me as if I had always been possessed by this lyric clarity and grace of sight, as if my life had always possessed this quiet haven." Don might easily have used Ratty's words to describe this birthday gift: "*That's music I never dreamed of, and the call in it is stronger than the music is sweet!*" Soon afterward, his military training completed, he returned home and told his father he wanted to attend college.

In his second semester at the University of Florida, Don met his first real teacher:

> My freshman humanities teacher Gary Scrimgeour had a strong and vivid impact on me. I remember very clearly his walking into class that first day in 1959. I was eighteen, he was probably twenty-six or twenty-seven. Tall, blond, self-confident, slender, with an engaging English accent. He talked easily and volubly about things that were then to me mysterious and significant entities: books, painting, classical music, sculpture. I was dazzled, breathless, wholly admiring.
>
> Understand, I'd been in the army, I'd grown up in a violent home (my father was alcoholic), yet oddly a loving home (he was also a warm and caring man). In the army, in the last months, I'd been introduced to books and reading by certain of my barracks friends. Also, I'd one Sunday afternoon wandered into the post library to happen upon a book entitled *One Hundred Poems*

from the Japanese, by Kenneth Rexroth, and I was deeply en-
chanted, magnetized. Thus, that day in humanities, when Gary
Scrimgeour came in, I had had certain powerful experiences of
a kind hard to describe, but I had never *talked* about them, nor
had I heard anyone else ever do so.

Yet here he was, brightly and engagingly talking of things
I'd loved in some dim, private way and place. I was hooked. I
wanted to do this, too, to talk of what was obscure and central
in this attractive and compelling way, to make what was dark
become light.

Needless to say, I didn't learn to do so that term. I barely
learned the right pronunciation of the difficult names and styles
of art. But I learned enough to know that here was my real work:
to turn the full light of sympathetic intelligence into the depths
of hope and terror and beauty that was—and is—true art. Gary
Scrimgeour awoke this in me.

The Prayer

Just past the middle of Don's life, in 1976, his father died. Seven years would
pass before he piled his family into the car to make the long trek from northern New Hampshire to Tennessee—the littlest of us, in those pre-seatbelt
days, preferring to stretch out on the shelf below the rear window. Arriving
at last at the cemetery in Memphis, we located the neglected grave, and there
Don read his father a letter of forgiveness, along with the scriptural account
of Abraham and Isaac (Gen 22). He ended it by assuring his father that, like
Isaac, "I didn't die, Dad. I didn't die!" I find myself wondering whether he
hadn't been sure of this himself until now. Three days later, he was awakened
in the morning by a prayer known in Eastern Orthodox Tradition as the
Prayer of the Heart. It filled him and *prayed him* for most of the following
year as it led him to the Orthodox Church. This story is told in full in his
first essay collection, *The Grace of Incorruption*.

When at last Don entered the Orthodox Church in 1984, he found
himself drawn into a new reality— evident in her every act and gesture—
and he was delighted. For in many ways it was not new at all but a fulfillment, a coming true or making clear of things that had marked and guided
his life up to this point, and a coming home to "know the place for the
first time."[14] He had listened. And, in the prayer that came to guide him to
the Church, he heard clearly that one "true voice not broken by our inner
accents." Following its leading, he seemed to hear it again in the chanting
that accompanied each service.

Then, many years later, our son Rowan Benedict spoke in an Ancient Faith interview of having, in his youth, *listened* to the voice of his father's psalmic chanting in the next room as he would fall asleep each night. He said that something of its rhythms and sound had found its way into the Church music he had been composing. Had that one true voice crossed over and passed on to him through his father? Had Don's "conversion" become not only a gathering in—a harvesting—of his own early experience but a planting of new seeds for future harvests? Is this passing-on of the Voice simply a miniature of how the Holy Tradition of Orthodox Christianity always acts and moves through time?

Not codified or legalized, never imposed, nor even wholly consensual in all respects, Orthodox Tradition is centered in the living Christ, who is at the same time the solid ground on which we stand and the goal toward which we reach. Tradition teaches us to listen, not to a fixed formulation that we can come to idolize, but to the living voice that articulates it. C. S. Lewis, in his long search for Joy, writes of learning neither to attach his joy to the experiences that seemed briefly to produce it, nor to focus on his own joyous sensations, but rather to recognize Joy Himself and follow Him: not, that is, to "look for the living among the dead" (Luke 24:5; Lewis, *Surprised by Joy*). For the living Christ does not reside in man-made things, be they tombs or temples. And yet, as Lewis also intimates, by His grace, even those things may serve to start us on our way.

Thus Tradition's rich variety of living voices and enlightened perspectives is, indeed, one of its greatest strengths. Both the varied witness contained in the Old Testament and the infinitely more immediate witness recorded in the New (immediate because it witnesses to the infinite as personal Presence)—both give essential dimension and *life* to their gathered writings. And in these writings, if we truly listen, the singular voice continues to sound, for the writers are also listening to it. He is always calling to us wherever He finds us, speaking to us—through the voices of those who love Him as they go on to speak to others—speaking, that is, with the voice of the One they love. And our careful listening *for* and *to* that voice draws us into the one relationship out of which our own personhood will be born.

Journaling about St. Isaac's *Homilies*, Don says that "the person who *is* these words becomes the person of Christ Himself." And the transformation "opens the great mystery wherein we, as readers, enter into the relation with St. Isaac *in and through the personhood of Christ Himself*. As St. Isaac seeks to know Christ, and as Christ beautifully manifests His love to St. Isaac, we—in Christ—come to know and love St. Isaac *in and through his knowing and loving Christ*" (chapter 18). This, I think Don to be saying, is Orthodox Tradition, beginning with the *Synelthontes* of Acts 1:21, those "walking-with ones" who were *with* Christ, within his circle, throughout his ministry, Crucifixion, and Resurrection. This circle of "being-with," Don also called *inwardness* (for more on this, see the glossary).

We are free, however, to refuse Love and in doing so to lose our way—by which I mean to take our *own* way, the alone way, as our first parents did, as Judas did: the way of preferring our "self" to God, our will to His; the way of feeding our God-given hungering in our own way, directing that hunger, not to Him but to something else that we imagine to taste better or shine more brightly. Tediously the same wherever it occurs, this misdirection of our God-given hunger is always disintegrative, a path of ongoing dying rather than living.

I pray that I may not take such a way here, for I believe the writings in this book offer us an image of the God-seeking rhythm and grace required for the effort of *living*—perhaps it would not be amiss actually to call the collection a dance, as antinomy is a dance. Don's dance, and in a small way mine, through him—or his through me?—with God. For in His Dance, to use C. S. Lewis's words, "all the patterns [are] linked and looped together by the unions of a kneeling with a sceptered love."[15] The image calls to my mind the time Don and I, dressed in our country clothes, waltzed rather elegantly together at a county fair in Vermont. I think he wore a big straw hat. I would wish for this book to taste something like that. Don was never really inclined toward leadership, yet that time we danced at the fair he led me with "merry bubble and joy." Even more important, he led me to the Church with the same sort of sure and quiet grace.

The Church

If there can be said to be a turning point where Don began to shape his own way more deliberately, his entry into the Communion and ways of the Orthodox Church was it. The title given to chapter 4 is his own: Inheriting the Orthodox Tradition. Practically, it involved his adoption of a clear center for his life and clear patterns of behavior not of his own devising—a rule of prayer that grew longer and longer, rich in Psalms; and a serious, if mostly private, ongoing ascesis. He would, for instance, remain, usually awake, with a group gathered in his home until it naturally dispersed, but no matter how late it was or how early the next day must begin, he would then go upstairs for his hour or two of prayer. He never imposed this on the rest of us in any way. His inheritance also involved years of regrasping his prior work and thought in the light offered him by the Church. He understood the Tradition he was entering into not as a set of rules or fixed practices, not as some sort of safety net, but as a new, compelling, and in-timate relationship of love with Jesus Christ, based in the heart rather than in the head. That is, he understood his new faith as a relationship modeled by the Church's *knowing* of Jesus Christ in an intimate, unmediated way, as a bride knows her husband; a relationship that, by virtue of God's infinite love, is open to all.[16] Poet Cleopatra Mathis has described this time for Don as "some crucial piece of his identity falling into place," writing that "The light of the man he was simply shone brighter."[17]

I believe Don was concerned not to pressure me to follow him, so we didn't talk much about his experience with the Prayer and the Church. Over time, I came to attend most Sunday services with him and little Rowan Benedict (who began serving—and, at some long festal services, sleeping—at the altar when he was four or five). I know Don prayed for me, if only because I can't imagine him not doing so. Perhaps it was all too new and private for talk. Or perhaps I simply wasn't listening, a little shocked myself, and much absorbed in various New Age activities, my study of therapy, and my clients' horrific ongoing suffering from childhood abuse. Whatever he studied and learned in those early years, he came to value highly the ascetic path of Eastern Orthodox Christianity as a path leading clearly toward a relationship with God that bears fruit as genuine person-hood in God's likeness. He understood it as a path with long experience in knowing who God is; exactly what it was that our first parents did in sepa-rating their wills from His, and how to counteract the human impulses on which they acted. And perhaps above all, it was the way that God opened before him and led him forward on, in response to his deep and hard-won willingness to forgive and seek forgiveness of his father.

Eastern Orthodox Christianity was a way that showed him there *is* pat-tern, there *are* rules, in all relationships—in this one relationship above all. Don might even have thought of them primarily as good manners—man-ners that, like all worthy ascetic practices, involve lifting up others before ourselves and emptying ourselves in all that we do and imagine ourselves to be, so that God may fill us and all that we touch. For His good manners are such that He will not do so without an invitation. He wants no slaves. In this way the life-giving antinomy between ourselves and God, created and Creator, human and Divine, can be held in the stillness of perfect balance in our hearts as we wait in love for Love to resolve it into a perfect unity between us—uniting our kneeling with His sceptered love, to use Lewis's beautiful image. Within the Tradition of the Church, then, Don had before him a clear and rich antinomy to work with: "a living law written on soft hearts," in the words of Fr. John Konkle.[18]

Since he did not enter the Church until well past the middle of his life, there is material in this book that predates his Orthodoxy. My claim here, and what I would like the book to show, is that, throughout his life, Don was being drawn into embracing the fullness of God's statutes: God's "songs," and the deep choreography of the dance they invite us into. I would claim also that we all are so drawn and called. But, as this is Don's book, what we will find here is something of how *he* responded, how he used everything he was given—even the violence and fear and unbelief—to become a person in and of God. This happened for him because he listened, and because, listening, he received God's songs straight into his heart.

Poet Cleopatra Mathis has written this memorial tribute:

> Don's commitment to poetry and his commitment to God were intertwined. What else had he been teaching us, the poets at all the conferences, but how to pray? Not a prayer of asking, of wanting recognition and success, but of searching a way into the deepest self, of allowing access to the best that self had to offer. What is poetry, he taught me, but patient meditation, words borne out of silence and listening. Someone has pointed out that silent and listen have the same letters in English. At each conference, Don urged us to be quiet and listen to the words of our fellow poets, to be silent in the force of emotion they conveyed and let our response be guided by that careful attention to the other. Whatever we would learn that week, he said, would not be from narrowing our focus on our own work, but from an openness that allowed us to see the whole endeavor of being alive. That attentive silence would teach us what we needed to know about our own poems. This, I realized gradually, was the essence of prayer, an abiding endeavor in Don's character, because as we direct ourselves toward the poem's center, its source, we spontaneously begin moving toward a higher level of life. Our senses are sharpened, our self-knowledge increases, and the love of God and others becomes one and the same.[19]

II. Foundations

Foundations must of course come first if you're going to make a house. I vividly recall doing this by hand when we built our house in the Vermont woods: mixing the cement in a small mixer run by our generator and carrying it off in a wheelbarrow to shovel it into the holes in the concrete blocks we'd so carefully stacked. At eleven that evening, as we all sat down to eat, not quite finished but famished and wholly exhausted, Don leaned forward over the table and laid his face quietly on his full plate. We couldn't stop laughing.

To establish a strong Orthodox foundation for this work of his to stand on is a much easier task, also more serious in many ways, but it should never rule out the joy of divine comedy. I briefly put before you two acknowledged Fathers of the Orthodox Church, one ancient, St. Maximus the Confessor (ca. 580–662), and one modern, Fr. Alexander Schmemann (1921–83). Three other Holy Fathers that I know of were fundamentally important to Don, but their work is so present throughout the book that I have let them speak for themselves: King and Prophet David (10th–9th century BC); St. Isaac the Syrian (7th century AD); and Fr. Pavel Florensky, a Russian priest-martyr of the twentieth century whom Don (with many others) considered also to be a saint.[20] And I take some liberties inspired by Fr. Thomas Hopko and add a few important points from C. S. Lewis's *Surprised by Joy* as well; for more than once Fr. Tom referred to Lewis in his Orthodox Dogmatic Theology class (with a wink) as "Holy Father Clive."

I know that Don read and was inspired by St. Maximus, because we participated together in the early 1990s in an extended church study group concerning Panayiotis Nellas's book *Deification in Christ: The Nature of the Human Person*.[21] It was led by our dear friend Nil Nellis (now Fr. Nilos of Kaslo, British Columbia). St. Maximus is one of the five Church Fathers upon whom that excellent book is based. Although I have not found that Don wrote about him, I think it quite likely that he went on to read more of his work after the group ended. Fr. Alexander I'm guessing he had not read, though it's possible. I don't know how I missed reading him during the time of my study at St. Vladimir's—possibly just homework I didn't do as a busy commuter from the North Country—but his *For the Life of the World* has recently become for me a compelling over-and-over Audible read mostly because of his deep, difficult-to-take-in-quickly, but wonderfully clear presentation of God's intention for us to live in the world eucharistically. We are to direct all our hungers to Him rather than to the world, and to praise and bless Him not only for their fulfillment but for their very existence and strength within us (or so I take it).[22] For only in this way can we avoid consuming the world and one another and be filled instead by God to become persons in His likeness. Our first parents' failure to take God's way is what we know as the Fall, which to this day, with cumulative effect, inclines us to worship ourselves rather than God. These two very different and centrally Orthodox thinkers and writers offer an excellent conceptual ground, and a wholly Orthodox context, so I believe, for Don's explorations of antinomy and personhood, which form the intellectual and spiritual core of this book.

St. Maximus the Confessor

> *It is [man's] vocation to make manifest in his own person the great mystery of the divine purpose in bringing into existence things divided—to show how the divided extremes in created beings may be reconciled in harmony, the near with the far, the lower with the higher, so that through gradual ascent all are eventually brought into union with God. —*St. Maximus The Confessor, Ambiguum 41

One day, as I was beginning work on the book and finding antinomies to be such a recurrent theme, I found myself remembering and pondering an idea I'd first encountered in Fr. Tom Hopko's dogmatic theology class about five fundamental oppositions or divisions that God had implanted in His creation, though I think I never knew its source.[23] Turning to my friend and spiritual advisor Fr. John Konkle, I learned that the source was St. Maximus the Confessor.[24] He directed me to a blog, *Ambiguorum Blogis*, by Fr. Michael Butler, from which I quote:

> One of the more intriguing passages in St Maximus the Confessor is found in *Ambiguum* 41, in which the Confessor lays out *humanity's role in sanctifying the world* by mediating five pairs of distinctions inherent in the created order. Because of the Fall, mankind became unable to effect these mediations, but Christ, through the very fact of His incarnation, became Himself the mediation, which we can effect *in Him*, which is to say, in loving Him. The five distinctions are:
>
> 1. Between the uncreated and the created;
>
> 2. Among created things, between the intelligible and the sensible;[25]
>
> 3. Among sensible things, between heaven and earth;
>
> 4. On Earth, between paradise and the inhabited world (the *oikoumene*);
>
> 5. In humanity, between man and woman, or the masculine and the feminine.[26]

"Humanity's role in sanctifying the world." What a high calling! How often in our self-examinations and confessions do we turn our thoughts in directions such as this? Our time on earth is *not* merely about feeding our hungers (though we must of course eat to live), nor balancing our personal conflicts or our budgets, nor healing our afflictions and hurt feelings (though it makes good sense to do those things as best we can), nor about raising healthy children (though if we are married we are called to do so to the extent we can), nor fulfilling our personal potential (though the gifts God gave us should surely be gratefully honored and put to their best use), nor having a good time (though we are indeed called to Rejoice!), nor saving enough for the pleasurable retirement we feel we've earned, surviving as long as possible, and, at the very best, dying repentant and confessed, not too painfully, and not alone; nor even successfully renouncing all that we understand to be sin and learning to get along with others in a peaceful and loving way, though that's closer.

Rather, it is about enacting another sort of peace, God's Peace: *in and through Christ*, the second Person of the Holy Trinity—the Tri-Personal God, Father, Son, and Holy Spirit, one in essence and undivided. It is about actively affirming, blessing (a point much stressed by Fr. Schmemann), and sanctifying the *whole* of His creation through our grateful love for Him, its Maker and Poet. This enacting must certainly begin with ourself, by tending our own garden with great care. But unless we wish to live a life that is really a dying within our own self-willed, loveless, and isolated garden, our enacting must—and *will* if we direct all our hungering toward God—extend beyond ourself by overcoming all the fallen but powerful inclinations within ourselves that lead us to affirm and protect *only* our own, or our own *against* all others, even against God. Most important of all—we must learn to remember that our little garden is indeed a gift of God and therefore a way—*the* Way—given us to enter into a communion with Him in whom all humanity, indeed all creation, is united. For we are all "called to share consciously in the life and glory of God," who created all and loves all.[27] But we are also entirely free to ignore this call and embrace death instead.

St. Maximus explains it this way:

> Now man has been set over all things as a kind of [workshop, *ergasterion*[28]] holding everything together, and has been appropriately placed in creation as a natural mediator in his own person between all the things which are at opposite extremes through any kind of division. Thus man possesses by virtue of his nature full power to bring about union through the mediation [he is able to effect between all the extremes[29]], since in the different aspects of his own nature he is himself related to all

these extremes. In this way it is his vocation to make manifest in his own person the great mystery of the divine purpose in bringing into existence things divided—to show how the divided extremes in created beings may be reconciled in harmony, the near with the far, the lower with the higher, so that through gradual ascent all are eventually brought into union with God.[30]

St. Maximus goes on to show how man is meant to accomplish his vocation on each of the five levels named, thus "bringing into unity in his own person those things which by nature are far distant from each other," "until the whole of him then coinheres wholly in the whole of God, and he becomes everything that God is except for identity of essence."[31]

But man chose not to take this way. Instead,

> . . . he abused the natural power given to him for the union of what was divided, using it instead to create divisions, and was thus pitiably in danger almost of lapsing into non-being. For this reason new forms of nature were devised, and, in a paradoxical way beyond nature, that which is utterly immovable by nature moved without moving. . . . God, that is to say, became man, in order to save man who was perishing: uniting in Himself the natural divisions throughout the whole nature of the universe, and *revealing the totality of the inward essences which are expressed in all particular things, and through which the union of what has been divided naturally takes place,* He fulfilled the great will of God the Father by recapitulating all things in Himself, in whom they had also been created [italics mine].[32]

PROTOPRESBYTER ALEXANDER SCHMEMANN

Fr. Alexander Schmemann, in *For the Life of the World,* may be thought of as taking up the tale at this point, revealing the new light in which resurrected humanity was now, in and through Christ, the God-man, able to live and act:

> The first, the basic definition of man is that he is the *priest.* He stands in the center of the world and unifies it in his act of blessing God, of both receiving the world from God and offering it to God—and by filling the world with this eucharist, he transforms his life, the one that he receives from the world, into life in God, into communion with him. The world was created as the "matter," the material, of one all-embracing eucharist, and man was created as the priest of this cosmic sacrament. (22)

It is Fr. Alexander's clear understanding of exactly what the first sin actually was—its unmaking of our true eucharistic calling and priesthood in that calling—that most excites me about his approach and illumines for me much of what Don means by the antinomic process and its power to lead us to what St. Maximus called our God-given "role in sanctifying the world." Everything was given to our first parents, everything God created was blessed for their use and consumption—except for the fruit of that one tree, which, unlike every other fruit of the Garden, was offered not as a gift to man for his own consumption but for Life, on behalf of all and for all. It was to serve as a reminder of our human mission to mediate all of God's antinomies, in each of which we are all antinomically involved: That is, we are *created* but with a noetic opening to the *uncreated*; *sensible* but having the capacity to reach toward and perceive the *intelligible* insensibly (see glossary); *earthly* but destined for *heaven*; born in *paradise* but self-exiled to the *oikumene*, the "world"; and *human*: both male and female (for, many persons, we share one nature, humanity). Spanning them all, mediating them all, even challenged by them all, we are to love God *as ourself* (not as we love ourself but *as being* ourself), as being *who we are*. And, in so doing, we are to unite all in His love. When God *is* ourself, by our own will, that's when we become truly persons. But when we deny His will and choose ourself and our own hungers over and against Him, we ongoingly break both ourself and His entire creation, failing of our priestly calling.

I want to tell you here about my own first exposure to the possibility of redirecting hunger to where it belongs. Don had recently returned from a trip to Russia led by Matushka Mary (Schmemann) Tkachuk to honor the first thousand years of Orthodoxy in Russia.[33] On August 23, 1988, the group visited the incorrupt relics of fourteenth-century St. Sergius of Radonezh and Don was deeply moved by the experience—as was I by his telling of it. I tried to tell my mother about it and she responded by making comments about the marvels of waxwork. An old and deep-rooted anger began rising in me, so great that I excused myself, left the room, and could do nothing but pray tearfully before my icons. The result of my prayer was a sudden and clear understanding that the love and affirmation I was wanting from my mother were much greater than anything she could give. I had it all backwards. That love I hungered for, I saw, comes from God, and it fills us so that we may give it to others. To my surprise, my heart felt suddenly full, the anger disappeared, and I found I could easily do as I felt myself to have been instructed. For the next and final decade of my mother's life, I visited her regularly, once or twice a week, even hitchhiked the two hours when the car wasn't available, and we enjoyed one another thoroughly. At the end of my mother's life I was with her, playing Brahms's

Requiem on her CD player, when she sat up suddenly, her mouth and eyes open wide in astonishment, then raised her arms toward the upper corner of the room as if for a welcome embrace, and quietly passed on. Our hungers belong to God and are for Him alone.

Fr. Schmemann writes about the tree from which Eve took for herself the forbidden fruit, the tree given us so that we might be truly like Him, wholly free:

> Not given, not blessed by God, it was food whose eating was condemned to be communion with itself alone, and not with God. It is the image of the world loved for itself, and eating it is the image of life understood as an end in itself. . . .
>
> To love is not easy, and mankind has chosen not to return God's love. Man has loved the world, but as an end in itself and not as transparent to God. He has done it so consistently that it has become something that is "in the air." It seems natural not to live a life of thanksgiving for God's gift of a world. It seems natural not to be eucharistic.
>
> The world is a fallen world because it has fallen away from the awareness that God is all in all. The accumulation of this disregard for God is the original sin that blights the world.[34]

It will be clear, however, especially when we read Don's reflections on St. Isaac in the book's final part, that we still have access to clear pathways for remaking that original choice moment by moment in our lives. And I suggest that the antinomies we encounter in Scripture and most strongly in Psalms, in the patterns of Orthodox life and liturgy, in poems, even in the rifts and breakages of our families—and surely everywhere—are a way that God sings His rhythms to us to teach us to dance *with Him*. He sings them to inspire us to seek the unifying center where we will always find Him and from which we may, in Him, be restored to our true human vocation to make manifest in our own person "the great mystery of the divine purpose in bringing into existence things divided."[35]

When Fr. Alexander speaks of living eucharistically—that is, blessing and giving thanks to God, over and over, for being and providing our true food—I think we are to understand that, indeed, everything *is* food, all of it, even now in our fallen state—with its conflicts and sadness, its failures and enmities—if we can but bring ourselves to thank God for our life and love our way through it. And I suggest that, even though Don did not always use this language for it, this is what he means throughout the book when he writes of living antinomically—as he himself did: that is, by engaging the oppositions and impossibilities and disappointments and even the disasters the world presents us with, and bringing them into the "workshop" (*ergasterion*) of our heart where Christ lives (as we witnessed St. Xenia doing in the book's preface).

Just so, may one become a "natural mediator in his own person between all the things which are at opposite extremes through any kind of division." And just so, does our communion with God's creation become a Holy Communion. For, as we receive it as food, in Christ, who has trampled down death by His own death for our sake, and as we offer in return our love and thanksgiving to Him who gave it, we too overcome death in our daily living, and the world becomes food again. In this way we ourselves become living, blessed food that genuinely nourishes others, as St. Xenia, through her willing foolishness and self-deprivation, nourished so many; and as so many other saints have done.

PART ONE

Listening for My Life

I was alone in my life,
fully and strongly alone
in the light of this sudden extraordinary clarity,
listening and listening for my very life.

On Becoming a Person

A Personal Narrative

*". . . if I make my bed in hell, behold,
Thou art there."*

PSALM 139:8, KJV

Late May, 1994

WE'RE SITTING ON THE upholstered porch swing, Cutter Davis and I, both age eight.[36] I can still look down and see my 1948 sneakers, black canvas hightops with long dirty-white laces, broken and tied in two or three places. The summer day opens beautifully before us; it's midmorning, and we're reading comics. That is, I am reading aloud, one balloon, sometimes only one phrase, at a time—and Cutter is looking hard at the words I'm pointing to, then saying them aloud after I say them. Cutter can't read and I'm teaching him how.

I've no idea, now, how we arrived at this. There's a wisp of memory of my being surprised that he can't read, and my saying that it's *easy*, you just *do* it; and then we're on the porch swing. Morning after morning, all through that summer, Cutter and I would sit and practice, and, slowly, he became able to say the words simply when I pointed to them. A good two hours before lunch, we'd stop for the day, for the summertime intensities of play could be only briefly transfigured by the intensities of verbal comprehension.

No one had told us to do this. We discovered it because I wanted him to read the comics I loved and to enact them with me as our play. It was necessary to me that he know how to read; and I came to love the process of doing this, the vivid words, the long patience, the quiet sitting together in the intense summer mornings, our being so intimately together in something so other than ourselves. I loved the words arriving alive in us.

The following summer—July 4, 1949—he will get us three kids out of bed at one or two in the morning, after several hours of strangely growing violence, and herd us down the stairs. He will point to our mother standing up against the hallway wall, biting both her fists in the advanced stage of terror while blood flows from a cut in her temple.

"There's your mother," he'll tell us, slurring the words. "There's your mother."

My father has been drinking somewhere for hours; the car lurches to a sudden stop in the driveway; and instantly my twin brother, my big sister, my mother and I freeze as Rage slams shut the car door and walks fiercely up the porch steps. The front door crashes open and terror seizes all four of us. This is my father called Rage.

I cannot remember the next several hours. I'm sitting upstairs in the dark as my father's harsh yelling and the sound of things breaking punctuate long stretches of terrified silence. My brother and sister and mother are down there. After a very long—maybe half an hour long—stretch, a time so long that my terror eases considerably, I go down, too, avoiding the living room where I see my father sitting on the couch and staring out a now darkened window. In the kitchen, my mother stands at the stove where nothing is cooking, while in the dining room my sister and brother sit numb at an empty table looking down at the tablecloth. No one talks, no one moves, no one acknowledges I'm there.

I go to stand in the archway between the dining room and living room. My father slowly turns his head from the dark window to me. His Irish blue eyes are sad, clear, and exhausted. He pats the couch next to him, an invitation to sit. I walk right through my terror and straight across the room, picking up a magazine—the *Saturday Evening Post*—as I sit down on the couch next to him. I open the magazine on my left leg and his right, and slowly I turn the bright pages, saying, "Look at this, Dad, look at that," pointing to one picture, then another and another.

His warm voice sounds in my ear. "You're the only one not afraid of me." And it's almost a soft song.

In the summer of 1957, my mother and sister and brother and I moved to Florida while my father stayed in New Jersey. He stayed in the north and moved us to Florida, I would learn two years later, so he could rent a large house in Montclair, New Jersey, for himself and his then 21-year-old mistress, Joan. What he told my mother was—he'd be selling on the whole east coast, including in the south a great deal of the time, and living costs were considerably lower in the north Florida town of Gainesville than in Denville, New Jersey, and besides, the University of Florida was right in town and Nora, David, and I could attend college very cheaply as Florida residents. A plausible enough lie at the time; he was to be in Florida at best maybe two weekends a month, usually only one.

Interestingly, he didn't simply abandon us. In the grip of fierce desire, he nevertheless kept paying our rent and buying our groceries. After a few months, my mother took a job in the admissions office at the university, less for the very modest income and more for something interesting to do: the students to talk with, their families to help. They all loved her and she them. In two years, the income would become essential for survival; and she kept the job for the next twenty years.

The income became essential this way: The summer after my freshman year I was nineteen and my father had me work in his company in New Jersey. So in June 1959 I flew north to his Montclair home and there I first learned of Joan. He told me about her on the way in from the Newark airport.

She was nervous at meeting me, breathtakingly beautiful, streetwise, and strong: and going on eight months pregnant. During the ride in, he had said, "She didn't want an abortion." I was rocked, so stunned that I became silent, shut down, and yet courteous. Joan and I shook hands in the kitchen, a room larger than our living room and kitchen together in Gainesville, a blue and white room looking out on a large lawn and garden: a lovely late June afternoon.

"Welcome, Donald," she said. Her voice was rich, warm, and clear with no least hint of bravado or bluff: and with the tiniest touch of clearest beseeching, Forgive me, forgive me.

I looked into her deep brown eyes and I nodded. It was all I could manage.

My father's drinking was very bad all that summer. (In Florida, he still kept up the fiction of the sobriety begun in 1949 but actually ending in 1956.) Joan turned to me for solace—where else could she turn?—and she wept in my arms countless times, while I lightly stroked her long black hair and said what meaningless kindnesses I could. The night her and my father's baby was born, I drove her to the hospital. (Years later my mother would tell me that the neighbors drove her to the hospital on the night my brother and I were born.) When I got back from the hospital, my father was back—passed out on the living room couch. I got him up and into bed, always a delicate job, for if you woke him too much too quickly, he'd become violent.

In the morning, he was, as always, shakily contrite. "Did you get Joan there in time?" His words were neutral enough but his tone was unmistakably a plea. "Yeah, plenty of time," I said, my voice as free and light as I could make it of any condemnation. And somehow I didn't even feel much except some irritation last night at having to be up at three a.m.

"Well, I guess I'll go over," he said, relieved. He dropped me at the company on his way to the hospital.

The baby was beautiful, a boy. "What'll his name be?" Joan asked me when I visited that evening, so delighted and radiant, "George thinks Jeffrey's a nice name." I looked at the baby and fell in love. A day or so later, Joan and the baby were home, and I had his name all ready to tell her: Geoffrey. All summer I'd been reading—devouring, really—Louis Untermeyer's paperback anthology, *A Concise Treasury of Great Poems*. Chaucer was the beginning of English poetry and his first name was spelled *Geoffrey*, and the baby should have a name of great beginnings. Joan was delighted and my father was pleased I'd thought of it.

In another week I became Geoffrey's morning babysitter while Joan and my father went to the office. (Many mornings, my father would be sleeping it off upstairs.) I loved the baby, especially after his morning nap when, on awakening, he'd be beaming to see me. At noon, Joan would come home and I'd go to work at the company, loading and unloading trucks of siding, occasionally helping Frank, the warehouse man, deliver a shipment—and once we drove to Boston and back, nonstop for twenty hours. Always with me was Untermeyer's anthology.

The poems were, of course, an escape. The nearly incomprehensible sonorities of Milton—immense sounding waves of self-assured

significance—held and focused me on things far beyond the painfulness
of my life, on things whose vastness and stability and truth made what was
little, false and broken in my life lose its fierce grip on me. I no longer had
a family that made sense; but I had what Robinson Jeffers called in one
of my constant poems, read a dozen times every day that summer: "The
honey peace in old poems."[37]

In another sense, Milton's great poems plunged me directly into my
life precisely because they—like my life—made only vague and disastrous
sense to me. I would read many times that summer this passage from Chapter 1, Book 1 of *Paradise Lost*.

> . . . But his doom
> Reserv'd him to more wrath; for now the thought
> Both of lost happiness and lasting pain
> Torments him; round he throws his baleful eyes
> That witness'd huge affliction and dismay
> Mixt with obdurate pride and stedfast hate:[38]

I understood only a small fraction of what I read—that is, I got phrases
like "lost happiness and lasting pain" or "huge affliction and dismay"—but
nevertheless even the fraction gave some voice to my life and some shape to
my feelings. But I understood almost none of it: not the poems, not my life.
And so therefore I started to write poems; and they were about peace we
cannot understand. Like this one:[39]

STAY

Incredibly beautiful, cool lovely
breeze, warm sun's cry
out of thoughtful blue skies.
Sounds combine into
a lush euphony which voluminously
wells up to a gay,
young song of peace and
unreal gaiety and happiness pervades
into every pore of life.
Exit all strive!
Away all sorrows!
Maybe some tomorrow

you'll return to me.
But now I am awash
with a fabulous sea
of happiness; a light heart
resembling a child's
created out of pure, mild
sensuality;
a lushness of calm and wild
sensations combined
in scenes of radiant
creations.
This beauty is so rare;
so it shall depart.
But now I do not care;
I have created a light heart.
So I sink into my ocean
of beauty;
this balm, this lovely lotion
which soothes all
worries and cares and grief
and pain. . . .
I am trying, Lord, I am trying!
Have patience with me.
I must stop crying.
I am soaring on high
on beams of love I do not
understand,
Only a sea of love, a land
of beauty. . . .
But, God, this day!
this wondrous day!
Stay . . . stay . . . STAY!

Just before I went back to Florida, my father and I talked, he sober and therefore vaguely depressed, me inarticulately vague and therefore intense. I was starting my second year of college in a week at the University of Florida, and he had said all summer that I should major in business administration, that anything else risked economic collapse and personal failure. (His siding business was to last another two years.) But I'd begun to write poems (of a sort)—and to read great poems, or at least to read *at* them. And I wanted to understand something about it because I was deeply in love with it all.

"Dad, I . . . I want to study poetry in college," I began. My hands were clenched together, fingers tightly interlaced.

Some brief passion swept his tired face and was gone. Was it embarrassment?[40] He picked up his newspaper, opening it. "Well, son, if you want to, that's fine."

Thunderstruck, I saw that the conversation was over. *Is that it?* I wondered, getting up to leave. *Is that how things go, you just say it'll be this way, and then it is?* I headed for the door. His voice reached me in the archway between the living room and hallway.

"I'm very proud of you, son. And I don't understand you."

In a few days I was on the airplane heading back to Florida. I was never to see Geoffrey again.[41]

Some eighteen months earlier—in January 1957—I'd been in the US Army bootcamp at Fort Jackson in Columbia, South Carolina. I was seventeen years old. I'd joined the Army Reserves because I'd refused to apply for college. High school studies had been a disaster for me, one long catastrophe of incomprehensible books and humiliating tasks: books and tasks obliterated into unintelligibility by the inner and outer storms raging in my life. Now I was engaged in meeting demands that quenched my rages by a massive and violent indifference. The sustained fury of army bootcamp—its grueling physical exertion, its absolute submission to rigid code, its bitter conditions of thin squad tents in freezing weather, and wretched food hurriedly gobbled, its weapons and ceaseless yelling and doubletime marching night and day, exhausted, angry, cowed, yet murderously competent—all this was tonic to me, for it drove me out of my mind where I did not want to be, out of my rage and despair at a childhood where I had seen my mother gripped by terror as blood flowed on her face.

High school became for me a long series of fistfights, a few I would lose and many I would win. When I'd lose, I would curl up in a ball to protect face, stomach, and groin—until the victor's rage was slaked and he'd walk away. When I'd win, I'd rain down blows on my fallen opponent until his face would start bleeding: then I would stop.

My senior year in April—just after my seventeenth birthday—I had my final fistfight. My strategy in fighting had long been to let my opponent hit first, for I knew that the first punches were almost always misaimed through fear and so were usually mistakes, because they'd always leave the hitter wide open: and then I would strike, without mercy, savagely. This fight began (as always) over nothing, a misstep in basketball and a misspoken curse. In an instant, we were fighting—rather, he was throwing a barrage of punches while I was easily avoiding all of them, a now familiar pleasure of engagement arising in me. Then all at once he slipped and fell to his knees just beneath my cocked right fist, his face a mask of suddenly terrified beseeching. I reached down with my right hand and gently touched his face, my fingertips just brushing his cheek. And then I turned on my heel and walked straight home, ignoring the startled silence behind me. A week later I enlisted in the army.

Now, as bootcamp daily broke in strong waves all about me, I was lifted by their intensities right out of myself. The sergeants encouraged our inevitable fistfights, probably on the grounds that our blooding of one another deepened our will to violence, increasing our *taste* for it. Just as inevitably, my turn to fight came, which I of course welcomed—not knowing (how could I know when I so desperately wanted not to be in my mind?) that what had happened to me last April had happened at depth. I laced up the boxing gloves, surprised and then stunned to find all feeling in me ebbing entirely away; and I was all at once left high and dry—and uncannily *clearsighted*. For as I stepped into the ring made by thirty or so others and went toward my opponent, I could see—vividly, sharply—his genuine fear and simulated anger. He threw two, ten, twenty quick punches, a windmill with no tactical point; and I could no more bring myself even to threaten (let alone harm) him than I could lift up the squad tent he and I both lived in. I reached out and clumsily grabbed his wrists and pinned his arms to his sides. "No," I said to him. "We're not going to do this." Then, again, as in April, I turned on my heel and walked firmly away. The few weak jeers and catcalls did not really disperse the sudden depth of silence behind me.

The clearing of sight stayed and grew through the rest of bootcamp. Former buddies and barracks pals began giving me distance, but I didn't mind and welcomed the room. The waves were far less intense. Toward the end, my sergeant said to me, aside, "Sheehan, I thought you were going to soldier for me." "So did I," I replied truthfully. I had no idea what was happening to me.

In the final week, I was awakened at four-thirty a.m. by the CQ, dressed quickly in the cold and headed out to walk across camp to the motorpool. I had become a driver and I was to get a jeep to bring the company commander to our bivouac in the field. The dawn had now well arrived, and I started up the long hill that separated the camp and the motorpool. As I walked up the hill, an idea broke through my long intellectual blackout, as if carried on the very light itself of the newly arriving sun: all this agony I could end in a moment, by my own hand, with the pistol in the holster on my belt, a matter of the merest seconds. I didn't *have* to endure this; therefore I *could* endure it. Never before in my life had I had an *idea*, and this one shook me to my depths, like a dog shaking a bone.

I stopped, consciously deciding not to shiver in the cold February dawn air. I didn't *have* to do all this; and so I *could* do all of it. Suicide's *idea* gave me for the first time the *experience* of choosing my life, of choosing to be on this hill—and *not* dead—and to be walking where I was walking and to *know* that I and no one else was doing this. I was alone in my life, fully and strongly alone in the light of this sudden extraordinary clarity, listening and listening for my very life.

In college, I would read Sartre and Camus, misunderstanding everything through them. But first I had to name my baby brother.

Two months later, on April 2, 1958, I turned eighteen years old. I was now stationed at Fort Benjamin Harrison, located just outside Indianapolis, Indiana, attending the US Army Finance School and learning payroll procedures and financial accounting. In high school I had done especially poorly in everything mathematical—yet because I had entered active duty in the Army Reserves at Gainesville, Florida, I had thus joined a unit whose sole purpose was military finance and accounting. Therefore I had come to Finance School to become a bookkeeper and payroll clerk.

The first day of eight a.m. classes, when I opened the textbooks, my heart sank and my mind froze. The long lists of figures and tables of computation might as well have been Greek, so incomprehensible were they. As a result, I simply did not hear what the instructor was saying. Fortunately, someone else asked him to say it all over again: "Sir, I don't understand."

"How hard is it?" he said, slightly irritated and greatly bored—and massively hung-over, as if he'd quit drinking about three a.m. and had slept in his clothes until seven-thirty or so. "The Army is changing the payroll system," he repeated, "and by the time you finish in June, the new system'll be in place.

But the textbooks we have are for the old system, which is completely differ-ent, and we won't have any new textbooks until late June, after you all are out of here. So you're going to learn a system you'll never use."

He shook his head slightly, in wry resignation to the Army's idiocies. "If you want to know why they didn't get the textbooks out three months earlier, you can write a letter to your congressman or maybe President Eisen-hower, *they* might know." He snorted in bitter amusement, then winced at the effect on his headache.

"So I don't give a damn if you learn it or not," he concluded, "because it's not worth a goddamn." Such was our teacher's wisdom.

In the barracks, the outlook on our studies was surprisingly different. The platoon was made up of men three or four years older than I, most of whom were now in or already through college. In 1958, the Korean War draft was still operating, and young men in colleges were seeking job placements in the Army Reserves where actual combat was fairly unlikely. The prevailing barracks view therefore was: it may be crap, but it'll get you the job descrip-tion—the MOS—that'll save your ass. The barracks outlook seemed at that time the cannier wisdom, but our instructor's was probably truer.

I learned enough of it to pass, just barely. What I learned more deeply I was taught in the barracks by my college-educated pals: a love for books. To stave off massive boredom, they all read omnivorously, and they men-tioned titles and authors to me that I'd never heard of—James Joyce, for example, or *The Winter's Tale* and *A Midsummer Night's Dream*, or Wil-liam Whyte, *The Organization Man*, or Sartre or Camus. I was extremely confused by it all and often embarrassed by their constant dismay at me: "Oh, come on, Sheehan, you haven't read *Othello*?" But when we went out drinking in the Indianapolis bars I was about my father's business of alcohol and violence, and I gained something like their amused respect by becoming something like him.

Yet I never re-crossed the line back into actual violence, a line drawn, it seemed, quite permanently last February.

I didn't open the books they continued to give me, as if I couldn't risk failing to comprehend what I read. The Sunday afternoon of the week of my eighteenth birthday I found myself alone (I'd told no one, somehow not want-ing to emphasize the fact that I alone in the barracks was still a teenager). It was the first warm spring weather, and I wandered out and strolled aimlessly around the post, finding myself in about a half-hour at the door of the post library. I liked this being alone; it was feeling very like walking the hill last February in the South Carolina dawn—only very peaceful. I looked at my hand as it reached for the knob and turned it and pushed open the door: and this image of my hand at the door passed straight into my heart.

Inside, the room was empty except for the woman sitting at the desk, who gave me a pleasant nod and went back to her book. The room was washed in a warm spring light. I wandered vaguely toward the shelves on the left, away from the desk, suddenly very unsure, and I stopped and turned to the reading table where a cream-colored cover lay, *One Hundred Poems from the Japanese*, by Kenneth Rexroth. Still standing, I opened the book to midpoint and read:

> I have always known
> That at last I would
> Take this road, but yesterday
> I did not know that it would be today.
>
> —Narihira (ninth century)[42]

I turned the page and read on. I sat down into a stillness and depth I never knew existed, every word carrying the clearest grace of comprehension. I turned the page again. I was overwhelmed. What I did not understand in them were the very things not meant to be overmastered by understanding but things to be obeyed and loved and treasured. The "I" of the poems rose up out of them and claimed me as if I had always been possessed by this lyric clarity and grace of sight, as if my life had always possessed this quiet haven. I turned to the first poem and began slowly to read them straight through, differently yet deeply held by each one.

I was startled by a touch on my shoulder. The woman from the desk spoke. "I'm sorry, we're closing." I looked over at the windows and the sun was way down and the sky was fast darkening. "Do you want to check this book out?" she asked. I stood up, surfacing from depths. "No," I said, "no, I need to get back." She smiled.

"What time is it?" I asked, disoriented.

"It's eight o'clock," she answered. "You've been reading that book since twelve-thirty."

I looked down at the book on the table, and I knew at once that it should stay here and not come with me. Where would I put it?

I looked back at her. "It's a good book," I said, and then I headed out.

As I reached the door and turned the knob, she spoke once more. "We're open every day from noon to eight. Come back again." I didn't go back.

If I make my bed in hell, behold, Thou art there.

At the end of June, 1958, I was released from active duty in Indiana and I headed back home to Florida, still in uniform as I arrived in Atlanta to meet my father.

Last January seemed years ago now; and as the night plane from Chicago touched down in Atlanta, I wondered (but not at all consciously) whether my father would recognize me. As we taxied to the terminal, an image floated a moment in my mind: the cold Carolina hill I'd walked and the first Japanese poem I'd read—an image more felt than seen—and then it was gone. The cabin lights switched off at the terminal, and as I rose I caught a glimpse of my face in the darkened window, thinner, stiller, the fire and bluster gone: a face now more actually *composed*. I scarcely recognized it.

But my father at the gate had no trouble recognizing me. And as I embraced him, I got a bad jolt: he'd been drinking. I was nine in 1949 when he'd gotten us kids up at two a.m. to see our mother bloody from his fists, and for these past nine years I'd wholly believed in his complete sobriety. As we ended our long embrace and stepped back, I had to steady him—and instantly I was overwhelmed by his intense vulnerability: and I was pierced with love for him.

I drove from the airport at his insistence (impressed by his new Ford Thunderbird), while he closed his eyes and I followed signs. When we entered the hotel dining room in downtown Atlanta at around ten p.m. and were shown a quiet table by the wall, my father was joking and graceful and urbane and savvy, a master of the social circumstance. The *maitre d'* greeted him—and then me, after my father's introduction—with an elaborate and canny suavity, calling me (in an accent I didn't recognize) "the young captain," and I was entirely out of my depths.

We sat at a table covered with a white damask cloth and softly burnished silver, having drinks—me nursing a Scotch and soda (a taste so recent it was not yet acquired), my father taking practiced sips of straight Courvoisier brandy. He looked across at me.

"You're surprised I'm drinking, aren't you?"

The words barely began to indicate my state of mind and feeling, which was more like grief. But I simply nodded, trying not to cry. The Japanese poems and the walk uphill were now vanished utterly from my heart and mind.

"Well, let me tell you something," He picked an invisible crumb from the table, searching for words, and went on. "About two years ago, Clif and I—Clif Johns, you remember him, don't you? He came to the house in

Denville a hundred times, he and Annie, his wife, you remember them?"
I nodded.

"Well, Clif saved my life. Back in forty-nine, when your mother and
I split up, I really hit the skids, and I wound up in a Boston flophouse after
about a ten-day drunk, and that's where Clif found me, God love him, and
he took me to his house down in Jersey, and that's where I dried out. He and
Annie—a terrific-looking broad—gave me orange juice and chocolate candy
until I could hold food down, and I could walk again without falling on my
ass, and then Dixie took me over to an AA meeting—she was a lush who'd
gone on the wagon and had a life again, you know what I mean?"

I nodded, a bit quieted now by the seeming honesty in my father's eyes
and voice.

"I never knew why Clif and Annie did this. I'd ask him sometimes,
and he'd just say, 'You're a good guy, Georgie, you'd do it for me.'" My
father shook his head in disbelief at love. "You know, Clif spent six days
tracking me from Kingston to Boston, about four days behind me, and
stopping at joints he figured I'd hit." He lifted his eyes to mine. "He was
one helluva good guy."

The waiter appeared, asking were we ready to order. My father waved
him away—graceful but clear—not wanting to break his remembrance.

"Anyway, Clif saved my life, and after that we worked together, doing
deals for this joint or that joint, and we did pretty good, him and me, good
enough for Clif and Annie to buy a house near Boston and for me to get all
of us out of Kingston and up to Sherborn, near Clif, and we were a *family*
again, weren't we? I mean, a real *family*, you know?"

"I really loved Sherborn," I said.

"Yeah, me, too. But then Clif and me had a sweet, sweet deal open
up for us in Jersey, a chance to set up our own operation—and not have to
beg some asshole for shit leads that never work; *a real chance.* So we did
it, you know? Because if you don't move fast when the track's open, the
pack'll trample you right the ** down in the dust, you know what I mean?"
He took a big swallow of brandy, breathing air for a chaser, and glared at
me for an answer.

"I know what you mean."

"So we did it. And it worked, and I mean *worked*, and I never took
a drop of booze, not a single drop, for six years. I worked like hell, so did
Morris, and the business kept growing to beat the band, and we kept getting bigger, and finally we had a chance to tap the Atlanta market—and I
mean tap it *good*, we could *smell* the big money just around the corner, we
could *taste* it."

The waiter hovered again at the table. My father turned his head. "No, I'll call you."

"Very good, sir." He turned back to me.

"Then two years ago, a little more, Clif and I were sitting here, right at this goddamn table, having dinner and talking about the deal we were closing the next day—a whole string of siding joints in the city—and Clif was sipping wine and suddenly he stopped talking, and his eyes got glassy, and he said, 'George, *Christ!*' and he dropped the wineglass and clutched his chest and leaned sideways against the wall there by your arm, and he was dead. Just like that, *bam*, gone, a massive heart attack. An hour later, I had to call Annie up in Wayland (I'd told the cops I'd do it, not them), and I sat by the phone in the lobby for almost an hour, and then I went into the bar and ordered a double-brandy and drank it down in two shots like it was ** water, and then I called Annie. I couldn't swallow Clif being dead, so I figured I'd swallow brandy and make myself dead—at least so it'd not hurt so ** much."

He shook his head slowly in an ocean of grief. Then he looked at me once more. "He saved my ** life, but I couldn't do a goddamn thing for him. So I started drinking again. Do you understand any of this?"

There were tears in his eyes and in mine now. "Yes, I understand," I said.

Two hours later I was lying in my hotel room bed when the prostitute my father had hired for me knocked on my door. As I let her in, she gave me a surprised look and then a long, hard kiss. We smoothly but quickly took off all our clothes, I helping her with her clasps in the back. As we lay down on the bed, she said, as if this were now the first order of business:

"Who's that old guy who hired me? Why are you two together?"

"He's my father," I said.

"Come on, don't bullshit me," she said, her twenty-year-old streetwise voice suddenly alarmed—even panicked—at some dimly understood violation of family bonds.

"Nah, he's just a guy in the business trying to show me the ropes," I said. "He likes me."

"Well," she said, first relieved and then moved, "that's really sweet, I mean really, really sweet." Her voice was all at once a lyric from some long-forgotten dream of disinterested love, a lyric something like my Japanese poems, neither a child's voice nor a woman's, but profoundly a person's. She held my face in her hands. "You're kinda sweet, too," she said. And beneath the heavy mascara and painted brows, I could see her eyes shining and shining.

If I make my bed in hell, behold, Thou art there.

When we kids were little, our father would delight and terrify us whenever he sneezed or coughed. For he'd roar and stagger about, clutching his chest as he sank into a chair, ending with an extravagant curse—an altogether strong performance for us. "Don't do that, Daddy," we'd say, not meaning it at all. And he'd shudder dramatically, saying he was not long for this world, not long at all. It was wonderful.

In early September 1958, as he drove me to the Newark airport in his white Thunderbird, my father said, "I want you to take care of Geoffrey and stay in touch with him even if Joan and I break up—I want you to be his brother."

I looked out the window at the crumbling Newark neighborhood, the boarded up windows and the dirty streets. "Okay," I said, not having the least idea how I could even begin to do that. And I couldn't, I couldn't, to my great grief.

In mid-September 1958, I found in the first weeks of college that I did not know how to write. I saw (dimly) how single words became brief phrases— for the Japanese poems from last April shone still in my mind (though I'd not read them since that Sunday of my eighteenth birthday)—but I had no idea how phrases were made into sentences, or how sentences became paragraphs. And now I was expected to write whole essays on complicated books. A kind of frozen panic gripped me all term; and only the delicate kindness of a faceless instructor in composition (faceless because I was ashamed to look at him all semester) kept the panic from unfreezing into flight. Kindly, gently, he would show me the broken or missed connections, the great gaps in articulation, the illogic or a-logic of my meager writing: and every so often he'd delight over a phrase or two and I would be cheered for a few days. But he could not give me the great principles of coherence, the archetypes of wholeness and intellectual strength without which no one can write. He could not give me personhood.

But at the start of second semester in late January a new teacher entered my life: Gary Scrimgeour. Tall and slender, long blond hair waving onto a high forehead, old clothes indifferently worn, thick glasses nevertheless showing alert brown eyes: and a radiant smile as he greeted us that first morning of Freshman Humanities in an English accent I'd heard only in movies. He seemed genuinely delighted to be there with us, and I was instantly awakened from my four months of glum panic. He stopped a moment at my name, looking over the top of his class list and smiling at me.

"I know your mother," he said. And then I remembered my mother telling me last week about a new instructor she'd met from Australia who was beginning this term, and how he'd been in despair at finding a place to live, and how my mother had heard just that morning about an apartment in our building complex suddenly free, and how he'd been overjoyed and went over immediately to rent it.

"And I know where you're living," I said. He beamed.

I had never had a teacher like him. He threw himself passionately into both his and our explanations of Plato, Shakespeare, Goethe, Bach, Renaissance and Impressionist art: as if his very life—and ours—depended on our comprehending with depth and accuracy of feeling and idea the very fullness of Western philosophy, literature, music and art. He was at once for us a *living* voice, one that had been created to love us by the texts he had learned to love and one that therefore bestowed creativity on those who through him learned to love the texts in return. He often read aloud, and we listened and were moved, for it seemed as if Shakespeare and Goethe were loving us. I was astonished, awakened, overwhelmed—as if my Japanese poems had been swept up into this massive rush to ecstatic comprehensiveness that was our humanities course: a rush I felt not as speed but as fullness.

Then, in the third week, I had to write a paper and I plunged into the depths of depression. I skipped Monday and Wednesday classes so as to sit in the library, blank pages before me in the blankness of my wretched mind. And that's where Professor Scrimgeour found me late Thursday afternoon, and the paper was due the next morning. He sat down next to me at the reading table; we were alone. "Where have you been?" he asked in a library quietness and a genuine concern.

"Trying to write," I said softly, "and I can't," sliding over to him the single page with its illegible scrawl. I was profoundly ashamed and trying not to cry.

He read the page. Then, with a judicious carefulness I welcomed with all my heart, he softly began, "Well, you're certainly bright enough"—and the words were great balm to me, for my page had shown me only my own depthless ignorance—"and you're trying to say something important about *Faust*—in fact, something very important." Dim light began to break through my three-day depression.

"You know," he went on, "if you want to learn how to write, it's really quite simple. Whenever you read something—anything—this, say," and he slid towards me my well-worn Untermeyer anthology of poems, "and you come onto something that's *really true*, stop right there and look at how that true sentence is formed: and then write one *just like it*, only saying something different, something of your own." He had his finger on a randomly opened page, and I leaned toward him to read Untermeyer on Keats: "Keats's short life was a flash of powerful ecstasy, and the intensity of his nature is everywhere in his poetry. The verse is vivid and definite, lavish with a feeling of textures, with minute felicities of touch and taste, 'filling every sense with spiritual sweets.'" "Don't you see?" he continued. "The 'flash of painful ecstasy' gets repeated in the 'intensity of his nature'—you see the two 'of's' binding together the two phrases? Then the 'with' phrases are all alike, and at the end the 'touch and taste' alliterate, I mean begin with the same sound—and then he works in a quote from I guess Keats that also alliterates, a nice touch."

He stood up and I looked at him. "I've got to go," he said. "I'll see you in class tomorrow?" I nodded. He turned to go and then turned back. "Oh, and do the paper over the weekend and bring it in Monday." He smiled once more. "It'll go well."

I watched him walk away from me and then I turned back to Untermeyer's sentences. My paper would be only slightly less wretched than the ones I'd written last term. But a key to the principles of intellectual wholeness had been put into my hands: and I knew, now, how to work the key. The whole of the art lay in the act of listening. . . .

. . . Listening. I'm sitting in the backseat of my best friend Neil's 1952 convertible, it's the summer of 1956, and I'm sixteen and Rosie next to me is sixteen, and she's wearing tight bluejeans and a bright yellow sweater that clings to her high, shapely breasts, and her full lips are vivid with the reddest lipstick I've ever seen, and her short blond hair is brushed back into a DA,[43] and it's nearly ten o'clock now on this warm late-July evening as Neil swings his low, throaty Ford onto a lonely back road several miles out from Boonton, New Jersey, and we roll to a stop at the edge of the dark woods.

I cannot now remember the name or face of Rosie's girlfriend sitting up front with Neil, for all my intensities are held in Rosie: who now turns to me as I put my arm around her shoulders, leaning her lovely mouth up into my kiss, and my head begins to swim as oceans of desire surge up in me and sexual ecstasy engulfs me. My hands roam from her shoulders to her bluejeans to her bright yellow sweater as I now unfasten her bra in back and move myself over her.

She suddenly straightens up and leans sharply away, clasping my hands in hers. The car radio is playing, I'm all at once aware.

"Listen," she whispers strongly. "Listen to this song!"

Through the haze and heaviness of my lust I begin to hear—what? I cannot now remember; but probably Elvis Presley, who'd burst into all our teenage worlds that spring and summer.

I shake my head to clear it. "What's so great about that?" I ask, not wanting to leave the ecstasies, wanting (oh, so much) to go on plunging into the ocean surging still in me but now just beginning to ebb.

"What's so great?" she asks in genuine disbelief. She reaches out to me to press her hands to my cheeks: and they're cool to my hot face. "Just this: what we're feeling now is *there*, it's *there*, it's *in the song*—but better and harder and stronger than we are. Please listen, can't you listen, please?"

I listen, at least I try, and after a bit I glance over at Rosie, and in the faint light from the car radio—and the immense summer moon—I see her in profile, her lips slightly apart as she concentrates on the music, listening as if her very life depended on it: and it does. And all at once I feel a wave of affection for her, a wave from another ocean than ecstasy, a wave that seems to clear the very air I'm breathing, and so I take a deep breath.

"Neil, let's go," I say aloud, and he and Rosie's girlfriend finish a long, long kiss, and she softly leans back, her arms outstretched on seatback and car door as Neil turns the key and the rumbling Ford instantly catches.

On the way back to Boonton, I watch Rosie, and she smiles at me once, and this absurd wave of affection keeps on running deeper in me. Neil and I had picked them up an hour ago, and we leave them at the same corner we'd met.

I turn off the radio as we drive back home. I want to listen to the sound of the night air rushing by.

A small group of us in the humanities course became Gary Scrimgeour's disciples, a relationship he treated (I now see) with good humor and great tact. He neither mocked nor flattered us.

Almost a Soft Song

(FOR DON SHEEHAN)

Cold Carolina hill that I walked
when I got my first idea: I could live,
I could choose to.
First Japanese poem
Turned the doorknob of lyricism.

I caught my face in the window,
passion gone, composed.
I hardly recognized it.

I met my father again:
he was drinking.
I steadied him.
He was so vulnerable;
I was pierced with love for him.

I have always been aware
that one day I would
Take this narrow path,
but did not know yesterday
that today would be the day.

True affection
—a wave from an ocean
different from ecstatic hungers.

—*Matthew Brown*

2

Poems

"Whereby Light and Pain
Round into Grace"

small labors
steadily undertaken

in the humility of failure
and in
the fullness of confession

. . . wherein the activity of
light

moves with
the motion of pain
that, vivid as
rhyme,

sharp as lyric,
etches its
intricate way into words.[44]

A Comedy

(A POEM)

FOR DAVID KELLER

PROLOGUE

"La traccia vostra è fuor di strada."
I crabwalk sideways, backwards,
Never straight to the line. Careful,
I tell myself, *your track*
Is off the road.

I come back
When the trees begin
Seething new leaves
And black mud is running
In the gutter: Spring!

Ten year old boys shriek
Obscenities in the street
And end their vicious games
In fights—a raw wound
Streams hot blood red.

No questions? Fine, his letter said,
For two men in white cashmere sweaters
Are carrying a smashed harmonium
(I think) by my table as I sit
Here in Paris and conjugate verbs.

I loll on my couch and learn
To speak, too, my brother!
But to
What purpose, what hope
We cannot see or say.

"Hope," I said, "is the certain expectation
Of future glory, it springs forth from
Divine grace and precedent merit."

I go out again, O,
The temperature is thirty degrees,
It's the tenth of May and
Everything blooms and blooms! Poetry
Is a form of suicide, O.

Plunk, plunk, here we are again. Back.
A boy watches his mother's head
Gush blood, his father mad
Again, the rug out on the lawn, sis-
Ter and brother crying . . .

"But why are you going back to such misery?
Why don't you climb the delightful mountain
Which is the beginning and cause of all joy?"

Who is this young boy?
And What does he augur?
Whose is the head
(heh, heh)
We must set in order?

I.

The hour you walked with the father
Into his mad wishes
Is the same hour, though later,
The mother buckled
And broke. Mangled house!

You understand, my son?
(And from out of the mud a face

Appeared asking *Who are you?*
And I knew the face
And cursed it.)

The angel wipes fog from his face,
Stepping off leagues!
We wait, very afraid . . .

"The pilgrim in his terror begins to doubt whether Reason is a
safe guide. Without venturing a direct question, he tries to as-
certain whether his companion has full knowledge of the road
they are to travel. The sage assures him that he has probed every
depth of sin—that he has gone to the very bottom of Hell."

Just the two of us here, heh,
And the way seems dark?
I'll take good care of you,
Son, I know the way.

See that bitch in the corner,
Son, the gray haired one?
She runs the ass in this town,
Has since she was twenty one.

And the blond over there,
The one in green,
That's her new chick.
Makes you cream.

And O that redhead's hands
Are like fire!
Remember the time you and me
Drove to—where was it? . . .

I remember the way—
A strange simplicity.

II.

"When the mind is like a hall in which thought is like a voice
speaking, the voice is always that of someone else."

Always this silence in which
No voice familiarly speaks
Right words of right origins
Is like the midnight pall

Of a day of ceaseless shouting
Of phrases without meaning
Of words made meaningless
By the need to see, to hear,

To think one true thing truly—

Tell me, father, does what drove you,
And drives you now in your last mad days,
Drive me? Do the hands
That once tore a stuffed chair to shreds
While a child watched a rage
He would finally come to feel
Only in the need
To see and hear and think—
Do these hands drive mine?
And does the mind flooded
With brandy, brandy, brandy
Until the body breaks down
In a fierce exhaustion of the nerves,
Like wire snapped from a bundle of sticks—
Do I think with this mind?

O, sweet father, can we survive?
Tell me, if you know.

III.

"We now learn that the damned, while aware of the past and indistinctly cognizant of the future, have no knowledge of present events on earth. Just how much the 'present' embraces we are not told."

It's the summer of 'forty-nine
And Bacchus is enthroned.
Out of school, I'm home
For each of my parents' crimes.

"George," she says, "I'm scared
You're going to hurt the kids."
"Honey," he says, "whatever I did
Won't happen again." The Irish smile flares.

The same old song for fourteen years,
The helpless, undying lies.
Dinnertime, I watch my mother's eyes
Watch the clock. The same old tears.

IV.

"The suicide uses his freedom of bodily movement only to deprive himself of it, robbing himself, by his own act, of that which corporeally distinguishes him from a plant. Such a sinner, then, his wicked deed externalized, may aptly be figured as a tree or bush."

Plunk, plunk. The blues of 'thirty-five.
The trick was not to stay alive
But to want to, to feel
As though fear was not the real
Air one breathed (Roosevelt—Papà!)
But the illusory made visible, the
Nightmare moving through confusion into day,
Made bright as day and as ghastly.

It would not work, the pitiless sun kept shining
And the air was real and fear kept prying
Open skulls by the score. O, *surrealiste,*
Your collage is a ghostly theorem, *manqué, pauvriste,*
To the suicide's smallest act, sheer
Filigree to his intricate, disastrous fear
That the sun shines and will, the air
Is real and will be, fear is where
And what one breathes and will breathe,
Hears moving through the night and sees
Seething in the leaves. Trees—!

V.

I dream my loves
And curse my blood,
Time isn't hope or despair.
But O sweet father, we're not
Getting any younger or better.

"Undoubtedly," my brother writes,
"Greatness is within my grasp.
I wonder what kind?"
Plunge on, old raft, plunge on!
A barrel of laughs!

And then I said, "Sweet father,
Where are we going?" And, "My son,"
He said, "The way is dark

And few have had the strength,
For the slightest lapse is death
And the paths of light are lost;

Once before I tried this trip
Down through the broken walls,

Our sister's sweet voice in my ears,

Her song wound with shimmering light":

O infinite knowing   know
Only we survive   our shocks
Saying we know   we know not
What it is we   rush to
Down on the endless plains
Where nothing will move   or has
But the sense of what we must know
To survive the sense of where we have gone
Psyche I was born I   call and call
I am your thousand gestures and voices
You cannot sense   as distinct
You can only seek me hoping
I'm somewhere within and on
The way you are going and must
If you want to survive what you know
What you think
You know
Which are not the same things at all
Though
It all seems the same   the same

It's the summer of 'fifty-nine
And we collapse the last decade
In the past where we restage
With different scenes the same crime.

This year's mistress is twenty-three
And I am nineteen and sick
Of the high-wire balancing trick
Of amorality.

"Don," she says, "I'm scared
He might kill me sometime
When he's mean drunk, raging blind."
I touch her sleek black hair

And let her choke on her tears.
I've nothing to say, I try
No longer to live every lie,
Not to find out every fear . . .

VI.

The first snow is falling lightly
In a mid-December gray.
My two day fever's finally broken,
I'm up today.
But I'm not yet strong.

Lines I wrote two months ago
Fall under my gaze.
But their rhymes and wish
Have escaped my mind,
They embarrass, daze:

"Twelve noon. I've been up an hour.
Coffee, cigarettes and silence
Drift in wisps of dreamy elegance
And mask what's going sour

Slowly: simple conversation, ease,
Delight, desire for spiritual success.
Soon I'll shave my stiffening face, dress
The creaking frame with which no one's pleased

And go out and recharge my anxieties."

What was it? . . . Last night
I dreamed I taught a class
In which my closest friends sat
Waiting some word and I could not
Even remember their names.

Later a lovely woman
Wrote a report in which
She noted I had not worn
A necktie while teaching.
Greatly afraid, I awoke.

VII.

What word, my brother, my twin?
(We were on a lonely plain
Like a man who finds a long-lost road,
And, till then, going-on was vain.)
I turned
My ashen face toward him,
Awaiting his word . . .

"When you were a child and thought as a child
Hell was midnight downstairs, fear
Firing rage, glass breaking
And the shrill phone ringing. Shouts everywhere.

And a sudden silence, and later having
Almost to be yanked back into sound
As the thin sun ebbed upstairs
To that queer clock of your face run down,

Your eyes without time. It was when
You'd walk into rooms where so much
Rage was flowing that your eyes would
Look through and beyond, as dogs will clutch

Tearing a bone and not see it . . .
Summer evenings, you'd lie on the lawn
Gazing up at the trees whose boughs
Hung down, and for hours hum songs

Tuneless and crazy while inside
I'd pull together my child's dreams
In which we'd walk effortlessly
Past horrors . . . Twins? It seems

We haven't lived two seconds the same."

VIII.

A year or a day, my sister,
My lovely voice?
And how far have we come?
Must we keep starting over,
Going back again and again?

It's forty degrees outside,
Warmer tomorrow. Spring
Saturdays are more than clockwork
As the reborn trees get bigger.
Speak to me clearly, speak now.

*It wasn't easy, no, none of it, for you fought scarcely at all, moon-
ing most of the time, silly and passive as daydreams. And when at
last you woke up, you fought—how shall I say it?—vapidly, without relevance, a sixteen-year-old's painful posings. But, la la, I'll
drop it, there's little point now. Except O it was ugly, I bore a terrible weight, and I got no help at all, that's clear to me now. And
bright as day—listen now—I remember the time we drove up-
state, it was summer and the highways were packed—the fourth
of July, I think—and driving was very bad, treacherous and fast.
And it took us five hours to go a hundred miles, and after the
tenth tavern we left the road at sixty, hurtling up a grassy slope,
careening through bushes, over fallen trees, somehow keeping*

upright, bumping and rolling to a gentle stop in mid-field, the car
still rocking, the radiator hissing in a stunned silence. Then your
thin nasal screams—that child's sound!—and father savagely
cursing! Mother bled quietly
. . . Ah well, I could sing this same song forever, I'm so well re-
hearsed, don't you think?

Yes, dear sister, you are
And we thank you, all of us do,
For singing it to us again.

It's washed our dark tale
With a clear clean light.

Refreshed, greatly changed, we go on . . .

IX.

Feeling nothing
I wonder how I'd feel
If I had to,
If something
Broke the walls around

Me down. . .

. . . And I remember the great hill
Rising behind our house, how
On late summer days, dry, hazy,
We'd all start up it, five, six of us,
Through the back gate hanging crazily
On its hinges, up the old road now fallen
Into the dust, here and there old tar
Chunks bubbling in the August sun,
And up to the broken tractor rusted
Paper thin by raw winds, snow, rain,
And perch (one of us in the hard iron scoop

Of the driver's seat and turn the useless wheel
For a moment or an hour . . .
Then back on the weed-choked fading road
Up past the tin cans broken glass
The mounds of twisted rust and junk
Shoveled into the half standing cellars
Of houses blown down by hurricanes
In the 'thirties and never rebuilt,
Up to where the trees started
And the grass would be thick green still
Instead of dust beige like below
In our yard, the thin August color,
And we'd run the last fifty yards
To the top, all of us shouting
Me first Me first
Shoving laughing as the first one
Would fall face down to drink the stream
That bubbled a few yards brilliantly clean
Before going underground further down,
And I remember the time I was first
And how the water was so sweet
I thought I'd never tasted water before,
While the others tried pulling me away
As in my mind's eye rose solid
Burning
The broken cellars, walls leaning . . .

X.

"Once again we touch on the puzzling question of the imperfection of our earth. The real and complete universe exists only in
the mind of God. What we call the world is only a shadow of the
divine Idea. It is the product of the skies working upon matter.
Now, as we have been told before, matter, for some unexplain-
able reason, is faulty; and the skies are continually changing."

Customs room, the Paris airport,
A bearded man elbows
Through the crowd.
Wait! It's the brother!
He begins to speak:

"When we were small boys, you thin
As a rail, I chubby,
We suffered our sister's scorn
Like the lash. Bloody

Our dim silly child's minds
Each blessed time she loosed
Her savage tongue. *We're not
Responsible*, says Proust

Somewhere, *for nervous states.*
For the past I concur.
She couldn't have known, I guess,
Why she made us suffer

The things she couldn't endure
Alone. Suffering the worst
She became our separate hells
And gave wholly of herself—ah, the curse

Of giving for love what's hate!
We are what we've learned
How to do, *c'est la vie*, eh?
And she got what she earned:

A symbol you are, dear Psyche,
Sweet sister, meaning more
As idea than ever you meant
In life—a total metaphor,

Bloodless and complete.
So it goes, *va bene*, I suppose."
(He turns away, plunging
Into the crowd that flows

Out into bright Paris streets.)

XI.

The mother looks back and muses:

. . . Well, somehow it seemed
Things were predisposed
To run down and quit,
That the ruins
Realized the shape
Inherent all along
In the act of plugging in
A washing machine
(I said to myself)
Now screw-loose and rattling.
I examined every nut
In my hand afterwards and
There was nothing left
Of me . . .

Who knows?
The madman tiresomely insisted I knew.

So later on I thought of
The martinis and rice crispies
And of the roast that once rotted.
That? No? The car door then?
The green bananas . . . ?
No? What then? Eh?

It is madness to explain.
The result is all.

Mildly I'm here now.

XII.

And couldn't we have guessed
it'd finally all come to this:
the occasional letters,
quick notes and postcards,
the unreal snapshots and
the long-distance calls
and polite, brief visits—
and the imagination's helpless
meditations on what is
painfully obvious
about it all now:
the simple suffering,
the sharp regret,
the clear waste
of immensest love?
No, not then surely,
above all not then,
for even to conceive
that one's agonies
could issue in nothing
except some slight tokens
(and not even tributes)
to love, life and hate
is literally unthinkable.
For the final nostalgia
(as someone says) that
we should understand,
is part of another
possibly deeper belief,

that there is or was
something to be understood.
And so, sweet father,
your fifty-eight years
(the "almost six-decades"
You wonderingly say)
gather about you like
obstreperous children
now grown into strangers
smooth, mannered but vague.
Unkind but not cruel,
your years and ours
move now around you
in an odd kind of dance,
arranging themselves
into a tentative scene
from some intricate masque
whose meaning eludes
as its music's unheard,
but which allows us at least
some last lingering looks.
Let the masquers proceed!

Our sin, I see now,
was simply that we
(like everyone else)
never once disbelieved
that attractive half-truth
that claims what we do
is what we are. So
as we all strike
some truly typical poses
and enact in dumb show
this last curious scene
of our little playlet,
I ask you, dear reader

(and who else at this point
can I appeal to?),
to pay strictest attention
to whole, not half truths . . .

. . . It's a summer late afternoon
At a small New York resort,
the lake's glaring surface
dies into mere brilliance
as through the window
of a too-costly dining room
we sit watching some sailboats
endlessly crisscross the lake,
their crisp sense of direction
a transparent bravado
of full, rakish sails and
aimless, spumy wakes;
and we too have drifted
through two intricate hours
of that odd conversation
only a family can have
who know one another
too well to be chatty
but themselves not enough
to accept lightly the trick
of forgetting one's loves
(which are close to one's hates)
in order to live
both in and beyond them—
the toil of smooth sailing!
the work of pure play!
And so, sweet father,
you lurch to your feet
to glare down at the game
we've so miserably played,
and poised for an instant

in that maddening dilemma
of dishonest feeling or
forced, joyless sprees, you
raise up your brandy
in mock elegant salute
and gaze slowly in turn
down into our souls
whose spiritual voices
have fallen into silence
from listening to yours
grown hoarse with the shouting
of impossible demands;
and all in that instant
sailing quite, quite alone
out over those depths
we could not negotiate,
you see the very mud at the bottom
of our aimless churnings
and know then you have
to curse yet forgive it—
knowing that all flesh
at last can desire but
its own degradation—
and there, where dilemmas
lose all power to madden us
in the far vaster insanities
of the soul's wars with the flesh,
you lower your brandy,
the wind dying in your sails
as the instant now rushes
impossibly toward speech
whose merest ripples of meaning
(let alone deepest currents)
are literally unspeakable;
and . . . you start swearing,
sweet father, you swear

the basest of base words,
whose savage unmeanings
abolish what prompts them
by debasing language itself,
and reveal—precisely nothing.
Outside, the sailboats continue
to crisscross the lake
while we pick our way
through a labyrinth of hushed
voices and shocked looks,
as out from the silence
of damask, silver and glassware
drifts a murmured cliché
whose arresting half-truth
freezes us in tableau:
". . . four sheets to the wind. . ."

XIII.

A mauve twilight, an open field,
Heavy thickets. Two figures speak:

Tell me, have I everything I want?
Yes, but you've nothing you need.

Why do these branches needle my face?
They are the way you have to go.

What is that moving there up ahead?
Where? I saw nothing.

There grinning, dancing, waving, bowing—
Pass by! Pass by!

AN EPILOGUE

To close the unbearable gap
Between what he was
And what he thinks he was,

Rightly remembering all the while
What he is and wants to be
And thus to have been—

This is the task he set himself, this
The road on which he walked
In a kind of constant hallucination,

All the while saying (in two languages,
Neither his): "Ah-ha! It is done!
I've hung pleasing curtains, found

A most comfortable chair, set an odd
Tongue to wagging, dined very nicely,
And rung major themes in my minor key,"

His fussy voice booming so magnificently,
He felt, that no one could hear
The sniggerings and snide jokes

He constantly heard in the *crack-crack*
The scenery gave off, nor could see
The sword of imminent collapse

Suspended over that radiant stage
Where danced the terrors of his life,
And angels sang softly in the wings.

"Here," he said, "all terrors terminate,
Fears end in the image of them, end
In that single illuminate text

Where we can be ourselves wholly,
Happy as can be." Ah, see him digging
In his garden, dreamy, singy, just as he likes & lives.

χρὴ δέ σε πατρὶ...κτίλον ἔμμεναι
"But you should be gentle towards your father."[45]

We Have Begun

TO MY FATHER

Who once in a mad drunken rage
Cut open my mother's head,
Dragged me downstairs to see,
Shouting: There's your mother! And fled
Nowhere, gripped by his paralyzed rages
Against his terrible demon of fear,
Smashing his years' hollow frenzy,
Cheeks rigid with icy-sick tears,

While I open-mouthed stood,
Drowning in the blood of her head,
My nine years locked in the fear
Born of the need to be dead.

Like Chinese boxes, we open one
Gift from our ghosts, then another,
Their years dying to live only once.
And that was not my mother.

Fall

Now the bitterest of weathers begins—
The concrete skies, the sharpening wind.
We have begun a beginning at an end.

Out of the wreck of summer you come,
Bringing death and desire still one.
Before love, so much dying to be done.

The crippling seasons of the buried past
Die slowly, hard; they cannot last
In the heart—and cannot die fast.

The dying fall mocks the possible spring:
It is an idiot babbling love, promising.

Winter Song

Pale sunlight lies along the frozen snow,
Mud is locked in place,
I've unloved a few more things
I couldn't face:

An eye so mad with fear
It couldn't see,
A love so sick with need
It ceased to be—

Abide! Abide! there's an end
To what we give.
None of us are very strong,
We live and let live.

Ice cracks the thin branches
Off the trees,
Another winter of record cold.
What doesn't freeze?

The Silence of Cold

"The sun was not the sun because it never shone . . ."
—Wallace Stevens[46]

Cold and motionless as the grey winter day,
the shadows freeze
in place with their arms awry.

In the absence of color
blacks and whites fitfully,
mournfully twist into greys.

The silence silently plays
upon the leaf hopping and scraping along
on the hard-crusted snow.

It is night all day.

And the stillness becomes colder.
And the winter becomes older.
And spring is crying loneliness
in the frozen shadows.

A last twist of icy wind slices across.
The silence stiffens.
And the wind dies.
The nothing returns
and remains; the leaf hops and scrapes
over the cold, dead ground.
Again and again.

The Last Match

The night triumphs, the light collapses;
and once again, groping, lost, I strike
the last match—and hope it will catch.

The light, flickering and weak, reveals
itself, the night, the monstrous shadows,
whirling and chaotic in the room.

With trembling hands, lest it go out, I
hold it higher, and stare at the night,
the shadows, knowing that, at last,

they will stop and will arrange
themselves; they will be myself; the night
will become day, the shadows part of it.

But now there is but the match: it is
all of me, all there can be. So
I perceive this; and this perception

is enough, this knowledge is enough,
this match suffices. This becomes obvious.
One must see the obvious to see: and see and see.

Tell Me of Love

Tell me of love, my old one,
    Tell me of love, my father.
—Love is a fire you burn in, my son,
    A fire that burns in a moment,
    A broken flame yearning, yearning,
    Burning in brightest light.

Tell me of hate, my old one,
  Tell me of hate, my father.
—Hate is an ice you freeze in, my son,
  Ice that locks tightly,
  Splinters of ice turning, turning,
  Twisting in coldest light.

Tell me of death, my old one,
  Tell me of death, my father.
—Death is a child so old, my son,
  So old he never is young,
      Never with fire burning, burning,
      Never with ice, twisting, turning,
  Laughing in blackest light.

How should I go, my old one?
  What should I do, my father?
  For I'm so afraid of fire and ice,
So afraid of twisting and burning, old one—
  What, what must I do?

Laugh in the hottest of fires, my son,
  Laugh in the coldest of ice.
For the child not laughing is killed in flame,
  He's twisted and locked in ice.
But do not laugh too loud, too long,
  As I have, my child, my son.
  For I've loved and hated and still lost all—
  And I laugh in the blackest light.

Then It Was Love

Like a shouting, fraudulent drunk,
  Tough on hoped-for courage
I roared love at you, love and love.
  And it was hope.

Then I got you wild drunk
    On the belief I didn't have.
You pulled houses down, mad with it.
    I was stunned.

Kicking apart your lies you found
    Feet to walk with.
Your eyes burning with my love,
    You came to me.

And it was hope. Then it was fear
    Where belief should have been.
I was frozen by the fact of giving
    What I didn't believe: myself.

Afterwards it was love, touched into life,
    A believing beyond hope, beyond belief.
It was to know you, to love myself.
    But it was hope

    First
And to be drunk, to need to be drunk,
    To shout out the voice
Of the terrible need to give up the fraud

I couldn't give up: it was my hope.
    Then it was the chill fear
To give. You gave, teaching me to take of you
    And thereby to take

The voice of my need and speak
Love. And it was myself, still and certain,
    Honest in the knowing of you.
It was shouting and fraud. Then it was love.

April 1963[47]

Park Bench

He is on that peeling park bench
Days long, sunlight sifting through cloth
To warm those spring-locked braces
Clamped on his senseless spindles of legs.

His back bunches in muscle at his neck;
His arms move in a held rage of strength.
Glass-eyed pigeons strut up to peck
Popcorn he inches out with a crutch.

The mauve and yellow crowds plunge past
His bench swirling to the park's pools,
Zoos, roller-coasters and bumper-cars.
His eyes stay pale as a pigeon's.

The park drains out as the hot day sags
To a stunned, cool five o'clock.
Then lurching upright, he snaps the springs,
Locking the dead flesh rigid.

He crutches stabbing and swinging
Past the loud waves of fuchsia flowers
And every so often he stops and remembers,
And his pale eyes glitter to a hardness.

ca. 1965

Richard Eberhart at The Frost Place, August 1980

I am thinking
of Richard Eberhart,
full of clear grace,
speaking,

in the August haze
of the New Hampshire mountains
where Robert Frost once worked and
wrote,

and describing
the moment when
sixty years
ago

one bright, terrible Minnesota summer
his mother
died, his father lost a
fortune

and how such actual
catastrophe,
such indubitable suffering,
sprung

him into
poetry's toil
wherein the activity of
light

moves with
the motion of pain
that, vivid as
rhyme,

sharp as lyric,
etches its
intricate way into words:
grief

gripped a boy of sixteen,
turning him
toward syllables' mazes,
while

in the New Hampshire mountains
Frost at forty-five
used black on
gray

to make accessible
a grief
like granite,
like

glacial erratics
permanently hard and nothing hidden,
words of this place
where

sixty summers later
Richard Eberhart,
master of light's ways,
graces

the air with
poems wherein pain
is a fine tracery of lines
that

hang in this New Hampshire mountain haze
a net
of brightest
connections

that makes lucid the way
whereby light and pain
round into
grace

Sysladobsis August, 1982

It's the summer of 42—*my* 42.
Here at the lake in Springfield, Maine
We negotiate again our family life
Arranging free-time from a tiring game

Our 2 ½-year-old insists we play:
Shambles Parchesi, dice and men thrown
Round the board as he yells ONE-FIVE-TWO
(Or some other three). Picture two grown

(We like to think) adults, a boy of 13,
His lovely older brother, clear, kind,
Regarding us—Carol, me—as once again
As with him we seek—is it strength? mind?

(It *can't* be) to stay afloat in games
Where rules are ceaselessly remade
By the only one of us who easily cries
Really laughs and isn't at all afraid

To claim the love he needs—here
We all are, bent to our game.
Many questions rise—what's this game we play?
Is anyone ahead? why?—at the same

Time others slither darkly up
Into view: Is the lake really colder
This year? Is my breathing worse?
Am I supposed to *like* getting older?

Dinners here are an elaborate affair.
Taking turns, we fire up the stove,
Burning last year's birch, the gas-
Lights cheery in the deepening mauve

Of evening as we create the casseroles
We're too busy to make at home.
The stove keeping steady at 375
Turns out a perfect pie. And no telephone

Shrills its voices into our ears.
By turns we wash the day's dishes
In hot water from the stove
With cold from the pump—all the wishes

Of the nineteenth century heart!
Babar is the bedtime passion now
As (in turns, of course) we half-read
Half-tell of mean Rataxes, good Babar, how

They always find their way to
Sweet accord. And sleep finally falls.
I close the book and blow out the light.
Outside, unraveled moonlight falls

Where now loons everywhere call and recall.

This Is Where I Start

This: my father sees my pain,
Agonizes with me in my suffering.
But he is helpless to ease my agony.
Except this: he always and always loves me.

The hour I walked with my father and mother
Into their afflictions and agonies
Is the hour I broke my heart:
This, this is where I start.

January 2, 2008

Almost Enough

All I know is that the wisteria bush
By the side of the house in the thin
Cold autumn air where light is dying
On branches that are now like bare wire
Against the empty sky, is almost enough.

ca. Late Autumn, 2009

Those Unspeaking Stones

Teaching the Permanently Valuable

Spring 1976

Editor's Note: The 1970s marked a turning point in Don Sheehan's life—a turning away, not from the lyric art (especially poetry) that had transformed his relationship with his life and his world, but from various aspects of the career track on which it had thus far led him. In 1972, he decided (with my full support) to leave his tenure-track job at the University of Chicago. Inspired by impulses more hippie than holy (though the mix in those days was a complex one), we made the ritual slow pilgrimage to the West Coast in our VW bus with three-year-old David, whose nighttime bed platform (eventually painted purple) spanned the back of the passenger seat to the dashboard, on which we kept a jar of growing sprouts during the day. Arriving in the Bay Area, we stayed with friends and flirted with the New Age. I worked in a health food store, and Don did some day care work, took David to new movies like *The Yellow Submarine*, and most likely read and wrote a lot.

Then one day a single red leaf on an autumn tree caught our attention and brought New England to mind—how much more elegantly it embraces that autumn transformation!—and Don found himself thinking about teaching again. So we began a leisurely trek back East, taking the southern route this time. We limited ourselves to two or three hundred miles a day and made an effort to stop at every playground along the way (where

David made us several new friends), abandoning that plan only when we got to Texas. We visited Don's mother in Florida and my father in Washington, and there Don came across an ad for a position teaching English at a small New England alternative college with no tenure system. He interviewed for it and was hired. So for the next five years, he happily pursued the studies and shared the knowledge he loved in a way that satisfied his desire to cross the usual academic boundaries and draw from many wells. In 1976, however, the college changed presidents (along with its founding commitment to liberal arts), and Don, asked to explain how he could contribute to the new curriculum that was to focus on political activism and community organizing, wrote the following letter in response.

A Letter to the College President

I'D LIKE TO SUGGEST something. My sense of my own skills and talents and capacities might be useful to you. I think if I had a clearer sense that you and I were talking approximately about the same person (namely, me), then we'd probably have more to say more clearly about me and the College. So I want to tell you some things about myself. Then I want to ask you a question.

As for dynamics of teaching, I think I'm good at a certain style of attention to others, at listening to some (not all) ranges of expression. . . . It has to do with (among other things) ideas and the energies of ideas, especially esthetics and especially pre-contemporary esthetics; with the discontents due to cultural-psychic-spiritual abandonment (as opposed to violently active oppression and direct assault)—that is, most of the people I meet; and with disarming the more rampant forms of academic egotism by not asserting my own at any given moment. At very best, I can sense people becoming better with me; at worst, I don't exist for them, or exist ambiguously—hence, uninterestingly; most of the time I can help create non-competitive classroom situations, which is usually pretty useful. The general ethics I lump all under is Good Manners—a thing I take seriously precisely to the extent I don't see much of it.

But the point is, all this is not a construct of mine; it isn't a chosen or consciously willed kind of behavior, it is simply what I am, it is what flows from me because of the kind of person I am. It is a useful kind of person to be *in certain contexts*. In other contexts, it probably is not. I'm not good, as I said yesterday, in fact I'm awful, at "defending" my ideas, at presenting them in contexts of debate and struggle, *because that's not my own relation to my ideas*. Instead, in such a context, what I'm good at—that is, very stilly listening to and toward the center of another's expression—becomes something "inconsistent," chameleon-like, "dishonest" (as you often called me last fall). And I suppose in such contexts I am. But I—or anybody— can't will myself to be another person.

This doesn't mean I can't or won't discuss myself or my ideas, it only means I won't—because I can't—fight for them. And so I simply pull away from situations or contexts of fighting, only partly because I "want to," mostly because I have to, with all the inevitability of *being* somebody.

As for my materials, after fifteen years of study I know a lot about literary history and structures and styles. My education—that is, what I can *use* every day—is far wider than a good many, if not a great many, of the people who teach literature. My strongest feeling about literature is that it asserts a structure of value nowhere else so asserted—philosophy is a special (highly mental) case of value; organized religion is a charade of value. Here's the point: only literature teaches us that the world we move in—the political, historical, presumably "real" world—is defined more by *what is missing* than what is present. What's missing is the places where we say—*and mean every word*—something like this:

> But man is a noble animal, splendid
> in ashes, and pompous in the grave, solemnizing
> nativities and deaths with equal
> lustre, nor omitting ceremonies of
> bravery in the infamy of his nature.[48]

And we *mean* not only the words but the rhythm, the antique ring and resonance. Or this:

> Were I (who to my cost already am
> One of those strange, prodigious creatures, Man)[49]—

Or this:

> Men must endure
> Their going hence, even as their coming hither:
> Ripeness is all.[50]

The point is, as we push our baskets around the supermarket or wheel our cars into the gas-stations or turn on our TVs to watch the news or a kids' show or (God help us) a serious drama, what we experience in relation to *man is a noble animal* or *those strange, prodigious creatures, men*, is, very precisely, culture shock. What in the world has the supermarket to do with nobility? Or my guiding question, where in the world—that is, where in the supermarkets, the newspapers, the government, the churches, the universities, right politics, left politics, official politics, TV, movies, magazines; in short, where in the whole dense, corrupt spectacle of technological reality do we find the order-of-being implied by *Men must endure their going hence even as their coming hither?*[51]

And so, the study of literature is a break, is a radical moving toward a sphere wholly apart from that reality where phrases like *ceremonies of bravery* or *infamy of his nature* have no place or are out of place. For a reality where those words are out of place is one I call a corrupt reality. And the study of literature must detach itself from that corruption, must withdraw from that reality, if it is to be powerful and true and vivid and urgent.

Detachment, withdrawal—hard words. Yet what we call our morality (but which is really our corruption) is experienced as a sequence of carefully nurtured confusions and often literally stunning obstacles. And literature, especially classical literature (by which I mean the Greek and all later Hellenic energies, all the way up to Eliot and Pound and now Charles Olson), *pushes back* against those constructs of confusions we call our society, pushes back so that we can see—glimpse fleetingly—what is missing, what is simply *not here*, so that we can then begin the task of making those things present and here and alive. That is, literature—and that alone—teaches us what to make, because it teaches us what is permanently valuable; it is, so far as I can see, our one potent source for building the Just City.

This is *not* the creation of a cultured elite, *not* the literary PhD-as-God that the fifties hatched (one more corruption). Because what I see as the study of literature is not a plaything of a leisured, privileged class, but the urgent eleventh-hour rescue of human essentiality.

There are two things I hear at the center of certain very strong student voices right now: that the still approximately intact fabric of our lives could very soon simply collapse; and that what is missing in that fabric is a *sacred language*. These two facts seem to me at the center of what literary—more widely, humanistic—education should be about. Paul Valéry wrote: "We civilizations know now that we are mortal. . . . We sense that a civilization is as fragile as a life. The circumstances that would send the works of Keats and Beaudelaire to join those of Menander are by no means inconceivable; they are in the newspapers." Many many students sense this; and go something beyond this grotesque reality, to find "separate realities" in the Guru Maharaji or in Jesus-communities; but only to find there new simplifications and distortions being imposed, new confusions being carefully nurtured, new obstacles created.

What I conceive the study of literature doing right now is speaking, first of all, to those two senses: of social collapse, of sacred language, and doing so with clarity and power and depth and richness. Such a study would not be "easy," it would mean, among other things, learning difficult languages (if one were seriously committed), it would above all mean entering what Pound calls *the mysteries*: "Our time has overshadowed the mysteries by an overemphasis on the individual."

My ideal syllabus would begin with the Greeks, that is, with the sources. (In the original language, if possible; for I insist our essential languages must be kept.) There, as a recent scholar has written, we can see the terrifying dialectic at work in, say, fifth-century BC Athens: the restless energy of achievement, of ceaselessly *doing* something, over against the profound sense of mortality and piety and submission to necessity. The dialectic has two words: *polupragmosune* ("much-doingness") vs. *hesychia* ("calmness"). And these words resonate very deeply to our situations and dilemmas and tensions; they are present in our field of possibilities and they can be *retrieved* (as Heidegger says) and brought vividly and urgently and significantly into our present. Then, Christianity—all its literary shapes (Dante and Milton above all). Then the whole European mimetic tradition.[52] Up to Ezra Pound's *Cantos*, that immense re-creation of the whole.

American possibilities are very great. I see American Indian texts, such as:

> Every part of this earth is sacred to my people. Every hillside, every valley, every clearing and wood, is holy in the memory and experience of my people. Even those unspeaking stones along the shore are loud with events and memories in the life of my people. The ground beneath your feet responds more lovingly to our steps than yours, because it is the ashes of our grandfathers. Our bare feet know the kindred touch. The earth is rich with the lives of our kin.[53]

This to be seen with the Hesiodic *Works and Days*, or with this from Sophocles (as Creon tells the attendants to take the blinded Oedipus indoors):

> But if you no longer respect the sons of men, revere at least the all-nurturing flame of our lord the Sun and do not nakedly reveal such a pollution that neither earth nor holy rain nor light can accept.

Another thing—the last time our civilization collapsed we lost far, far too much (in the fourth century AD, for example, there were fifty plays of Aeschylus's; now we have seven). And among other things, what a genuine education in literature could teach is "survival skills," as they say, only what

would be saved would be far more important, because more humanly essential (that is, of the essence) than what's usually implied.

This only scratches the surface. Excuse the haste, read between the
lines, etc., etc., sensing only the best.

But my question for you is: Does this strike you as something you want
in your school? Am I the kind of person you want?

> *Editor's Note:* In January 1978 the college officially closed, owing
> its teachers a fair amount of back salary. Over a few of the years
> that followed, the two of us created and operated the *Center for
> Archaic Studies*, published several issues of a journal, *Archē,* held
> conference-like events, and created a second alternative elemen-
> tary school to replace the one that hadn't survived the college's
> demise. The family lived on Don's unemployment benefits and
> various employment of my own until he was offered by the Town
> of Franconia, New Hampshire, a position managing the newly
> purchased Robert Frost Farm. His salary, initially provided by the
> Federal Comprehensive Employment and Training Act of 1973
> (CETA), soon came to be covered through fundraising, and Don
> served, for the next quarter-century, as Director of the Frost Place
> Center for Poetry and the Arts offering seminars and workshops
> in poems and writing poetry that drew international acclaim.
>
> Through all of this, I don't believe that his vision concern-
> ing the importance of "real" education changed, except perhaps
> to reflect over time, often invisibly, his deepening knowledge of
> the loving God, Poet of heaven and earth, who spoke Creation
> into being by His Word and embedded His statutes within it.
> Having taken to heart a determination not to repeat his father's
> failures in supporting his family (or possibly to emulate his suc-
> cesses against all odds!), Don found ways to "plant" his edu-
> cational vision in whatever good soil offered itself. This meant
> teaching and lecturing at a number of different venues of higher
> education simultaneously, including adult learning centers
> (where he loved the keen motivation of his older students). All
> the while he continued to direct the programs and lecture fre-
> quently at The Frost Place. From 1989 until his retirement in
> 2004, he added a third employment as Senior Lecturer at Dart-
> mouth College, where he taught freshmen to think and read and
> write with great care, older undergraduates to learn Latin (and
> occasionally Greek), and graduate students in the Master of Arts
> in Liberal Studies program in their explorations of a wide range
> of literature, from ancient to modern.

4

Inheriting the Orthodox Tradition

Late 1984

I CAME TO THE Orthodox faith in a way whose meanings are for me probably endless. My alcoholic father died on April 26, 1976, in Memphis, Tennessee, a year or so prior to the demise of the college where I was teaching. In the spring of 1983 I decided—for a series of concurrent and powerful reasons—to visit his grave, something I hadn't done in those seven years.[54] So the four of us, my wife Carol, myself, and our sons, David and Rowan Benedict (then ages fourteen and three), got into our car and drove some seventeen hundred miles from New Hampshire to Tennessee. At my father's grave, much happened for me. I had written him a letter the night before in the motel while everyone slept. Next morning at the grave, Carol and David knelt with me as I read the letter aloud (Rowan preferring, after long hours in the car, to skip around among the gravestones). I had written about love and suffering and my needing no longer to be attached to the pain of our life together. The letter ended in my offering and asking Dad's forgiveness. "For," I said, "the heavenly untwisting continues for you, in me because of you; it must so act, that what you do now, after death, changes what I am now, in life." It was a Wednesday, I recall.

It was the middle of what I came to know later as Holy Week, for in the Western churches that Sunday, April 3, 1983, was Easter. We stopped in New York at St. John the Divine for Easter service, then drove home on Monday. On Tuesday, April 5, I was awakened before dawn by these words spoken within me, filling me: "Lord Jesus Christ, Son of God, have mercy on me, a sinner." I wrote in my journal: "This prayer was humming and

81

singing in my mind, as if Something were 'saying' the words to me." While daylight softly came I lay fully awake, silently saying the words over and over, times past any counting.

I arose and found a crucifix of Carol's, one I had a friend carve for her one Christmas because she had dreamt it vividly, and I sat before this holy image saying over and over this prayer. Other thoughts, images, words, ideas would clamor for a moment or two, but the prayer's stronger words simply—and lightly—overrode them, and all was still. The day got on some-how, I went to work and did and said things (I guess). But the prayer in me never stopped. In the evening I got the crucifix again and sat in silence and let the words have their way in me.

For the next three weeks or so I said the prayer in my mind hundreds and hundreds of times a day, some days into the thousands. In the morning and evening when I sat before the holy crucifix I began to read the Bible. At hand was an Anglican Book of Prayer and I followed its daily lessons. Then in the College library in early May, walking in the stacks, I suddenly stopped and took a book off the shelf, and it was *The Way of a Pilgrim*.[55] I read a page, then another, in transfixed amazement, for here was my experience of the last five weeks. The prayer, known as the "Prayer of the Heart" or "The Jesus Prayer," has been the basis for all Orthodox contemplative practice since at least the fourth century AD. Later I remembered that, long ago, I had read and loved a short story, *Franny and Zooey*, by J. D. Salinger, in which a character talked of this book and this prayer—but I never supposed the book was an actual one. And now I held it.

A new world swam into view. A footnote told me of *The Philokalia*, "the great collection of mystical and ascetic writings of the Eastern Orthodox Church, over a period of eleven centuries."[56] I found in the library the Palmer-Kadloubovsky volume on the Prayer of the Heart,[57] and I knew I was coming home then. I began to read all I could on the Orthodox Church in my library, and a wise friend several weeks later gave me Vladimir Lossky's book on mys-tical theology.[58] I didn't yet know I wanted to *be* Orthodox. I knew only that what was happening to me made sense only in Orthodoxy.

I kept on praying and studying. Morning and evening I sat for some forty-five minutes reading Scripture (lots of the Psalms), above all saying in silence the Holy Name of our Lord. I'd once been given some myrtle-wood "worry beads," and they now kept a kind of brief-count of the prayer for me during the day. Days and weeks passed into months, and the inten-sity of prayer seemed impossibly to be growing, not lessening, as the habit of prayer steadied and settled my life.

As another Easter approached I began to wonder: maybe I should visit an Orthodox church. Certainly there wasn't one anywhere around here (I didn't think to look for one), probably not even in New Hampshire. Maybe when I'm next in Boston I'll see if I can find one, I half thought. Then one evening in early May, 1984, I opened the phonebook to check something and my eye fell upon the listing for the Orthodox Church of the Holy Resurrection, Berlin, New Hampshire—about one hour away. For some days I hesitated, knowing that a deep purposiveness was opening before me, and yet wanting, in some way, to take the next step in full deliberateness, in stillness. And so I prayed and in that state of mind and spirit, I called Father Vladimir—that kindly man!—and as we talked I told him I'd been reading quite a bit about Orthodoxy and I felt my heart was calling me.

Chrismation

When I walked into the church, that third Sunday in May, I was home and I knew it. I won't try to describe my experience; the joy of the Orthodox convert is in essence as incommunicable as any mystery of our faith. I wrote this on the evening of September 7, the day before I received Chrismation as an Orthodox[59]:

> The convert's joy is ephemeral and perfect. Ephemeral: for this blush of love can happen only once and very briefly, before the full weight of the Church's immense life has filled every tiny corner and cell of one's life—some slender quicklight of loving, and not the full, rich, universal conflagration that is God's love in the Holy Church. Perfect: because all our lives we try to recapture—or grasp once—that bright first intensity, when for the tiniest instant at that intensity's heart the Kingdom of Heaven opens perfectly and fully.

After my Chrismation, my private prayer changed quite a bit as I replaced my privately created prayers with those of the Church, finding again and again the Church's wisdom in prayer to far exceed mine. I also began to use the Prayer of the Heart less, and now I say it silently during the day some two or three score times, no more, and not hundreds or thousands of times, as when I began. I think God is having me let go of my own private spirituality, my own little enclosed world of prayer, my own spiritual drama.

In Igumen Chariton's *Art of Prayer*, St. Theophan the Recluse (1815–94), who lived in that great flowering of Russian Orthodox spirituality in which Dostoevsky so deeply participated and from which he drew, writes of what he calls "the fire in the heart":

Stand with your mind and attention in the heart, being very sure
that the Lord is near and listening; and call to Him with fervor:
"Lord Jesus Christ, have mercy on me." Do this constantly in
church and at home, traveling, working, and at table, and in
bed—in a word, from the time that you open your eyes till the
time that you shut them. This will be exactly like holding an
object in the sun, because this is to hold yourself before the face
of the Lord, who is the Sun of the spiritual world.[60]

Spiritual Sobriety

"But," says St. Theophan, "whoever strives to maintain and increase this
warmth for the sake of its sweetness alone, will develop in himself a kind
of spiritual hedonism." In other words, if such experiences of sweetness
become something *you create for yourself*, then they will quickly lose all
their sweetness and you will become like an alcoholic with liquor. "Therefore," St. Theophan continues, "those who practice sobriety pay no attention to this sweetness." What do the spiritually sober do instead, then?
They "try simply to stand firmly rooted before the Lord in complete surrender to Him, giving themselves up into His hands." Sobriety is the spiritual practice, in other words, in which not merely alcohol but all addictive
substances and states of being—including certain inward consequences of
prayer—are surrendered wholly into God.

The Divine Liturgy each Sunday and feast day became for me what C.
S. Lewis (I think) somewhere calls *sober ecstasy*[61]: the direct experience of a
sobriety that is simultaneously an ecstasy. The clouds of incense, the engulfing Russian bells, the steady perfections of sacred chant and choral song, the
processions and solemn entrances, obedient simplicities and complex coher-
ences of ritual, gesture, and tone formed over centuries of slow and profound
practice: the Orthodox Liturgy is a living spiritual art form whose meanings
are endless and all of them joyous. To step *inside* this art form, as participant
each week in its unfolding, was for me ravishment.

For within the Liturgy I could perceive—not all at once but with growing
clarity of outline and detail—the meaning of the ancient *filioque* controversy.
This controversy culminated in the year 1054, when the Orthodox Bishop
of Rome chose to separate himself and his entire See from the other Orthodox bishops (the bishop of Rome in turn becoming the Pope and his See
the Roman Catholic Church). At doctrinal issue was—and still remains—the
Roman introduction into the Nicene Creed of a single phrase, changing this
crucial sentence of belief—"I believe in the Holy Spirit, who proceeds from

the Father"—into a new sentence: "I believe in the Holy Spirit, who proceeds from the Father *and the son*" (in Latin: *filioque*).

In the original Orthodox form, the Holy Spirit directly enters human life, while in the Roman revision, the Holy Spirit becomes, instead, a relation between Father and Son and thus becomes something only secondarily accessible to us.[62] Among other things, the *filioque* transforms the Church itself into a barrier between individual believers and Holy Spirit. For if the Holy Spirit is primarily a *relation* between Father and Son, then the Church's *primary* purpose becomes the institutionalization of ways in which to close and mediate the distance between the Holy Spirit and the individual. But if the Holy Spirit proceeds directly from the Father into the individual's life, then the Church becomes the arena of this living encounter. In place of the elaborate Roman techniques for reaching toward the always distant spiritual life, one therefore finds in Orthodoxy the direct experience of that life: simply, mysteriously, and immediately. A central Greek idea from Orthodox theology is one without real counterpart in Roman doctrine, an idea that holds that the sole aim of every believer's life, is *theosis*, "becoming God."[63] The Liturgy is where this essential process begins, unfolds, and completes itself. Slowly, dimly, I was beginning to see what this process might be.

My guide into the Liturgy was Father Vladimir Sovyrda. Several days after I entered the Orthodox Church I wrote this about my experience during the ceremony of Chrismation:

> I felt clumsy and little and helpless—the Church seemed immense and alive and quizzical and a bit remote, as if for the first time She were turning Her sacred gaze upon me and saying intently, *Now, who is this?* And yet Father Vladimir's hand upon my head as I knelt was everything I could have asked for: clear, firm, open, warm, assured.
>
> Father's voice in the Liturgy as he chants the ancient words of divine praise is rich, shaped, awake. His kindness as a confessor sometimes almost breaks my heart with his depths of sweetness. He is also a recovering alcoholic. . . .

Tradition

In Orthodoxy, there is a single idea that has guided vast areas of its practice, feeling, and thought for some twenty centuries. It is also an idea that has preoccupied almost every major poet and painter in the West throughout our century. The idea is *Tradition*. The Orthodox Church generally uses a capital letter to talk of Tradition (unless one is referring to something that is simply an accumulation of particular local practices over time). What is meant by the word? First of all, Orthodoxy means by the Tradition the faith which Jesus Christ gave to the Apostles and which each generation since has given to the next. This faith is based on a *knowing* of Jesus Christ by the Church, His Bride, in the way that husband and wife know one another, a way that is intimate, unmediated, and, by virtue of God's infinite love, open to all. When the Church sees caricatures of Christ offered up in His place, She recoils in horror: "That's not Him!"[64]

But, writes Archbishop Kallistos, Tradition means something even "more concrete and specific than this. It means the books of the Bible; it means the Creed; it means the decrees of the Ecumenical Councils and the writings of the Fathers; it means the Canons, the Service Books, the Holy Icons—in fact, the whole system of doctrine, Church government, worship, and art which Orthodoxy has articulated over the ages."[65] Where the liturgical services of (say) the modern Roman Church can be comfortably fitted into one or two slender volumes, the current Orthodox service books run to over twenty very substantial volumes. *Orthodoxy remembers her past*: that is the first fact. But it is not the mere fact of remembering the past that's essential to Orthodox Tradition. What's essential is how and why the past is so fully remembered. For it is in the *way* of remembering that Orthodoxy holds the fullness of Christian truth. And this way is ruled by the heart rather than the head.

The End-Point

As I knelt in the cemetery in Memphis, Tennessee, on that morning in 1983, I was remembering. What I was remembering was not my father and our life together, for I knew then that what I sought was to release both of us from that past as an experience of pain, violence, and failed love. What I was doing was deliberately placing myself at what Mother Maria, the great contemporary Orthodox nun and theologian, calls the *End-Point*.[66] We live our lives, says Mother Maria, in the progress of time unfolding moment by moment, into the years up to our death. The End-Point toward which we are hurtling—so very quickly!—is a point, she says, "or transition, when all that is ours is left behind, and the new has not yet begun." At that End-Point, there is nothing left of us "except our sins, and the cry for mercy." To become conscious of this End-Point is to become aware of everything we do not—and cannot—know, have mastery over, possess. At this End-Point we are stripped absolutely of everything; and our minds, our powers, our possessions fall away forever from us. The Prayer of the Heart—*Lord, Jesus Christ, Son of*

God, have mercy on me a sinner—is, says Mother Maria, "a prayer of the End." We live at this End-Point at the same instant we live inside the progressions of time; we are—when we awake—in both at once.[67]

I see now so clearly how I was trying that March morning in Tennessee to place myself at the End-Point. And a tiny glimpse came to me in the moment I found myself writing to my father: "The heavenly untwisting continues for you, in me because of you; it must so act, that what you do now after death, changes what I am now in life." Across the great abyss between life and death, through that impenetrable door between the realms, there is communication because there is communion. Love survives and is far greater than death because our loved ones—and the One Who Is Love—continue in that loving to love us. Just days later I awoke into the Prayer of the Heart, those Orthodox words that, after mind and body and soul and spirit have slipped away from us, remain in and as our heart.

To be mindful of death, says Metropolitan Anthony of Sourozh, is not to live in terror and helplessness. It means rather: "Be aware of the fact that what you are saying now, doing now, hearing, enduring or receiving now may be the *last* event or experience of your present life."[68] So often we live provisionally, he says, making quick, rough drafts of what later on we will write truly. "If only we realized whenever confronted with a person that this might be the last moment either of his life or ours, we would be much more intense, much more attentive, to the words we speak and the things we do." Nothing else but mindfulness of death will give us this attentiveness and intensity; nothing else will give life to this vivid depth and profound clarity. "All life," continues the Metropolitan, "is at every moment an ultimate act." When we begin to experience our moments so, then we let fall away everything inessential and begin to hear the profound Orthodox call to repentance.

"Have mercy on me, a sinner," we pray. "The call to repentance," says Mother Maria, "is the call to leave behind all temporal achievement, good or bad. . . . To leave behind all possession, of matter or of mind, at the very instant of leaving."[69] When we linger in achievement, or when we hunger for applause, we are continually forming schemes for increasing our achievement-wealth, thereby deepening our guilt. Of course our work is horribly imperfect: but its imperfection, says Mother Maria, "lies prostrate, before Christ, at the End-Point," while we are free to engage what the next instant of time is already bringing us. We must do this work as it comes to us, but we must leave it behind at the very moment we make it ours and thereby complete and fulfill it. Such is the activity of repentance, she says: "an attitude, immensely positive, an attitude forwards, keenly alert, and of love for the Paraclete."[70] If we did not repent, we would have no proof that we had loved truly and fully and deeply. The form this call to repentance took for me was the call into a rule of prayer.

Noetic Healing Begins in a Rule of Prayer[71]

I began that first morning of April 5, 1983, simply with the Prayer of the Heart, silently repeated over and over in my mind and heart as I sat before a crucifix for about three-quarters of an hour or so. When a few days later I had added the daily Bible readings from the Anglican Book of Prayer, I had begun to search for the *shape* this rule of prayer should take. A few more days passed and I began to pray for others, for my family and friends at first, then for those whom I didn't directly know except for hearing somehow of their affliction or grief. I had no idea what I was doing, and I told no one anything at all of what was happening to me. Was I obeying in this what the early Christians called *Disciplina Arcani*, the Discipline of Secrecy, whereby the rites and practices of the faith were concealed from a hostile world? Does every conversion reproduce the entire history of the faith? I knew I was following something, that I was "hearing"—but that's not the right sense—some very faint but very clear voice, one I could easily have ignored but somehow would not. I remember experiencing my mind those first days as a profoundly shocked, even stunned bystander, one scarcely innocent but not exactly guilty, either. If I had voiced it, my mind would have said to me, "But how *dare* you do this; this is absolutely shoddy nonsense, completely fraudulent and probably dangerous; and how *can* you leave me like this—and what about Carol and David and Rowan?" But all the anxious contempt and self-pity and fear of the mind's clamoring was simply no proof against what was happening to me. For what was happening was my coming into a rule of prayer.

A rule of prayer is characterized above all by *rhythm*, and the experience of a rule is that of submitting to the rhythm of it. You pray at certain times and in certain words; and these times and words begin fairly soon to give a definite pattern to one's days.[72] My first weeks of prayer were wholly solitary; every now and then I would wonder whether I was having a nervous breakdown of sorts; but such thoughts were quite insubstantial for I in fact felt very well indeed. Then I found *The Way of a Pilgrim* and the volume from the *Philokalia* and all at once remembered a brief and inexplicable dream from two years previously, in which a friend handed me a large book in Greek, and as I began to read the title it changed into Russian, and I couldn't read it. But then the world of Orthodox prayer swam into view. My experience now began to make tremendous sense because I began to feel the spiritual contours of it, its underlying rhythm. And when months later I entered for the first time an Orthodox church, I *heard* this contour and rhythm in the steady chanting of the Orthodox voice in prayer.

I was not alone, nor had I ever been. I was inheriting the Orthodox Tradition.

Alcoholism and the Invisible World

TWO YEARS OR SO after I became Orthodox, I received minor clerical orders—specifically the order of Reader—in the Orthodox Church.[73] Two weeks after that, a man I knew of but hadn't met came to my house, uninvited; I had a few guests whom he knew. He was—as I later learned he often is—drunk and abusive, for he was an alcoholic, and he somehow knew of my recent "tonsure." That evening, reeling but standing so as to look down on our little sitting circle—he began a stream of anti-Christian mocking. The nature of his derision, aimed entirely at me, was familiar enough: how could a virgin birth have occurred to a biologically human female; did I suppose that Mary engaged in sexual intercourse with Joseph after Jesus's birth; why are Christians so terrified of erotic sexuality, especially the Christian saints. Put as questions, they were of course statements.

This man had lost all access to a profound understanding that Righteous John, Wonderworker of Kronstadt, has articulated this way: "Establish in your mind and heart this truth: that the invisible plays the first part in the whole world, in every being; and that when the invisible leaves a certain being, the latter loses life and is destroyed: so that the visible in beings, without the invisible, forms but a mass of earth. I and all men live through an invisible first cause—God."[74]

Now, to someone possessing perfect spiritual organization (say, a saint), the relation between visible surface and invisible energy is everywhere and always experienced as simultaneously *shaped* and *useful*. By "shaped" I mean that the saint experiences this relation as something that possesses definite pattern and clear, distinct rhythm. What gives expression to this pattern and rhythm is for the saint a life of prayer, a life in which certain words and ideas *not of his own devising* are repeated—and usually sung or chanted—throughout the hours of each day. The clarity and firmness of this daily cycle of prayers therefore becomes for the saint the most perfect expression of this relation between a life's surface and its in-forming depth. Repeated through days and years into a lifetime, sounding with the simultaneous familiarity and freshness of birdsong, the cycle's firm shapeliness tells how and why and when the visible world every day arises from the invisible energies. Thus, the usefulness of the shaped relation is vividly apparent. For if every instant of visible life is charged with invisible energy, then that relation which permits this fact to be felt most directly and most steadily becomes the most clearly *useful* relation. For the saint, this is first of all a practical matter.

What struck me the next day was the connection between anti-Christian mocking and alcoholism. Alcoholism is a sickness on all four levels of human existence: the physical, the emotional, the mental, and the spiritual or *noetic*. On the first level, the alcoholic becomes physically ill very soon in the disease, and grows progressively sicker as the condition deepens. Certain internal organs of the body are directly attacked—above all, the liver— while the whole physical system deteriorates steadily. The shaking hands and the swollen face are signals of a physical life in deepening crisis. The emotional derangements parallel the physical ones. The alcoholic quickly becomes at once disturbed and disturbing, experiencing hostile and fearful feelings that simultaneously create the same feelings in others. This emotional derangement explains why the alcoholic seizes and holds the psychic centerstage in any social setting: anger and terror are emotions so extreme that, in most social circumstances, they will engulf all other feelings. Alcoholics may drink alone, but they emotionally crave a relatively sober social setting to provide the triggering conditions for the release of their hostility and paranoia. Certainly that deliberate artifice of feeling we call courtesy is wholly destroyed in alcoholic emotion (that this guest in my house had not met me before made no difference to his desire to dominate). The result is inevitable: anger or fear, or both at once, are created in the alcoholic's circle of family and friends. Much has been written on the process termed *enabling*, whereby the alcoholic's circle supports the disaster that is unfolding through a complex series of denials of and adjustments to it. This process can also be rightly seen, I think, as emotional usurpation.

The intellectual disorders of alcoholism follow a similar pattern— but with a significant difference. The body breaks down in linear fashion (though the speed and mode vary for each person). The intellectual disorder, however, is not linear but spiral. Ideas become for the alcoholic very hard to hold in place; but the power to use language socially is often increased by the use of alcohol. This is a common enough experience: a glass or two of wine, for example, and suddenly our ability to talk French is wonderfully enlarged. This step-up in the social use of language suits, perfectly, the alcoholic's emotional will to power. As alcohol makes permeable the barriers between conscious mind and unconscious emotion, social language becomes saturated with personal need. The experience is very powerful, for it effects a union of sorts between language and feeling. The alcoholic often grows more and more articulate as unconscious feeling finds linguistic pattern. But, of course, what the alcoholic can articulate is only his own terror and rage. And in time his circle reflects these feelings back to him, the alcoholic begins to articulate *their* feelings—and so he usurps the emotional language of his circle.[75] They are therefore reduced to silence by his articulation—which further plunges him into deeper anger and vaster fear, and still greater articulation. And so the spiral opens in which language deepens into greater emotional expressiveness and shallower intellectual content. He cannot stop talking and cannot stop feeling. But his thinking is getting dimmer.

The spiritual disarray illumines the other three. The visible world of our lives—the endlessly intricate and vivid surfaces we ceaselessly experience through our senses—stands in strong relation to the invisible energies that shape those visible surfaces.

For the alcoholic, this shaped and useful relation between the visible world and its invisible energies becomes shapeless and uncontrollable. As his language becomes solely a means for emotional expression, his grasp on reasoned thought, along with the orderly patterns of courtesy, begin to dissolve. For such courteous thought gives form and even substance to our part of a bridge between the visible world and the invisible energies that inform it. These energies are (as the biblical and older literary understanding saw quite exactly) angels or messengers from the invisible God. And as the alcoholic's ability to thoughtfully reason fades or becomes disordered, he loses the sense of angelic presence in and behind the visible world and so begins to experience the invisible energies precisely in the form of the alcohol itself: that is, as something fluid, infinite, dark, and engulfing. A cruel parody of spiritual illumination then begins to unfold, one in which the saint's self-surrender in prayer becomes, for the alcoholic, self-obliteration in liquor. But as saint and alcoholic move toward their respective ends, the gulf between them widens and then even the parody collapses: the saint enters into the life of the living God while the alcoholic enters the living death of his own terror and rage—all the more alone as the spiritual chaos continues to act back upon the alcoholic's mind and emotions and body, further disordering the other three levels of life. And as his will to dominate increases, his helplessness spreads.[76]

That night, as our guest mocked Christianity, he was exhibiting alcoholic disarray on all four levels. For anti-Christian mocking of that sort is a disordering of actual, lived human life.[77] It attributes false physicality to spiritual relations by making literal what is invisible, at the same time it falsely spiritualizes the human body and "disappears" its actuality. Throughout much of the twentieth century we witnessed the Soviet government's attempts to make such mockery a part of daily Russian life. The attempt has, from most reports, largely failed. For example, before World War II, anti-Christian processions used to be held at Christmas and Easter in the streets of Moscow and other cities, crude and carnival and deliberately sacrilegious. Timothy Ware—who became Bishop Kallistos—quotes one Russian witness to these processions:

> There were no protests from the silent streets—the years of terror had done their work—but nearly everyone tried to turn off the road when they met this shocking procession. I, personally, as a witness of the Moscow carnival, may certify that there was not a drop of popular pleasure in it. The parade moved along empty streets and its attempts at creating laughter or provocation met with dull silence on the part of the occasional witnesses.[78]

Why has this mockery failed? It failed for the reason historian John Lukacs once expressed this way: "people will live if they must with oppression and suffering; they will not live long with untruth."[79] Anti-Christian mockery, like alcoholism, is essentially an engagement with untruth.

It would follow that an engagement with Christianity would be an engagement with Truth—and so I say it.[80] I am, however, also saying (1) that an engagement with Orthodox Christianity—with the historic Eastern Orthodox faith—is an engagement with the clearest and fullest Christian truth, and (2) that *only* in engaging Orthodoxy can the clarity and completeness of Christian truth be known and experienced. I am fully aware of the outrageous tone these assertions may have for some people, perhaps for many. So I want to be very clear in saying what I am *not* asserting. I do *not* assert that the truth of the world is known solely to Orthodox Christians and to no one else. For I am following here Bishop Kallistos when he writes, "We know where the Orthodox Church is but we cannot be sure where it is not; and so we must refrain from passing judgment. . . ."[81] Orthodox teaching holds that some outside the Church are very close to Orthodoxy, while others are very far away. But Orthodox believers are forbidden to judge another's closeness or distance because it is only our own relation, each one of us alone, that is our proper concern. The Orthodox Church seeks the conversion of everyone on earth to her. But she awaits this fullness in the chiaroscuro of history, in God's time, not in ours. Finally, as Bishop Kallistos says, "it must not be thought that Orthodox demand the submission of other Christians to a particular centre of power and jurisdiction."[82] The Orthodox Church is decentralized in organization and administration, with each and every church in all practical ways autonomous.

Alone on earth, what the Orthodox Church asks is total self-abandonment to the fullness of Truth, always invisibly accessible in her visible mysteries.

A Monk of the Heart in the World

St. Symeon the New Theologian

"It's not the habit that makes a monk;
the only true monk is one who lives in his heart.
Be a monk of the heart in the world."

—FR. ROMAN BRAGA

1987

LAST EPIPHANY, I WAS on retreat at St. Tikhon's, where I met Viktor, of Kiev. A devout Orthodox believer, he had emigrated from Kiev some six years ago. In Kiev he was an astrophysicist; at St. Tikhon's he is the caretaker, cleaning the floors and rooms and kitchens—and living a life deeply in the Liturgy of the monastery and seminary of St. Tikhon's. He wrote me a letter in late January. I'd written him after my return home, to thank him and his wife and son (a seminarian) for his hospitality. I'd talked in my letter of the beauty of the New Hampshire mountains where I live, of how God's love can be felt in these mountains and forests. Here's how he answered me [translated by his wife into English]:

> Dear Donald,
>
> Peace be to your home!
>
> It's pleasant to receive such kind letters as yours. My wife and my son and I came to love right away, that very evening, our

Christmas Eve. And we, I think, forever will keep the memory of that wonderful and holy Eve. That's why it was good to find out from your letter that you by God's mercy arrived safely home and already reminisced about our talks of Dante, about languages, about Kiev. . . .

Thank you for the kind and warm words which I believe come from your heart. We remember and hope that perhaps even this summer, God willing, we'll see you again.

It seems to me, that that majestic landscape which surrounds you in New Hampshire—mountains, woods, rivers, waterfalls, lakes, flowers, grass, and sun, and air, and the clouds floating above the heads—acquires a special beauty and expressiveness according to our spiritual state. Our flesh, its vain existence, that "vanity of vanities" prevents us from penetrating the innermost mysteries of nature and participating in its beauty and harmony. This happens despite the desire of the human heart, yet unfortunately it is often forced into submitting to that vanity. And only by the Savior's mercy are we freed from those vain nets of death, and then appears the marvelous truth of life's beauty. Then, finally, we realize how much greater the Creator is than the creation. "Taste and see that the Lord is good"—this is from the Psalter [33:8 LXX].

You've promised to read books by Symeon the New Theologian. I've read them recently and found there a lot of precious and spiritual material, that which an Orthodox Christian is so in need of now. I think that you too will enjoy familiarizing yourself with this saint, and then, when we see each other again, we'll gladly exchange our impressions.

Let the blessing of our loving Lord be upon you and your family.

Viktor

This is how I began to read St. Symeon. I dedicate this essay to Viktor.

This will be an introduction to selected main themes in St. Symeon, a kind of report on my first discoveries. I don't pretend it's anything greater than a mere report.

To begin: Central to St. Symeon's work is Orthodox apophatic theology, or mystical theology. This is a very great and very beautiful subject—one about which I want here to make only two simple (but I think essential) observations.

First: that God can be known only in surrendering our normal modes of knowing.

Second: that the operations of the Holy Spirit are not confined in time or place (for example, to the first apostles in Jerusalem), but they are active in every Christian's life: now and always—and unto ages of ages; that is, beyond our death.

I shall return to these two points. But I want to begin by emphasizing a very important fact about Symeon: For him, the details of his actual life were spiritually charged with meaning; and, thus, to record these details was, for him, to reveal the spiritual power that gave those details their meaning. To appreciate the importance of this fact, you must see it against the background of Orthodox monastic life.

In Orthodox monastic life, there is a strong and clear distinction made between one's *individuality* and one's *personhood*. *Individuality* is the assemblage of one's accidental qualities—color of your hair or eyes, for example, or skin, or social background, or family history. You may share aspects of your individuality with many other people; in this sense, our individuality is part of our common humanity. One's *personhood*, however, is quite different. In theological terms, your personhood is that which responds to God's call to *be*, to *exist*, in relation to Him. Hence, your personhood is made clear in your power to love. In this power you are absolutely unique and irreplaceable: you share your personhood with no one else—at the very moment you find it only in loving another, and ultimately in loving God.

To feel this distinction, consider someone you love. What is it you love? Is it their eye color or their hair? It is certainly signaled by these things—but what you love, finally, is not their *individuality* but their *personhood*: that is, you love what has *called you out* to them. And this is (of course) precisely what they love in you: your personhood.

Now, in the ascetic life of the Orthodox monk, what the monk seeks to do is let his personhood take over and consume his individuality. This taking-over and this consummation are acts of *ardor*: that is, they are processes in which individuality is *burned away* (for that's what "ardor" means) so as to reveal, purely and fully, personhood.

These processes of ardor may occur very slowly over a monk's lifetime, with few or no perceptible shifts: except for the sense (now and then) that certain aspects of one's individuality have been gone for some time. Or the ardor may work very rapidly—then indeed it's a flame of fire, a flame that burns up in *a moment's spiritual holocaust* an entire lifetime of enslavement to one's individuality.

Now, it is against this background of monastic life that the fact I mentioned before takes on its importance. For (to repeat) St. Symeon regarded certain details of his individuality as spiritually essential to his personhood. Let us return, now, to my two points about Orthodox mystical theology, and see how they operate in St. Symeon.

First, God can be known only through *the willing surrender of our usual ways of knowing.* St. Symeon in his *Discourses* writes this sentence: "Unless the mind comes to the contemplation of the things that are above thought, it does not perceive the mystical activity."[83] Symeon believed that the whole aim of Christian life lay precisely here: in the direct vision of Christ. He felt that we are in our lives as blind men are: we stumble up against things, and sometimes we experience pain and sometimes we feel pleasure—but we've no idea what we are really up against. To know *in truth* what we are up against, Symeon felt, we must gain our sight: which means, we must gain the direct vision of Christ. For Symeon, that direct vision arrived as the experience of light: a light beyond any human source and beyond any natural source such as sunlight. This light was not something he reasoned himself toward; in fact, when it came, it superseded rationality the way a single candle is superseded by the full blaze of a noonday sun. Symeon describes his experience this way:

> One day, as he stood and recited, "God, have mercy upon me a sinner" [Luke 18:13], uttering it with his mind rather than his mouth, suddenly a flood of divine radiance appeared from above and filled the room. As this happened the young man lost all awareness [of his surroundings] and forgot that he was in a house or that he was under a roof. He saw nothing but light all around him and did not know if he was standing on the ground. He was not afraid of falling; he was wholly in the presence of immaterial light and seemed himself to have turned into light. Oblivious of all the world, he was filled with tears and with ineffable joy and gladness. His mind then ascended to heaven and beheld yet another light, which was clearer than that which was close at hand. In a wonderful manner there appeared to him, standing close to that light, the saint of whom we have spoken, the old man equal to angels, who had given him the commandment and the book. (*Discourses*, 245–46)

This is an extraordinary account, vivid, lucid, powerful. Notice the key features.

- Loss of all awareness of surroundings— that is, usual modes of mental sensing are suspended.

- In this light he himself turned into light— that is, *he becomes what he beholds.*

- His emotions—filled with tears and filled with joy—are not contradictions but harmonies.

He concludes his account by saying this:

> Once this vision was over and the young man, as he told me, had come to himself, he was moved with joy and amazement. He wept with all his heart, and sweetness accompanied his tears. Finally he fell on his bed. At that very moment the cock crowed and announced the middle of the night. Soon afterwards the church bells rang for matins and he himself rose to sing psalms as usual, without ever thinking of sleep that night. (*Discourses,* 246)

Again, note: he wept—and a sweetness accompanied the tears. Emotions that normally conflict with and exclude one another (tears and peace) are in this experience fully reconciled. This seems to be one clear consequence that follows upon the knowing that is beyond knowing: our emotional life is in an instant completely healed, completely harmonized.[84]

Now, Symeon teaches that such experiences cannot be willed by us. Nor should they be.[85] What we *can* will is: a willingness to be open to its happening. And the way, says Symeon, for us to become open is the way of repentance, the way of following the commandments of Christ, the way of purification in the Holy Orthodox Church. Symeon says:

> Where there is the keeping of the commandments, there is the purification of the flesh, and from the cloud that besets the soul and prevents it from clearly seeing God's ray of light. Where there is purification, there is illumination. (*Discourses,* 248)

I repeat: "Where there is purification, there is illumination."

A side-note on the word "purification": its roots are *pur*, "fire," and the verb *facie*, "to make": hence, to purify means to make fire, to cause to be burnt away. Purification therefore is the way into personhood. Thus, in showing that God can be known only through going beyond knowing, Symeon uses the details of his individual experience as aspects or revelations of his personhood.

My second main point about Orthodox mystical theology is this: the acts of the Holy Spirit are not confined to one time and place (for example, the first apostles in Jerusalem) but are always and everywhere active in every Christian's life. Now this is a good moment, I think, to tell some simple facts of Symeon's life. He was born in 949, in Galatia in Asia Minor, of a noble family. At the age of eleven he was (said his uncle Basil) "distinguished by rare beauty and rare elegance." His uncle arranged for him to go to the imperial court at Constantinople to continue his education. But, at age fourteen,

Symeon met a person who was to determine his entire life. This was the holy monk of the famous Byzantine monastery of Studion, whose name also was Symeon (we know him now as Symeon the Studite). The monk's impact on the young Symeon was extraordinary. Years later, Symeon wrote that he "made known to me the state of my soul." What happened, clearly, is that the elder Symeon *called out the personhood* of the younger.

The result was, the young Symeon no longer wished to follow after the brilliant individualities of his life. At age fourteen, he begged his elder's permission to enter the monastery. Here is the deeper wisdom of the elder's response, a wisdom that lies at the heart of Orthodox tradition: the elder Symeon told the young boy he could enter the monastery at age twenty-seven—almost twice the boy's age. As guide, however, for those years, he gave the boy two mystical treatises by St. Mark the Ascetic—a spiritual master of Orthodox prayer from five hundred years earlier. (These two treatises are, in fact, the eighth and ninth selections in the *Philokalia*.[86]) These treatises became for young Symeon the anchor of his life. It was a gift, said Symeon, "sent by God Himself."

He read these texts, he tells us, "with longing and with attention," and three sentences from them he fixed in his heart. It is worth our while to read them, both for what they tell us about Symeon and for what they reveal about Orthodox spirituality. The first sentence was this:

> If you want spiritual healing, listen to your conscience, do everything it tells you, and you will benefit. (*Discourses*, 244)

A luminous sentence. It tells us that we have an inward voice of higher wisdom, an inner voice that speaks to us and we can hear it. Our spiritual healing lies in our doing *"everything"* our inner voice is telling us to do.

The second sentence, Symeon goes on to say, was this:

> He who seeks the acts of the Holy Spirit before he has practiced the commandments is like someone who sells himself into slavery and who, as soon as he is bought, asks to be given his freedom while still keeping his purchase-money. (*Discourses*, 244)

The primary injunction in this sentence is clear: you must follow the commandments of Christ, day in and day out, with discipline and perseverance if you seek the active presence of the Holy Spirit in your life.[87] The analogy the sentence uses, though, requires some care. If you *don't* practice Christ's commandments, then you are like someone who—after selling himself into slavery (that is, into the entrapments of one's individuality)—wants to get out by being bought by someone and keeping the purchase money for himself. That is, you are someone who wants his personhood without giving up

his individuality—that is, you won't pay the price. This second sentence, of
course, corrects for any potential dangers in the first sentence. You are to
follow your inner voice—but you are to carry out Christ's commandments.
You are to do *both* things, always and everywhere.

The third passage that the young Symeon learned by heart was this:

> Blind is the man crying out and saying: "Son of David, have
> mercy on me." He prays with the body alone, and not yet with
> spiritual knowledge. When the man once blind received his sight
> and saw the Lord, he acknowledged Him no longer as Son of
> David but as Son of God, and worshipped Him. (*Discourses*, 244)

In this progression, the blind man gains knowledge at the moment
he gains sight, and he abandons the social-historic individuality of the title
"Son of David" and replaces it with the true *personal* name of Jesus, that
is, the Name that signifies His sacred personhood. His eyes are opened,
and he actually *sees* Christ, and the process of prayer then culminates in
worship, in adoration.

These three sentences become for Symeon the basis for his life. For
fourteen years—until the age of twenty-seven—he lived and worked in
the brilliant and complicated world of Byzantine imperial court life. He
was (he tells us) "handsome in appearance, elegant in body, manners, and
style." No one was aware of his spiritual pursuits, he also tells us; and he
continued to manage complex employment for the Byzantine aristocracy.
But his morning and evening prayers grew longer and longer, especially
his evening prayer.

Symeon tells us about this time in his life:

> As he assured me by an oath, he did no more than carry out the
> simple command that old man had given him, every evening
> before he laid himself to sleep on his bed. So when his con-
> science told him, "You must perform additional reverences and
> say more psalms, and repeat "'Lord, have mercy,' for you can
> do it," he obeyed with eagerness and without hesitation. He did
> all these things as if God Himself had told him so. From that
> time on he never went to bed with his conscience reproaching
> him and asking him, "Why have you not done this?" So, as he
> constantly followed its demands and as it daily demanded more
> of him, in a few days' time his evening prayers became much
> longer. During the day he managed a patrician's household and
> daily went to the palace, engaged in worldly affairs, so that no
> one was aware of his pursuits. (*Discourses*, 245)

It was in this state of prayer-life that Symeon experienced his illumination of Christ (which I quoted before). This occurred, he says, while he was "living in the midst of the city and was in charge of a house and supervised slaves and freemen, and was carrying out all the duties and activities of ordinary life" (*Discourses,*, 248).

For Symeon, the Holy Spirit did not act once or in one place, but is permanently acting in the world and in the affairs of ordinary life. He himself was not living as a professed monastic; rather, he was living as a brilliant court-careerist, one clearly on a fast-track to material success. Yet at the same time he was living, since his fourteenth year, a life of prayer shaped by the teachings of the Orthodox Church. A concept articulated about a century before Symeon is pertinent here. St. Hesychios the Priest says, "It is easy to be a monk in one's outer self if one wants to be; but no small struggle is required to be a monk in one's inner self."[88] This perfectly expresses these fourteen years of Symeon's life: he was living, inwardly, the life of an Orthodox monastic.

The second fact I wish to mention about Symeon's life I shall do more briefly. Three years after he entered the monastery at Studion, he was made Abbot of the monastery at St. Mamas. The year was 980, and he was thirty-one years old at his election. St. Mamas was near Studion, and Symeon had continued his attachment to the elder Symeon as his spiritual advisor. When he assumed leadership of St. Mamas, he found a monastery in physical and spiritual decay. For twenty-five years he labored to restore St. Mamas, accomplishing near-miracles of administration both worldly and spiritual in nature.

The central body of Symeon's writings arises from his *Discourses,* which are Matins sermons delivered to the monks of St. Mamas. One quality that strikes a reader of the *Discourses* is worthy of comment: Symeon combines the administrative talents he learned in the imperial courts with his experience of God gained in mystical prayer. The result is a great and deep wisdom, a wisdom at once perfectly aware of the endless intrigues of political life and entirely open to the change of heart that Christ's light brings. A single example: "When in the life of a monastery, a new abbot is to be elected, and the most ambitious monks are pushing to the front while the truly virtuous monks are being swept aside, you must hold firmly to what is right, until it becomes impossible to do so. Then, Symeon says:

> [B]e merciful, compassionate, be lenient, take pity, and mourn
> over such people and weep tears. Since you have been vouchsafed
> to see clearly, represent in your mind the wounds of your breth-
> ren, how your [fellow]-members have been fractured, how the

whole body has collapsed. Entreat God with all your heart, with toil and tears, to stop the flow of so great an evil and to turn back the hearts of the brethren toward goodness. (*Discourses,* 215)

In other words, follow always and at once both the commandments of Christ and the way of contemplative prayer. He says, too: "You must examine yourself carefully to make sure that you are yourself free from all ambition" (*Discourses,* 217). One sees in Symeon's *Discourses* the sadness of a man beholding the destructive folly of ambition, the joy of a saint beholding Christ's light in the world, and the canniness of a confessor who has seen both things in his own heart; and the sadness, the joy, and the canniness are in perfect balance.

One final fact of Symeon's life. In the year 1009 the Archbishop Stephen of Constantinople challenged Symeon of St. Mamas—this sixty-two-year-old abbot who in a quarter century of devoted work had made his monastery a center of spirituality and learning—: Stephen challenged him to a formal theological debate at the palace of Patriarch Sisinnios. Apparently, Archbishop Stephen feared that Symeon was introducing a personalistic or individualistic form of worship, one that challenged *directly* the Church hierarchy.

At the distance of a thousand years, it is difficult to see what Archbishop Stephen found so troublesome. Certain issues of theology—for example, Symeon's view on grace and consciousness, or his teachings about the power to forgive sins—now seem to us perfectly consistent with central Orthodox teachings. The politics—court and ecclesiastical—are forever lost to us. But, whatever the cause, the consequence is known: Symeon was exiled in the year 1009, to a remote coastal town in Asia Minor. Near the town, he found the ruins of a small chapel dedicated to Saint Marina. A handful of monks from St. Mamas followed him into exile. One of them was from a wealthy family; and with this man's financial help, Symeon built a tiny monastery, and there he settled down to a life of prayer and writing.

Some years passed, and a new patriarch assumed leadership in Constantinople, Patriarch Sergius. Sergius reviewed the case of Symeon and immediately lifted the ban of exile and—by way of reparation—offered Symeon the post of Archbishop, still held by Archbishop Stephen. But Symeon declined the offer and chose instead to remain at St. Marina's, teaching and writing, and devoted to the life of prayer. In 1022, in his thirteenth year of exile, at the age of seventy-three, he died.

In his life, then, Symeon found validated two central propositions of Orthodox mystical theology:

- Full, open commerce between the present moment and the ancient spiritual past;
- This commerce is one in which, always, the vast, high past is flowing into the low, tiny present, even from Symeon to me; the Incarnation is an impossible actuality.

In this validation—this making of strength—the individuality of Symeon merged into the personhood of Symeon in such a way that certain features of individuality were not consumed but transfigured; that is, the fire of ardor did not burn away these features but made them radiant in a way we can still see a thousand years later, vivid and burning with ardor, as here:

> My dear fathers and brethren, as soon as I called to mind the beauty of undefiled love, its light suddenly appeared in my heart. I have been ravished with its delight and have ceased to perceive outward things; I have lost all sense of this life and have forgotten the things that are at hand. Yet again—I am at a loss how to say it—it has removed far from me and left me to lament my own weakness. O all-desirable love, how happy is he who has embraced you, for he will no longer have a passionate desire to embrace any earthly beauty! Happy is he who is moved by divine love to cling to you! He will deny the whole world, yet as he associates with all men he will be wholly untainted. . . . Happy is he who passionately embraces you, for he will be wondrously changed! (*Discourses*, 43)

In this process whereby Symeon's individuality became (in some senses) his personhood, a great mystery is accomplished: the mystery of sanctification. And the major and constantly repeated teaching of Symeon in his *Discourses* to the monks of St. Mamas is that this mystery is the secret process of every Christian life on earth. This work and discipline is the *only* real work of every Christian: a work all the richer and wiser if it appears poor and foolish to the world. For such a life, says Symeon, "though . . . without any visible glory . . . will be more glorious than all that is glorious, more honored and august than all that is honored" (*Discourses*, 43).

At the end of Discourse XXI, Symeon speaks movingly to a recently departed brother of St. Mamas, Brother Anthony, saying to him: "I know well that now you see clearly, having come out of the darkness and mists of this body. You see my soul in all its nakedness and its very thoughts . . ." (242). This is an extraordinary moment. As Symeon gazes into the living space where now is Brother Anthony, he sees—with what vivid shock!—the clarified gaze of Brother Anthony returning to him: and Symeon stands wholly revealed in this total and perfect gaze. We glimpse also in this exchange the one most perfect Face, the only completely true Eyes. "This is the One who is also (as we know) three Persons." Here, says Symeon, is "joy unspeakable, in the unutterable glory and brightness that is *seen* in the Father and the Son and the Holy Spirit and adored forever."

Finally, this: as Orthodox we all carry the name of an Orthodox saint; and to that saint we are joined in a love that is hidden, fructifying, and sustaining; and in this condition of love we every day pray for and find and receive love, and the whole of the Holy Orthodox Church is praying every day with each of us, mystically and completely praying.

And I think, too, that a second saint seeks each of us, a saint whose personhood is for us so bursting with light and with holy love that we can only gladly obey his call to love. For me, on retreat last Epiphany, this call came to me not from His Grace the Bishop, nor from his priests nor his deacons nor his seminarians (as illumined and spiritually rich as they all so very beautifully are). The call came from the caretaker, Viktor, a man humble in the world's eyes, a man of no ecclesiastical rank. I almost didn't hear it; I almost, in my normal, everyday, distracted and self-absorbed emptiness, missed it. But God had better things for me as I was busy making my plans. He was bringing me my life.[89]

7

The Transfiguration of Don Sheehan

HILARY MULLINS

"Your work at this conference," he would say at The Frost Place,
"is to make the art of at least one other person better and stronger
by giving—in love—all your art to them."

NINE A.M. AUGUST 6TH, 2004, at The Frost Place in Franconia, New Hampshire.[90] We are assembled in Robert Frost's old barn.

Don at The Frost Place, Franconia, New Hampshire.

It's the second-to-last day of the annual week-long poetry conference, and though lots of us are tired at this point, there's still a quietly-bright buzz in the air: every day here brings good things. But before the morning's lecture gets underway, Don Sheehan, founding director of The Frost Place writing programs, rises and walks to the lectern, clearing his throat to make his customary morning remarks.

At this point, Don, with the quiet assistance of his wife, Carol, has been running The Frost Place for almost thirty years, handling the multitude of various tasks involved. But I know very little about all that: the thing I have been learning about Don Sheehan is how, through all his teaching, he helps people bring forth their best and deepest selves and change their lives.

This morning he begins by noting the date: August 6th, going on to explain how it is one of the high holy days in the Russian Orthodox calendar, the feast of Transfiguration. This of course is not a common topic at most writing workshops, but his Russian Orthodox faith is a common topic for Don, and he begins to elaborate on the biblical story, describing how Jesus, on his way to Jerusalem to be crucified, taking three of his disciples, climbs a high mountain where suddenly he is transfigured by light, his face shining like the sun, his clothes dazzling white. The wonderful thing about this, Don stresses, is that this moment of Jesus's transfiguration is also a transfiguration of the world: the holy is *here*. Not somewhere else, but here, now.

Nine years it's been since Don spoke those words and he himself now is no longer here. And yet, I think of him almost every day. And looking back, part of what strikes me is how truly unusual he was, not only in the largely secular world of writing workshops but probably in most places he went. At the most obvious level, the reason for this was his devout Russian Orthodox practice. But it went far deeper than that, as did his gifts to those of us who knew him.

Though I am a Unitarian Universalist myself, I had the great fortune to know him first in his own context, tagging along with a friend one evening to what I thought was a Bible study class for members of St. Jacob's, a small Russian Orthodox congregation in Northfield Falls, Vermont. What I was expecting was a small circle, primarily women, gathered around the priest in chairs, nibbling cookies perhaps, leafing through Bibles balanced on their knees, commenting perceptively but mildly on lectionary passages.

What I got was something altogether different. For one thing, the people who came to the class that evening, men and women both around the table, were serious in a way I was not used to. That was partly a function, I'd guess, of the devotional character of Russian Orthodoxy, with its calendar structuring life around faith. But it was also Don himself. A scholar with a poet's heart dedicating the bulk of his energies to the Russian Orthodox

tradition, he taught by spreading out the fruits of his scholarship and invit-
ing us to take and eat. My own beliefs, theologically speaking, run along
more liberal lines than his did, but I knew right away on that first night in
his class, he was the religious teacher I'd prayed to find. So I kept attending
and sometimes too visited him and Carol in Sharon at their home, sharing
meals, spending time in the garden and, wonderful pleasure, spending time
also with the rest of their family.

Even then, Don was already ill, suffering with the beginning symp-
toms of the condition that three years ago [in 2010] ended his life, probably an undiagnosed case of Lyme Disease. And yet though I remember
him being bone-tired, he never lost his gentleness or his characteristic
bright clarity. He was in his mid-sixties then, with fly-away eyebrows
and look-clear-at-you blue eyes—a shy, soft-spoken man, reflexively self-
effacing, who appeared like the scholar he was in his well-used, rumpled
khakis and button-up shirts—except that because he and Carol were off
the grid on their somewhat remote hillside in the woods, he also wore
things like serious boots in the winter and a faded blue hand-knit hat to
keep away the cold.

And that is another key thing to understand about Don: money and
position were never his goals. This is clear, for instance, in the decision
he'd made much earlier in his life, before his conversion, to give up a tenure track job at the University of Chicago. In fact, even though he was at
Dartmouth, Don Sheehan was an adjunct professor—a low-rung position
on the academic ladder. But I doubt he regretted his choices—not because
he lacked ambition, but because his ambition aimed for what he thought
were worthier things. And this dedication of his to higher callings had a
tendency to rub off on others.

For Don Sheehan had a way. He was never one to call attention to himself, but in a room full of people, he was still someone you'd notice, not least
of all because of his unusually long beard, the kind older Russian Orthodox
men seem to cultivate. It draped down over his chest, a fluffy white wing
attached to his chin.

I don't mean to claim by this that Don was angelic exactly, but the truth
is, the man was so immersed in soul-work, he threw off a little light. And
he was always casting that light toward you. That was one of the remarkable
things about him: given his teaching at the church, and at Dartmouth, and
particularly as director of The Frost Place, he was continually in situations
perfectly rigged with opportunities for misusing his power and padding his
ego. But he passed all that by, leading in the humblest way I've ever seen.
And I don't think this was because he failed to understand power: I think it
was because as a man and as a Christian, he understood the best thing to do

with power is give it away. Not to dissipate it, as if it were a dangerous electrical charge, but to transform it into love, keeping the circles of its impact ever rippling out into the world at large.

Another element fundamental to this practice of self-extending was the way Don did not strike. Having survived a childhood that was at times shattered by brutal violence, he understood the multitude of diverse, often subtle blows we deal one another. And he made a practice of not passing them on. So, in class at St. Jacob's for instance, he never engaged in the far-too-common disheartening practice of chopping up or dismissing our responses. There were even times when I wished he would—a little anyway—be a tad more corrective perhaps—for instance, when it seemed another student's reading of a passage was clearly off the mark. But it was Don's habit instead to say yes and keep us walking with him, all the while modeling the way through his own fine work—essays and lectures that were deep and wide and reflective, pathways into marvelous complexities.

This approach of his he made explicit in The Frost Place workshops, starting off the week each year with these words:

> If you must make a flash choice between sympathy and intelligence, choose sympathy. Usually these fall apart—sympathy becoming a mindless "being nice" to everyone, while intelligence becomes an exercise in contempt. But here's the great fact of this Festival of Poetry: as you come to care about another person's art (and not your own), then your own art becomes mysteriously better.

And it was true. We were all always becoming mysteriously better under Don's tutelage. And happily, he had a way of making the work itself deeply satisfying, approaching writing not only as a believer but a lover too. In our classes at church, for example, passages from the monastic Saint Isaac of Syria or the chapters in First and Second Samuel were not abstract "texts" to be deconstructed: Don was no vivisectionist. Instead, he turned all the powers of his scholarship towards bringing out a passage's depth, approaching each one as real, as a lovely, created thing, like a chapel or a shaded pool, a place to be entered with reverence and wonder and pleasure.

Likewise, it seems to me that what Don did at The Frost Place was very similar, renewing poetry for others because he believed it too was real. And this is not just a pretty way of speaking. Where our secular culture denudes the sacred properties of poetry, of all art in fact, Don was deeply grounded in a tradition that has never lost its sense of the holy in art. As I understand it, for instance, a Russian Orthodox icon, properly prepared and painted, is not just a painting: it is a portal for the holy, an actual opening through which God moves toward us and through which we can move toward God, where indeed we are invited to do so.

The same goes for the written word; just as St. Isaac of Syria had explained in the seventh century, holy books in Russian Orthodoxy are understood to be places where the light of God shines through: "Those who in their way of life are led by divine grace to be enlightened are always aware of something like a noetic ray running between the written lines which enables the mind to distinguish words spoken simply from those spoken with great meaning for the soul's enlightenment."

The first time I read those words off a Xeroxed sheet in Don's classroom, they made the lights come on in me, as if a Christmas tree in a darkened room had just been plugged in, glowing suddenly with the light I'd always known was there in things I read and loved, bits of bright color weaving in and out of the branches, deep glimmerings from within all the recesses.

The psalms, too, were places Don brought us into the same way, teaching us the ancient chiastic pattern they're written in. That is to say, psalms move not only from start to finish in the linear way we're used to, they also move in a call and response fashion across the whole of the psalm, back and forth across the center, calling us, as we read, to pay attention to how the first and last verses are related, along with how the second and second-to-last are connected too, and all the others in just the same way, until we reach mid-point, which is the place where, one way or another, God appears, turning the poem in some way. But of course for Don, whose religious practice for years had included praying the psalms every day, this appearance of God wasn't simply a reference that functioned in the narrative logic of the poem: it was, just as in icons, the place where touching and being touched by God was actually possible.

To us this chiastic doubling-back-and-forth pattern across the center is so counter-intuitive, it can take some getting used to, but one inexact analogy is this: think of yourself again as a child, hopping along a slate sidewalk, coming down from every hop with one foot on each of two paired slabs—hop, hop, hop—until then you come to the center, the deepest point of the journey, where the presence of God wells up like a sweet water spring in a hollow. Then imagine lying down, here, now, in this marvelously still, green-grass place.

Now you might think from these kinds of descriptions that what I'm going to relate next is the story of my own conversion. But that is not what happened: I was certainly changed by Don's teaching, and I loved the way his tradition approached things that usually are understood as merely metaphorical, rendering them instead as vibrantly and powerfully real. But still, I have never shared his—or anyone else's—certainty about the workings of the divine. And Don knew this. Yet, in spite of that deep commitment to his own faith, he never cajoled conversion or conversely set me outside the walls in any way: these too were the sorts of corrections he did not engage in. Even while we were studying Isaac's lovely passage about the noetic ray glimmering in amongst the written word, and I said I'd experienced the same thing in, say, a poem by Frost, Don did not close the door. "Orthodoxy points to where the truth *is*," he said. "It doesn't say where the truth is not."

It was this sort of catholic approach that meant poets even more secular than I could benefit from Don's sense of the holy in poetry. We never talked about this explicitly, but my guess is that his daily contemplative reading of the psalms did lead him to find many contemporary poems to be empty, echoing forth a hollow space where he was accustomed to sensing God. And yet it seems he did sometimes see more in them too. For instance, once, on the wooded hill beside his house, I asked him, theologically speaking, for his definition of grace. He smiled in his unassuming way and told me he thought it was like the passage in Frost's poem "The Death of the Hired Man," where the farmer and his wife, in the course of deciding whether or not to take in their occasional (and historically unreliable) hired man, are talking about the definition of home:

> "Warren," she said, "he has come home to die: You needn't be afraid he'll leave you this time."
>
> "Home," he mocked gently.
>
> "Yes, what else but home? It all depends on what you mean by home. Of course he's nothing to us, any more than was the hound that came a stranger to us out of the woods, worn out upon the trail."
>
> "Home is the place where, when you have to go there, they have to take you in."
>
> "I should have called it something you somehow haven't to deserve."[91]

The last lines of course embody the generosity of Don Sheehan himself, a generosity he shared through all his teaching, be his subject a homily of St. Isaac's, a poem of Robert Frost's, or a theological concept he thought could bring something deeply good to our lives too. But he was remarkably kind in smaller, everyday acts as well, even in the very way he gave you all his attention in a conversation. And the sum total of all this of course is that this ongoing generosity of his quietly but powerfully influenced many, many people.

And because he knew the healing power this practice had for him as well, the mysterious way it had of making him better, he was always enjoining us to do the same: "Your work at this conference," he would say at The Frost Place, "is to make the art of at least one other person better and stronger by giving—in love—all your art to them."

In the end I think he stressed love so much because he knew and understood its opposite so well. He and I never discussed what went on in his home when he was a boy, but in an essay on the Orthodox concepts in *The Brothers Karamazov* (still easily found online) he referred to that history to make a point, writing, "I was raised in a violent home where, until I was nine years old, my father's alcohol addiction fueled his open or just barely contained violence, a home where my mother was beaten over and over (I remember her face covered with blood)."[92]

Nine years ago, on August 6th, 2004, when Don Sheehan got up before the morning's craft lecture and spoke, of all things, of the Transfiguration, of the miracle of the holy transfiguring the world, he turned next to its opposite, bringing our attention in his measured way to another event marked by August 6th: the bombing of Hiroshima: "This," he said, "we can refer to as a disfiguration of the world." Knowing disfiguration as he had in his own life, his phrasing was deliberate as quietly he urged us to choose transfiguration in our own lives, not yielding to the innumerable temptations to slight or demean others but instead to make the kinds of gestures that embody the practice of love.

This of course was how Don Sheehan himself transfigured the world as he traveled through it, bringing light wherever he went. And it was what he was pointing to again and again in everything he taught, just as he did each year at the beginning of The Frost Place Festival: "The key that unlocks all truth," he said, is "taking very great and very deliberate care with each other." This infinitely exacting, transforming task was his greatest lesson, the one that is up to us all to carry on.

PART TWO

Musical Disciplines of Lyric Art

In sum, "inwardness" expresses the first and most important antinomy: we become larger as we choose for our self and its desirings to become smaller; we are larger on the inside than on the out; in standing with Christ and confining our hungers to Him, whom the human race once tried to confine within the finitude of a tomb, we become infinite. . . . Thus, true inwardness, as Don writes, is a re-musicalizing of one's soul. —GLOSSARY

ANTINOMY MAY BE THE most important term to grasp in the writings gathered here, beginning with Don's and my different ways of understanding the matter of the book—something that I haven't grasped but suspect may be present. Antinomy is a reality in the world given us for our salvation, according to St. Maximus, not simply a literary device, and much more than a *paradox*. In *The Pillar and Ground of the Truth*, Fr. Pavel Florensky describes antinomy as "the experience of disjunction, the experience wherein human discursive rationality breaks helplessly apart in the face of—better, *in the teeth of*—harsh, dissonant realities. Such realities are the very ground of all biblical (indeed, all human) experience." He writes that "the *keeping distinct of the two terms while cohering their contradiction* is the path of Orthodox ascetic discipline, a path characterized by an always deepening love and a forever widening humility."[93] What Don calls in chapter 10 our "noetic beauty" depends on this, for "*earthly antinomy is the way that divine beauty takes root in us.*"

Chapter 9 discusses the polarity of strangeness and familiarity that exists between different historical horizons and their relations and reconciliations. "What we experience as difficulties of approach to the *Paradiso*," Don says, "are what Dante the pilgrim experiences as difficulties of approach to God." But as we approach a distant horizon with "long-guarded speechlessness," we may learn to hear "a voice other than our own." He concludes that in learning to know the *Paradiso*, "every age can come home to itself."

Chapter 10 considers the iconic face and the iconic poem as places "where touching and being touched by God was actually possible." Don examines the various poetic strategies in the seventh-century Akathist to the Mother of God that serve to articulate and resolve antinomies. He finds antinomies in this remarkable work down to the smallest verbal levels. With the enemy miraculously driven from the very gates of Constantinople, impossible contradictions are sung into unity, just as they are before the Orthodox celebration of Christ's Resurrection, quelling the people's fears through such subtle poetic means as rhyming sound or meaning; semantic rhymes with contrasting meanings but similar sounds, or similar meanings with contrasting sounds; verbs rhyming, held together by means of their common subject, each tiny poetic device sharpening into a sort of weapon for unmaking the trauma of the impending attack by simultaneously configuring and rejoicing in the healing noetic presence of the Holy Mother herself. For it is the heart's healing that her Akathist seeks, the awakening of its listeners' every capacity to heal the world's wounds within themselves as it calls on the Unwedded Bride and Mother of God (the greatest of all antinomies) to lead our "noetic re-making." In Don's words, "As the attentive listener is made noetically beautiful by the poem, he is thereby becoming free from terror's disfiguring attack on the noetic faculty itself."

Chapter 11 opens a window into the life and childhood home of poet Robert Frost. Suggesting that *home* is Frost's great subject, Don gives us the poem "The Thatch" as Frost's portrayal of the darkness and light of a home in mortal crisis. Sydney Lea has told me, "There is virtually never a syllogistic rendering of any of [Frost's] poems that has any cogency: indeed, in virtually all of his poetry, there comes a point where 'human discursive rationality breaks helplessly apart'" (here quoting Don). This poem handles the fracture chiastically. With the help of a virtual "class" (as Don left no notes of this discussion), chapter 11 shows how Frost used the formal pattern to render and reconcile in his heart the disturbing antinomies the narrator faced in this home "under thatch."

Chapter 12 is Don's most extensive and exact articulation of how antinomy and chiasmus work in Psalms and of how, in the psalmic unfoldment that begins (in Don's account) in First Samuel 16, the mind of David becomes the Mind of Christ (Don's Scripture-based phrase in that time and context for the *Nous*). The chapter is a revision of an essay published earlier to introduce *The Psalms of David*, here somewhat reorganized, with Fr. Pavel Florensky's significant and blessed presence to it restored. It is republished here with apologies for its earlier redaction. It is one of Don's best.

Chapter 13 reveals composer Benedict Sheehan's rich understanding and embrace of antinomy and chiasmus as he encounters them on several levels: in his own work of composition, in the Orthodox liturgical tradition, in the historically strong psalmic presence to the Vespers service (which his composition has revived), and in the placement, structure, and meaning of the service itself. Each evening, Vespers begins the next liturgical day by promising creation out of the darkness of nonbeing, and "from the descent into darkness comes a mysterious and gladsome light."

—*Xenia Sheehan*

8

Living the Harmony of the Cross

XENIA SHEEHAN WITH FR. MIRCEA GEANA

I. The Musical Disciplines of Lyric Art, *Xenia Sheehan*

DON USED THE TERM *lyric art* with a broader meaning than most classroom definitions would allow it. One of my favorite of his many beautiful sentences will be found in its original context in chapter 12:

> The mind of David may thus be understood as that long discipline of stillness wherein the ruining oppositions of actual experience are held within *the musical disciplines of lyric art*: held, until God Himself can be seen in the very ruins themselves: seen, and felt, and overwhelmingly and gratefully loved. This overwhelming and grateful love is the mind of David.

I have come to understand this as itself a small *chiasmus* (though I think not an intentional one). It is in fact a cross: a place where two opposing movements or perspectives meet and cross one another to produce a particular kind of *harmony*. This one describes the meeting itself, the suffering that has preceded it, the discipline that has enabled us to endure the ruin and now hold it, and the joy of grateful love that arises from that holding. I think of the young King David, quietly selecting the five smooth stones for his sling as he prepares to face Goliath on a battlefield bristling with spears, his "breathtakingly beautiful face, now wholly concentrated in perfect stillness."[94] This is chiasmus at work. From this, David himself gave us a body of lyric art that carries on its healing work to this day—healing us as it healed

Saul. Having arisen as song in the midst of the world's warfare, *Psalms* know the territory and hold open the pathways for God to position Himself at the heart of it, on the Cross of His Life-giving Resurrection.

Derived from the Greek letter *chi*, or X, the chiasmus is a verse pattern in which the first and final lines or portions of a given text connect or speak to one another (in such ways as repetition, opposition, emphasis, echoing, enlargement); then the second connects to the next-to-last; the third to the third-to-last; and so on, until a more or less exact midpoint is reached (often, Don has been known to tell his students, somewhere slightly past the numerical center). The pattern's midpoint provides a pivot upon which the passage's entire significance may be seen to turn.[95] Something to bear in mind is that with poetry we are generally *seeing* the poem two-dimensionally; that is, on a page. In reality, especially when it comes to chiasmus, it is helpful to think of the page as merely a flat representation of a process taking place in several dimensions. Don's graduate school roommates when I first met him were algebraic topologists who could express such things mathematically. He was fascinated by what they told him of their subject, and I doubt he ever forgot it.

Here is Don's sentence written in chiastic form, though still two-dimensional. I believe we are to imagine more:

  A The mind of David may thus be understood as

    B That long discipline of stillness

      C Wherein the ruining oppositions of experience

        D Are *held* within the musical disciplines
          of lyric art:

        D' *Held*, until God Himself can be seen in
          the very ruins themselves:

      C' Seen, and felt, and overwhelmingly and
        gratefully loved.

    B' This overwhelming and grateful love

  A' Is the mind of David.

We are to read the lettered lines (A and A', B and B', etc.) as bearing some significant relation to each other—again, echoing, matching, rhyming, even significantly opposing (as in the C lines, in which the experience of ruining oppositions is matched with a seen, felt, and grateful love—until we reach the center (D and D'), which may be thought of as the poem's heart. Both *from* and *to* this center, meaning flows, forming something like a whole living system. The center or heart is where Christ is: at the point of the chiastic crossover and, at the same time, on the literal cross, "in the very ruins." We are to take or follow our own ruining oppositions to that center, holding them in our own hearts, and there find His. And, in our loving gratitude, we are to take Him from that center to find our *nous* enlarged and strengthened; that is, made Davidic. It is the mind God gave to David as David learned to sing His harmonies. And it is the mind St. Xenia entered into when, she tells Don in the book's preface, "I fell down into my heart without my mind."

Reading this bit of text narratively from the center outward, the "musical disciplines of lyric art" (the first half of the chiastic center, D) are a holding place or a *keep* (here, it is the mind of David, but it could as well be ourselves, or the tomb of Christ as we'll see below) where ruining oppositions are kept or held for us, and by us, until we are able to bring them (receive them, endure them) together in union, or fruition. This comes about through our discovery (by way of disciplined stillness) of God's *presence* in the very ruins, and of our own being overwhelmed (the equal and opposite of the discipline of stillness) by grateful love for Him and acceptance of His Love for us in the midst of our ruin. So the second half of the center (D') is our endurance in this place of holding, our waiting in prayer for fruition to occur. We practice the long discipline of becoming *still* in the face of the ruining oppositions in our lives until we have learned to embrace and match them with our overwhelming and grateful love for God, and His for us.

I think this may be as simple as refraining or withdrawing from taking sides, from entrapping ourselves in a trench in which we feel we must fight for our life. I remember watching Don refrain in this way (sometimes even when I had wanted him to do battle on *my* side). Remember how, in chapter 1, he did it in his family too, where it was a terrible, ongoing pain. I believe we may each have such a generative work going on in the keep of our heart, perhaps even a single primary work that takes various forms over our whole life.

Only as I prepare this book for publication have I begun to identify certain of my own ruling antinomies: such as trusting, even believing, in an inward process (nowadays involving prayer) that generates hunches or insights, while in the same moment I fear the world's reception of them as nonsensical, irrational, "lacking in evidence." (This need for evidence was something of a ruling value in my childhood home, for which I am, a bit late, learning to be grateful to have in my constitution). Neither pole, however, conquers the other (nor should), and their opposition in me has intensified since I began publishing Don's work. But as I am, thanks to Don and the Church (especially to Fr. Tom Hopko), confident now in the truth of the "other" (and on the whole non-evidential) reality, it has become productive from both ends. And this is surely the sort of thing that Don—son of an alcoholic, Irish storyteller, loving, deeply intuitive, and well versed in the academic ethic (and no doubt, over time, in my own familial truth-telling rationalism as well)—faced and picked his way through over the course of his lifetime. The result was a good one, I think.

One's discipline of stillness in the face or fear of ruin is one's offering to God, rewarded in the lines of this found chiasmus with overwhelming love and gratitude—*our* love for God become one with *His* for us. It is a love that conquers (overwhelms), simultaneously, both the ruins we face in our lives and our own fearfulness or distress in facing them, freeing the isolated self to move toward personhood. And in the end this may all be a single act accomplished in a millisecond of time.

Such are *Psalms*, all of which, Don claimed, can be read chiastically, with the whole Psalter finding its center in Psalm 77[78], lines 34–38:

> 34 When he slew them they sought him and repented and rose up early in their prayers to God.
>
> 35 They remembered that God is their helper, the Most High God their redeemer.
>
> 36 So they loved him with their mouths but were lying to him with their tongues,
>
> 37 For their hearts were not straight with him, they were unfaithful to his covenant.
>
> 38 But he is compassionate and will be gracious to their sins and will not destroy them, again and again forgoing his wrath, never kindling all his anger.[96]

They remember God, seek Him, pray to Him, *want* to change (be redeemed). But they are broken and bent inside, lying, unfaithful. This is the antinomy of fallen humanity. But in finding our way, even for a moment, to the still center of our violent world, we are met with compassion, again and again, always. Here, in Don's understanding, is the heart of Psalms.

Chiasmus, as Don explains most fully in chapter 12, is the contrastive structure that most firmly and directly *holds* all of antinomy's contradictions—first, of course, having clarified what they are. Throughout these writings, we are called also to this work within our own hearts. I want to be clear about that as well, so I'll rephrase it: The work that ultimately matters is in the heart. This is not an obscure literary form but the fundamental work of humankind, as described by St. Maximus the Confessor: each of us "bringing into unity in his own person those things which by nature are far distant from each other . . . until the whole of him then coinheres wholly in the whole of God, and he becomes everything that God is except for identity of essence."[97] So it should not be surprising to find that chiasmuses happen on their own, without our intentionality. For, if we are about our Father's business, we will continuously be learning to reshape our experience—returning oppositions to Him as unities forged *within ourselves*, thanking Him for this food; or, if we aren't ready to take that step, simply identifying and holding the antinomies in the keep of our heart and, as we are able, offering them to Him for resolution.

II. Through the Cross, Joy

> . . . For, behold, through the Cross joy has come into all the world.
> Let us ever bless the Lord, praising His Resurrection.
> By enduring the Cross for us, He destroyed death by death!

—Orthodox Hymn to the Resurrection

Fr. Mircea Geana has graciously allowed me to include in the book a homily he delivered on the Sunday of the Cross during Great Lent, 2023, at Holy Trinity Orthodox Church in Springfield, Vermont. This is the church in which Don and I were married (for the second time; the first was in traffic court and lacked some important context and content, though it did include a judge intoning Scripture to us from a high podium! I wish now that I had listened—my brother-in-law and I were too busy restraining our laughter at the good man's Importance, and perhaps even our discomfort with the "religious" element). I don't remember exactly what the Church marriage (two sons and over two decades later) involved, but I know that our priest had a special blessing from Bishop Job to include much more than is usual when a secular marriage is blessed in the Church. For "the true form of the sacrament . . . is the entrance of the marriage into the Church, which is the entrance of the world into the 'world to come,' the procession of the people of God—in Christ—into the Kingdom."[98] In the full ceremony, the pair are crowned in glory and honor with the crown of the *martyria*—those who bear witness to Christ.

> And this means crucifixion and suffering. A marriage which does not constantly crucify its own selfishness and self-sufficiency, which does not "die to itself" that it may point beyond itself, is not a Christian marriage. The real sin of marriage today is not adultery or lack of "adjustment" or "mental cruelty." It is the idolization of the family itself, the refusal to understand marriage as directed toward the Kingdom of God. . . . [What]

breaks the modern family so easily . . . is the identification of marriage with happiness and the refusal to accept the cross in it. In a Christian marriage . . . it is the presence of God which is the death of the marriage as something only "natural." It is the cross of Christ that brings the self-sufficiency of nature to its end. But "through the cross joy [and not 'happiness'!] has come into all the world." Its presence is thus the real joy of marriage. It is the joyful certitude that the marriage vow, in the perspective of the eternal Kingdom, is not taken 'until death parts,' but until death unites us completely."[99]

I don't think Fr. Mark and the Bishop would have denied us this great blessing, though I know the actual crowns were omitted.

I include Fr. Mircea's homily here as an image of the fundamental *essentiality* of the cross to Orthodox Christians, perhaps to all Christians, and certainly to Don and to me. The cross points the way to understanding both the difficulty—the pain even—and the joy of escaping from our entrenchment in our own will so as to realign ourselves with God's and open ourselves to Him in the wholly free reunion with Life for which we were created. In doing this we enter into a relationship, a consummately beautiful dance, with Divinity. In the Judeo-Christian understanding, humanity rejected this from the start, and we continue to do so each time we choose our own will over His, preferring what has turned out, always, to be death. Through the cross of Christ—who is both God and man, having taken humanity upon Himself—we are again joined to Life if we will meet Him there.

Taking Up the Cross, *Fr. Mircea Geana*

"Whoever desires to come after me, let him deny himself, and take up his cross and follow me" (Matt 16:24–26; Luke 9:23). How many times have we heard this Gospel passage? And if you're like me, how many times did you hear this and think of it as a gentle invitation (as in, if you like, if you want to, if it pleases you . . . come follow Me)? But this is not a gentle invitation at all. It's a battle cry. How do we know this? Because the passage comes right after Christ tells Peter: "Get behind Me, Satan." Christ came to rescue us who were stuck behind enemy lines. He managed to reach us, and then came the battle cry: "If you want to get out of here, if you want to be rescued, to be saved, this is what you must do and we will do it together. Follow Me!"

"I will not, however, take you out by a secret passage free from all danger. The way out, the *only* way out, is right through the middle of it all.

Your only weapon is the cross and the only shield your self-denial, and most important, if you follow this path you will be with Me."

When I say your shield is self-denial, I mean that *if you deny yourself* the enemy can't harm you. You have removed the only ammunition that he can use against you. The devil will always tempt us with self-indulgence in whatever shape or form: food, entertainment, sexual temptations, possessions, the list goes on. But to deny myself is to empty myself of my will, my selfishness, my own desires, and to fill myself with Christ and a desire for Him and for His will.

When I say the cross is your weapon, it's not just to give you a beautiful metaphor. On the cross, Christ defeated death, man's last enemy. And, more important, through His death He gave us life. This means that through the cross we don't just fight, we don't just conquer or destroy, but we transform the reality around us. We pick up the cross—a brilliant light shining in the darkness—and we look at the world around us by its light. In that light I will see that every person I encounter is worthy of love and salvation. I will see that, through it, God can truly *make the evil good* by His goodness. But that transformation has to start first and foremost with me.

To deny myself is to renounce the delusion of this world. To "pick up the cross" is to carry it and be transformed by it. Then I can see that same beautiful transformation around me. We can honestly say that in the degree to which I am transformed by the cross, to that same degree I can help in the transformation of others around me. Otherwise, it's empty words. I would even say we can do more damage than good. But if you really want to help others, to be a ray of light, hope, and love to others, then you have to be crucified. You have to endure the mocking, betrayal, suffering, abandonment, mistreatment, and somehow not give in to it. It is the hardest thing you will ever do in your life.

The message of the cross has always been an extremely difficult one. It goes against any culture at any time. Today I will say it is even harder. Our culture elevates the personal will to the highest level. Because of that, the message becomes one that says: whatever you believe is right; however you perceive the world around you is right; however you identify yourself is correct; you know what's best for you and don't let anyone tell you any different. In fact, the expectation is that people should celebrate and applaud you for your convictions; and if they don't then you should distance yourself from them.

I don't think this could be any further from the Gospel. Where is the self-denial? In all honesty, I don't know what's best for me. I don't even know *who* I am supposed to be. What I do know for sure is that following my will and my desire is how I ended up in this mess, and that it is impossible for me to get out on my own. That's why Christ had to come behind enemy lines and say: "Follow Me!" Only in Him do I find myself and who I am supposed to be. Only in Him can I see clearly the reality around me. It's because of Him that I know how to love, how to forgive, how to live, and yes even how to die. But this comes through self-denial. I have to crucify my own will and put on His will.

And His will is glorious! His cross is glorious! Again, to the world this statement appears moronic, just foolishness. To those outside the Church this doesn't make any sense. You mean to say that you killed your God on a cross and now to show reverence to Him you bow down to the cross and you wear it around your neck and place it all around the church? Our answer would be: yes. But that's because the cross means something very different to us. When we look at the cross we don't do so to beat ourselves up, to cover ourselves in shame and guilt (there is an element of contrition and remorse for sure, but that's not the emphasis). The emphasis rather is the fact that our Lord went voluntarily to His death on the cross, showing us the extent of His love for all of us. On the cross we see Who He really is, and therefore Who we really are in relationship with Him. He is the Bridegroom, we are the Bride. He loves us with a fierce and passionate love, and therefore the invitation is to respond likewise.

St. Paul says in Hebrews that Jesus, "for the joy that was set before Him endured the cross." What joy is he talking about? The joy of being united with us for all eternity. He is the Good Shepherd Who lays down His life for His sheep. He knows His sheep and is known by them. Would we not follow such a One? Would we not desire Him with all our heart? Would we not lay our will at His feet, denying ourselves and picking up the cross in order to be bound to Him, united to Him as He united Himself to us? There is no greater struggle in this life, and yet no greater joy.

III. Resurrection, *Xenia Sheehan*

Consider: the cross of Christ is a focal point that forever *locates on the earth and in our lives* the place where the most intense betrayal imaginable—the creation violently rejecting its Creator—meets and joins with the most intense joy—Life Himself—in the Resurrection, and death is overthrown. This joining, proclaimed over and over in song as "trampling down death by death, and upon those in the tombs bestowing life," this is Orthodox Pascha.

The day after Christ's victory on the Cross, as Western Christians are preparing to celebrate Easter, the Eastern Orthodox Church is moving along a slow road toward Pascha.[100] Pascha itself marks the beginning of the Orthodox liturgical year, the time beyond time from which all time flows, and all joy. It may also be thought of as the chiastic center—the crux—to which the struggles that we embrace in humility will take us, and in and by which Joy transforms them.

The Orthodox Paschal celebration takes a full week of liturgical preparation (following the forty penitential days of Lent). On Holy Friday the Crucifixion has been accomplished, and the funeral is held in the afternoon. Then, in the evening of that terrible day when humankind has put its God, its Maker and Creator, to death on the Cross, the Matins of Holy Saturday is served. The next morning, at Holy Saturday Liturgy, the church's (and servers') Lenten purple clothing will be changed to white. Old Testament prophecies and prefigurings will be read (the children's favorite: Jonah in the belly of the whale; and other scriptural raisings from the dead). But even on this dark night, the Paschal music is tasted, and the first stirrings of the Resurrection are felt with anticipatory joy.

The crown of the Resurrection prophecies, however, has opened the Matins service of the previous night: Ezekiel 37:1–14. Of this Don has written:

> This reading begins with Ezekiel being set by God's Holy Spirit into the "midst of the plain" (ἐν μέσῳ τοῦ πεδίου, *en mesō tou pediou*) as if at the very heart of it; and the plain all around is filled with human bones, exceedingly dry and dead. Then God says to Ezekiel: "Shall these bones live?" And He commands him: "Prophesy to these bones; say to them: 'I will bring upon you the breath of life. . . .'" The bones then begin to move, each one drawing near its . . .
>
> *Its what?* The usual English translation of this phrase in Ezekiel is: "each bone drew near its joint." Yet the Greek word that the LXX translators used was *harmonia*: "each bone drew near its harmony."[101]

This is the chiastic reality of all of Psalms, Don says, in which,

> As we begin to let all the lines of the psalm live and move in their substantial and harmonic relation to the psalm's heart, the dry bones [of our incomprehension] can begin to arise into a new and vivid life. The Lord continues to Ezekiel: "I will open your tombs, I will put my Spirit within you, and you shall live" [Ezek 37:12–13]. Here, then, is the significance of the second stage in reading Psalms: as the "body" of the psalm arises from the chiastic heart, the psalm is resurrected into vivid meaningfulness. . . .[102]

The analogies here are rich and complex—the imagery and deep import of this moment on the brink of Resurrection, made incomparably richer in some, perhaps many, churches by good liturgical choreography: The tomb itself is in the center of the church—"as if at the very heart of it." It is the *keep* that holds and focuses our grief and pain, our memories of the Lord, our desolate need for Him, our hopes, our prayers, our awestruck wondering, our joy, and our love. Above all, it holds His Love for us! Don has suggested that in these moments He is both composing (prophetically, for David's sake) and singing Psalm 118 with us and for us, for it is, Don says, the "way of Resurrection."[103]

The people encircle the tomb to sing lamentations (most likely badly, for in an English-speaking church the Greek melodies and English words must bend to one another to find their *harmonia*, and it's a fervent prayer of the fallen, not a performance! I hope we never do get adept at it). Others— monks, nuns, or choir—chant the verses of the Great Psalm of Resurrection (118[119]) in alternation with the Lamentations. In short, it's a visible, audible, three-dimensional chiasmus, wholly resurrective in its meaning and result. It focuses in Christ's tomb our brokenness, our grief, our hope, and our love, and offers us impossible Life and miraculous Joy. Served in its fullness, assuming the whole of Psalm 118 were chanted and all the verses of the three *Stases*, I assume this act of liturgical architecture would take a couple of hours, as it should. The following day at Liturgy, the tomb, still in the center of the church, will fittingly serve as the altar for the preparation of the Lord's Holy Communion with us, and ours with Him; and His Resurrection is by this assured and confirmed as our own.

Much drawn to this liturgical moment, Don revisits it later in *The Shield of Psalmic Prayer*, saying that:

> The Matins service can thus be understood as one wherein *we*, the witnesses and beholders of the crucifixion, now enter the Tomb ourselves, so as to be with Him; and what we find is that He, in the Tomb, is praying aloud this psalm [118] in its entirety: praying so as to make crucifixion *become* the way of resurrection—to make violent death [to self] become the sole and perfect way into blessed aliveness that never ceases: *never.* (192)

I believe it can be said here that, if we think of the Tomb in this way, as the chiastic center of this greatest of all events, our entering into it in loving lament and praise may be understood as our own act of falling into our hearts, where Christ is. It makes our hearts themselves the place from which the blessed aliveness of Resurrection occurs.

The verses of Lamentations, like the psalmic *kathismata* (which divide the Psalter into twenty sections), are divided into three *stases* (each sung to a different melody of Greek origin). There are many translations of the Greek text. I have selected some crucial antinomic statements and incredulous questions in the translations used by the church I attend, Holy Resurrection in Claremont, New Hampshire. They offer us image after image of the impossibly possible event that is unfolding before our eyes—I begin with the first line:

THE LAMENTATIONS OF PASCHA

From the First Stasis

In the tomb they laid you, O Christ, who are Life. In amazement angelic armies lift up their song as they glorify your self-abasement, Lord.

Life, how can you perish or how dwell in a tomb? Yet the royal hall of death you now bring to nought, and from Hades' realm you raise the dead again.

King of all, O Jesus, who established earth's bounds, on this day you make your home in a little tomb, raising up the dead of ages from their graves.

In the tomb they laid you, you, O Christ, who are Life, death itself you brought to nothing by your own death, and you became the fount of life for all the world.

Like the sun when setting, to the tomb you descend, yet O Christ your Father's bosom you do not leave. What strange paradox, what wondrous thing this is?

As the sky's true monarch, as true king of the earth, though enclosed within the narrowest sepulcher you were known by all creation, Jesus Lord.

By your will we see you as a corpse in the tomb, but you live, O Word and Savior, as you foretold. By your Resurrection you raise mortal kind.

From the Second Stasis

All earth quaked in fear and the sun concealed itself, O savior, when, O Christ our light, you set, bodily, as the light that knows no evening was entombed.

Seeing you on high, never separated from the Father, yet below on Earth laid out as a corpse, the dread Seraphim, my Savior, shake with fear.

Humankind you formed, with your own hand you fashioned us, O Savior. Now, O Sun, you set beneath the earth, raising companies of mortals from the Fall.

Trembling Adam quailed when God walked in Paradise. He feared him but rejoices now as God enters Hell. As of old he fell, so now he rises up.

From the Third Stasis

Make haste to rise again, Word, abolish now her grieving, the all pure Maid who bore you.

Heaven's awesome powers stood amazed in terror to see you lying lifeless.

A dread and most strange sight is this, O Word of God, now tell us: How can earth cover *you*, O Lord?

All Heaven's angels tremble, Creator of the Cosmos, at your strange and dread entombment.

Peace unto your Church, Lord, salvation to your people grant by your Resurrection!

Each generation offers, my Christ, for your entombment, in hymns and songs, its praises.

Over and over, these services unveil the possible impossible, oppositions turning back on themselves, the pathway of life arising from death, having become possible through the Lord's willing acceptance of death for the sake of giving Life to us. I have come to believe that we are given all this antinomic literature within the Church Tradition as a way of enlarging and training our minds and hearts, over and over, to allow life's jarring oppositions and contradictions to draw us to the unity—the Life—that Christ means for us to have with Him, to show how this impossible thing we believe is indeed possible, has indeed happened, will indeed continue to happen in our hearts if we seek it. Further, I suggest that antinomy, and the chiastic form it so often takes (the cross-wise and heart-focused working of antinomy made visual—and audible to those with ears to hear)—that this may simply be a way that God reveals Himself to us in His creation. It is perhaps a mode brought into being at the Creation, surely in the knowledge that we would fall into misuse of the freedom so essential to our human calling and fulfill-ment: brought into being to draw us beyond the fears and desires and small comforts of our diminished (self-chosen) selfhood and offering us again and again, at every turning, the self-transcending choice of union, which is Life, with our Creator; that is, our personhood.

Wherever Christ the Risen One goes, the linear and the temporal change their normal directionality and even enlarge to be much more than they were in themselves, as He becomes their center of gravity. Perhaps this is why we will always find Him at the center and crux of every violent disorder of our own (or another's) making—as He chose to be when He accepted the cross for us. For there, on the cross, we surely are—alone and unwillingly if we are among His rejectors in placing Him on it—but there we will also one day find ourselves with Him, if we stand by Him in His rejection and thus enter with Him into His Resurrection. Can it not also be said that we are there every day with Him when we receive in gratitude the antinomies our life brings us and, exactly there, each moment of each day, allow His Resurrection to take place in us?

Journey of the Mind to God

A Reading of Canto 22 of Dante's *Paradiso*

WE MAY TAKE DANTE's Canto 22 as posing the problem of the whole of the *Paradiso*. Simply put, the problem is this: How are we to understand the experience it depicts? This problem is, at least initially, entirely our problem, not the poem's. We live in and are shaped by a century and a country that know nothing whatever about the general assumptions of Dante's poem. Where, for instance, shall we find in the cultural reality we inhabit even the slightest trace of that Thomistic comprehension of the universe so central to the *Commedia*? Where are the echoes to the Augustinian view of human life as a pilgrimage, a view that Dante's poem presupposes at every moment? Who of us speculates seriously and at length on the celestial hierarchies, speculation that occupies so very much of Dante's poem?

This problem is faced every college semester by every teacher of Dante. I shall remember to my dying hours the moment during the first week of a Dante course when a student blurted out: "You mean this guy believes in God?" Living in a post-Christian, post-literate, post-everything world, how are we to read—and to teach others to read—a long, complex text that everywhere assumes a Christianity practically no one remembers (certainly not Christians), a definition of reading as theologically urgent and a scale of perfection wholly unrecognizable as such?

I submit that this problem is the central one the *Commedia*, and particularly the *Paradiso*, poses for us: that is, recovery by means of historical scholarship of the intellectual-spiritual universe Dante inhabited is not really a solution. We may after a fashion outfit ourselves with the mental equipment of thirteenth-century Catholic Europe. But such forays (and they are extremely rare), even at their very best, are really tourism, not genuine recovery. For at the end, we take off our interesting garb and turn on the television news. We have not brought this poem a fraction closer to our lives. The *Paradiso* remains in its fastness, apart, seamless in its impenetrability. It may be that, for a moment, the very apartness of the poem holds us. But when we feel no returning gaze, when we cannot feel its eyes search ours and our lives, we begin to cease looking. And then the poem—the whole vast edifice—goes quite blank. At this point it may as well be written, not in Italian, but in Etruscan or Mayan or Linear A.

Is this what we want? Is this what we must accept? If the *Paradiso* slips in this way wholly beyond our reach (for the *Inferno* and *Purgatorio* will, I think, remain closer to hand), what shall we say of ourselves? Shall we say: there is something missing in us, something very great is gone from us we once had? Or shall we say: we do not need the *Paradiso*, we are not now who we thought we were, we are better, clearer, surer now? I do not think there is a third thing for us to say. I think we must choose which of these two things we want to say about the *Paradiso* and ourselves.

All my instincts, all my heart, tell me we must say the first: *something is missing in us, something very great is gone from us that we once had.* We may be better now than, as Western peoples, we were seven hundred years ago. But for six of those seven centuries we had the *Paradiso* within our reach. Are we to let the last hundred years of the *Paradiso*'s solitude deepen for us into full, final muteness? Are we (to return for a moment to the text at hand) doomed to imitate Dante's gaze at earth in *Paradiso* 22?

> . . . I smiled at its paltry
> semblance; and that counsel I approve
> as best which holds it for least, and he
> whose thought is turned elsewhere may
> be called truly correct.[104]

Certainly our century's thought has been turned elsewhere than the *Paradiso*; and our culture's smile of dismissal is no less complete.

I began by saying the problem is ours, not the poem's. But, of course, if it is ours then it is the poem's too, for the problem is precisely the relation between us. The most fruitful speculation upon our (and the *Commedia*'s) problem is that offered by Hans-Georg Gadamer in his very important book *Truth and Method*.[105] Gadamer says that a great work of art from the past does two things to us. First, it activates a *polarity of strangeness and familiarity* by virtue of the historical distance between ourselves and it. This distance,

Gadamer holds, is entirely useful, for it compels us to recognize the limits—or horizons—of the historical moment we inhabit. In the light of the distant artwork we all at once see very clearly that we are standing just *here* in our history and that the things close at hand are very familiar and those further off somewhat strange, while the things on the horizon's edge are only just perceptible. And the things from over the horizon, from out of the further reaches of our past, may not fit whatsoever into our landscape. At least, they may not fit without some shift of sight—on both our parts.

The second effect follows from the first. The distant artwork possesses its own historical horizon, its own patterns of assumption and habits of mind, feeling, and spirit. Thus arises the possibility of what Gadamer calls the fusion of horizons into "the one great horizon." In this process we must hold steadily to our own horizon, for if we begin by disregarding ourselves, we shall end by knowing nothing. At the same time we must learn to inhibit, says Gadamer, "overhasty assimilation of the past to our expectation of meaning." "Only then," he continues, "will we be able to listen to the past in a way that enables it to make its own meaning heard." For then is begun the dialogue that permits the fusion to occur. And as long as we do not attempt to abolish either our own historical moment or the text's—that is to say, as long as we remain truly courteous—the dialogue continues.

From this perspective, then, let us put once more our question to *Paradiso* 22: How are we to understand the experience you are depicting? We begin by noting that Dante is at the start in a state of sensory shock. An outcry like a thunderclap has left him like a frightened child needing a mother's comfort. This outcry is, we are told, the cry of outrage the blest give at the ceaseless corruption of church and monastic life on earth. Up to this moment, silence had reigned in this seventh sphere, Saturn's sphere, the place of paradisiacal meditation or contemplation. Dante has experienced this contemplative silence not at all as absence but as the full, rich presence of highest wisdom.

Silence and meditation: where are we to find within our historical horizon the call to contemplative silence? There are of course transplants torn from other, usually Asian, cultures, but they seem to suffer in our alien soil. What we seek, instead, are the contemplative forms rooted in our own deepest history; and they are there to be found, for they have never left us. For example, here is Thomas Merton, the great Cistercian monk [of our own time]:

The five senses, the imagination, the

discoursing mind, the hunger of desire
do not belong in that starless sky
(of meditation).

And you, while you are free to come and
go, yet as soon as you attempt to make
words or thoughts about it you are excluded—
you go back into your exterior in order to
talk.[106]

Firmly within our historical horizon, Merton writes with all our wars, distractions, and anxieties in mind and heart. Yet he can say, with Dante in *Paradiso* 22, that wisdom comes not in the mind's chatter but in silence.

From another direction, Heidegger offers an extremely interesting witness: "Out of long-guarded speechlessness and the careful clarification of the field thus cleared . . . the thinker utters Being, the poet names what is holy."[107] Here is the right accent: Long-guarded speechlessness, a carefully held silence that clears the field. And it has for us this pertinence, that whenever we wish to move toward the horizons of a distant artwork, we must move with precisely such long-guarded speechlessness if a voice other than our own, and other than the voice of our own time and place, is to sound for us. William Doty speaks of this as *phenomenological abeyance*, by which, he says, "we filter out our own signals and fine-tune both what the texts *were* saying in their own contexts and *are* saying within our own contexts today."[108] This abeyance, this long-guarded speechlessness, is what Thomas Merton and Dante of the *Paradiso* know as contemplative silence.

Let us now return to the opening of Canto 22. Beatrice tells Dante that here in heaven all is holy and that "whatever is done here comes of righteous zeal" (*da buon zelo*). Much of Canto 22 is then occupied with St. Benedict's angry denunciation of religious corruption. How are we to understand—not the denunciation—but the intense anger of it? Righteous zeal: all our experience of the last four hundred years rises up against such a thing being offered as a virtue. The centuries of private religious torment and sickening religious wars, the pathological certainties of the persecutor, the various reigns of terror in our national histories; all are manifestations of Christianity's righteous zeal. Yet the emotion lies very close to the heart of the *Commedia*. How are we to understand it?[109]

Let us sharpen the question still further. Santayana once lamented that, in Dante, "the damned are damned for the glory of God," and he continued:

> This doctrine . . . is a great disgrace to human nature. . . . [It]
> begins by assuring us that everything is obviously created to
> serve our needs; it then maintains that everything serves our
> ideals; and in the end it reveals that everything serves our blind
> hatreds and superstitious qualms. Because my instinct taboos
> something, the whole universe, with insane intensity, shall ta-
> boo it forever.[110]

In Canto 22 Beatrice tells Dante that "the sword of here on high cuts not in
haste nor tardily"—the cut is always precisely right. But where in Dante is
there a hint, even the merest echo of a hint, that the sword itself, and not
the timing of the cut, is the problem? Such an echo exists, of course, in the
fate of the virtuous pagans. Dante returns several times to the question of
why, for example, Cato is forever excluded from joy or why Virgil must
reside in Hell. The question is laid to rest for him in *Paradiso* 18, not by an
answer but by an invalidation of the question. Dante seems satisfied. Are
we? The matter is worth pressing, I think, because beneath the form of the
problem lies another issue.

I shall frame the underlying issue this way: what troubles us in the
fate of the virtuous pagans, and in the larger matter of righteous anger, is
also what, for a time, troubles Dante himself in the poem. What this is, is
the understanding of historical time. Within medieval Christian thought,
the thirty-three years recorded in the Gospels of Christ's life were ontolog-
ically realer and more actual than time before or after. As a consequence,
all historical time spiraled backward and forward toward and away from
those thirty-three years of history. In this spiral motion, time exhibited
now excessive brightness, now terrible darkness, consequent on the direction of will held by those acting in a given moment of history. Thus,
the substance of historical time is choice, or direction of the will, and the
paradigm of this view is of course St. Augustine's description of the Earthly
and the Heavenly Cities. Moreover, when this view of history is frozen
into a single moment, it reveals itself as the celestial-earthly hierarchy. We
are to envision here a vast hierarchy whose downward reach orders the
vegetative and animal kingdoms of earth, whose middle realm establishes
the personal and political orders of human life, and whose higher levels
orchestrate the angelic orders of heaven. The top is lost to our sight in the
radiance of God's pure order, while its base is lost in the invisibilities of
atomic patterning. Thus, while history is for us choice, it is also the spatial
reflex of our choice to rise or to fall in this hierarchy.

There is, of course, no gainsaying the enormous differences between our sense of historical time and this Christian medieval view. And,

following Gadamer, we must affirm the differences, see them as productive. For in so doing, we can begin to see an interesting situation: throughout the *Commedia*, Dante is himself struggling to cross some profound gulf between one sense of time and another. Everywhere in the poem, and with gathering intensity in the *Paradiso*, Dante is seeking to understand some new order of time, space, and substance. The outer dramatic form this struggle takes in the *Paradiso* is dialogue, and the characteristic accent this form has for Dante is shock. Sometimes the shock is carried by the conceptual message, but very often it comes to Dante through the medium of conceptual exchange in Paradise. Dante is continually startled by the way the blest understand his questions before he has asked them, sometimes well before he himself is even aware of the question. When he expresses his startled surprise, he is always told what St. Benedict tells him here in Canto 22: "If you could see, as I do, the charity which burns among us," you would understand. The way the blest of Paradise converse is from a ground of love, which is perfect and therefore unspoken comprehension. Each time this happens to Dante a conceptual shift occurs.

We may grasp this shift—and bring it closer to us—by asking a question posed by contemporary linguistics: do we understand a spoken sentence outside-in or inside-out?[111] That is, does meaning arise as the result of first hearing sounds, then decoding them, and finally constructing meaning or understanding? Or does meaning exist as some Gestalt, some total field underlying—or overarching—human beings involved in speech? If the latter, how does a specific act of speech activate and implicate that total field? The response the *Paradiso* makes is essentially dramatic. Dante the pilgrim is moving in the poem from the first conception to the second, from the notion of speech as the private creation of each speaker to the idea that, in and through dialogue, we are the creations of speech itself. This is also a motion from love as personal expression to love as the structure and energy of the world, in which we no longer speak love but are spoken by it. This is the love of the *Paradiso*'s final line: the love that turns the sun and other stars.

Once again Heidegger offers contemporary witness to this important conception:

> Man acts as though he were the shaper and master of language, as if language were his mistress. . . . If he acts so, then language becomes only a means of expression. And where it is only expression, language can degenerate into mere impression. Yet, even where the use of language is no more than this, it is good that one should still be careful in one's speech. But alone such care can never extricate us from the reversal, from the confusion of the true relation of dominance as between language and man.

> For in fact it is language that speaks. Man begins speaking and
> only goes on speaking to the extent he responds to, corresponds
> with, language, and only insofar as he hears language address-
> ing, concurring—running with—him.[112]

This perfectly describes the mode of dialogue exhibited by the blest of
Paradise. They tell Dante that they are steadily looking into the center of
language that is God and that, as they speak, they are saying again what is
being said at the center.

Such a conception of language carries with it implications about time,
space, and substance. In fact, we may say that this conception of language
is the ground for the view of history and hierarchy as patterned spiral. The
heavens exhibit to Dante the structure of nesting spheres, each closer to the
divine center. Yet, the blest say, all of them are equidistant from the center,
the greatest saint and the lowest of their kind are equally in the center. In
struggling to understand this, Dante is trying to see how a substance can be
simultaneously before his eyes and yet in this (to his eyes) distant center. How
can something be at once here *and* there? Language thus becomes for Dante
at once the mode of his struggle and its underlying content. I speak, and yet
what I speak is being said—has already been said, and will always be saying—
elsewhere, in the center of everything. Such is Dante's experience and such is
what he seeks to understand. For if he can understand how words in Paradise
work, he can understand space, time, and substance.

From this perspective, let us approach again the question of anger in
the *Paradiso*. Earlier, we called it an emotion. But in what sense is St. Benedict's anger in Canto 22 an emotion? When we say we are feeling something,
we are entirely private in saying so: such is, perhaps, the deepest psychological assumption our culture makes. But in this Canto—indeed, throughout
the *Paradiso*—another assumption about psychological life is being made,
and it is this other assumption that Dante is seeking to comprehend. When
Dante feels here the powerful desire to see Benedict directly and not in blaz-
ing images of light, he is told by Benedict: ". . . your high desire shall be fulfilled up in the last sphere, where are fulfilled all other (desires) and my own.
There, every desire is perfect, mature, and whole. In that (sphere) alone is
every part (of desire) there where it always was, for it is not in space, nor has
it poles." That is to say, the ground of every desire is not in us, nor is it in any
spatial or temporal location. The ground of all desires is wholly apart, in a
place that can only be pointed toward, not described: it is, says Dante, *là ove*,
"there where," a tiny but essential verbal gesture. In this ground are rooted
not only our own but everyone's desires; the medieval philosophic term for
this being-grounded is "fulfilled." Hence, within this conception, our desires are not merely private expressions, and thus we may say that when we
have feelings we are in fact expressions *of* such feelings and not their source.

From this perspective, *desire expresses us.* Anger, ecstasy, outrage, joy: in the *Paradiso* Dante is learning this new conception of desire. And the center and source of desire, like the center and source of language, lies beyond what we know as space, time, and substance: lies beyond, and is the place where all find their ground.

A thesis thus emerges. What we experience as difficulties of approach to the *Paradiso* are what Dante the pilgrim experiences as difficulties of approach to God. As we struggle to draw the *Paradiso* closer, so we see our struggle reflected—and grounded—in Dante's struggle to recall, re-present, his difficult "journey of the mind to God." The polarity of strangeness and familiarity is not only our situation but Dante's. Here, then, is a response to our initial question. *We are to understand the experience depicted in the* Paradiso *through understanding what we experience in approaching that depiction.* Such would be, I believe, a new and fruitful perspective from which to begin reading the *Paradiso.*

The value of such a thesis is that it permits us to approach the poem no longer draped in borrowed medieval finery: at heart, a ridiculous imposture anyway. From this perspective, my student ten years ago asked a much better question. At the same time, this thesis enjoins us against "overhasty assimilation of the past to our expectations of meaning," as Gadamer puts it.[113] The whole extraordinary structure of historical knowledge of Dante, slowly and selflessly elaborated over generations of scholarship, thus finds its real point and purpose as *phenomenological abeyance.*

I would further suggest, as a corollary, that every historical period—or horizon—finds in the *Paradiso* the perfect image of the mental processes it needs to undergo in order to comprehend the poem. In this sense, every age can come home to itself—can arrive at its own perfect self-knowledge—by coming to know the *Paradiso.* Thus, Dante in Canto 22 comes home and enters his own heavenly nature in entering the constellation Gemini. Here is the image of what our age has long sought: our home in ourselves in the *Paradiso.*

I shall close with two brief quotations, the first from one of Dante's most essential sources, Dionysus the Areopagite.

> We are protected in our protection of the writings;
> we are enabled to be protected by the writings
> by our protection of them.

The second is from our century [the twentieth] and is a perfect re-expression of this idea: Heidegger says, "The arts shelter the growth of that which saves."[114]

The Antinomy of Noetic Beauty

The Akathist and the Icon

Iconic beauty
is the arrival of divine reality
into the midst of earthly terror.

—D. S.

DURING THE SPRING OF 1987 I spent several weeks in the studio of Orthodox iconographer Vladislav Andrejev, learning from him the techniques and practices of painting the Orthodox icon. Our focus was simultaneously highly technical and deeply spiritual. For example, the long days I spent preparing the board to receive the egg tempera paint were likened by Vladislav to the long weeks of Lenten discipline. This likeness, Vladislav felt, was so profound that each deeply comprehended and exactly fitted the other. As a result, the end points of both practices—the iconic practice of preparing the board and the Lenten practice of preparing the soul— were likewise seen to fit together exactly. Thus, the finished icon became understood and experienced directly as the resurrected Christ Himself, as a Person ceaselessly and deeply and fully alive. And this iconic aliveness arose directly from understanding—and carrying out—the technical practice *as a spiritual practice*. In that long-ago spring, what I experienced can perhaps be expressed in this way: my hand became connected to my heart through a re-patterning of my mind, and in the process my mind was healed of very old and very deep wounds.[115]

The Miracle of the *Akathist*

In 626 AD, the ancient Orthodox city of Constantinople was besieged by barbarian armies. For several months, the vastly outnumbered Byzantine soldiers were defeated countless times in desperate sorties against the besiegers. The situation was approaching desperate when the Orthodox Patriarch led a procession along the great walls of the city, holding aloft the icon of the Holy Mother of God. That night (the chronicler relates) the miracle came.[116] A fierce storm with immense waves struck full force the barbarian fleet of ships, destroying most of it. By sunrise a full retreat had begun, and by midday the city was entirely free. At sunset, all the faithful filled the church and, led by the Patriarch, began to sing praises to the Mother of God. All night long, says the chronicler, they stood singing without once sitting down. What they sang was therefore titled the *Akathistos,* the "not-sitting-down" hymn.

The Greek text that comes to us from the seventh century exhibits extraordinary technical finish. It is twenty-four stanzas long, each stanza beginning, in sequence, with one of the twenty-four letters of the Greek alphabet: alpha, beta, gamma, delta, and so on, through stanza 24, beginning with omega. Each of the twelve odd-numbered stanzas also has twelve repetitions of direct praise of the Mother of God—each repetition beginning with the Greek word *Chaire, Hail!,* or, better, *Rejoice!* or *Be glad!*—for 144 repetitions over the twelve stanzas.

Furthermore, in each of these twelve stanzas, the twelve repetitions of *Chaire*-praises are organized into six couplets. These six couplets are organized in one or more of four main ways:

1. rhyme at the end of each of the two lines;

2. rhyme at midpoint of each line;

3. semantic rhyme in which words of contrasting meanings possess similar sound; and

4. words of similar meanings possessing contrasting sounds.

One further technical point. The twelve even-numbered stanzas all end with the word *Alleluia,* and all twelve of these stanzas are prose, not poetry.

A question therefore immediately arises. How can we reconcile the chronicle account of spontaneous prayer with this highly finished technical patterning? This question begins to lose a great deal of its cogency when we reflect upon the fact that organized prayer to the Mother of God is attested to at least two centuries earlier in the Byzantine Empire.[117] Also, the prayer that evening in 626 AD was being directed by Patriarch Sergius himself, a man long schooled in the techniques of organized prayer. The patriarchal presence is assuredly enough to account for the Akathist's astonishing *unity* of technique, while the long preparation in Byzantine religious culture is enough to account for the poem's *breadth* of content. But neither the unity of technique nor the breadth of content can begin to account for the poem's astonishing *depth*. The real question can be put this way: how can we understand the Akathist as an *iconic* poem—as, that is, a ceaselessly living *person* in the way the Orthodox icon is alive?

To approach a response to this essential question, let me suggest a thesis: the Akathist poem has as its primary aim the mental (better, *noetic*) healing of the attentive listener—and, in particular, the healing of the listener's mind from terror. It is this aim that made the poem—in its long cultural incubation suddenly fulfilled in 626 AD, especially suited to celebrating the miraculous liberation from a vast, encircling terror. The primary way the poem achieves this aim is by what stanza 19 calls *guiding the mind,* praising the Mother of God as "leader of noetic re-making."[118] I want to translate the Greek phrase of stanza 19 not simply as "guiding the mind," but more exactly and fully as *en-noeticizing the nous.*

We must first understand something of what the Greek noun *nous* means. Often translated as "intellect," *nous* is beautifully defined in the glossary to the English translation of the *Philokalia* this way: "The highest faculty in man, through which—provided it is purified—he knows God or the inner essences or principles of created things by means of direct apprehension or spiritual perception."[119]

The lexicographers then sharply distinguish the *nous* from the discursive reason or mind (*dianoia*), saying that the latter works by sequences of logical connections while the former works "by means of immediate experience, intuition, or 'simple cognition' (the term used by St. Isaac the Syrian)."[120] Thus, the definitive characteristics of the nous are swiftness and completeness. And in this sense, then, our word *intuition* covers a certain amount of the ground occupied by *nous.* But only a certain amount. For our word *intuition* cannot begin to carry the significance of "the highest faculty" by which God is directly and fully known. The nous, says St. Diadochos in the *Philokalia,* is the place in us wherein dwells the grace of God, citing the beautiful line from Psalm 44[45], "The King's daughter is all glorious within" (l. 13). The saint adds that this grace "is not perceptible to the demons."[121] The nous is our highest faculty in the special sense of *ennobling* us, making us "all glorious within" through its action of "entering into the King's palace" by our swiftly and fully beholding God as King (see Ps 44).[122] Our nous, then, in addition to being the faculty by which we know God, becomes *known to us* in the action of our knowing God. And in so doing, the nous begins to partake of the Divine King it is beholding.

In this way, we can see how the noun *nous* creates the need for the verb "*to noeticize.*" Or—perhaps better—we can say that the nous is an action we perform when we directly—and swiftly and completely—enter into the King's palace and thereby actively participate in the actions of the King. "To noeticize" is thus roughly equivalent to the more widely understood Greek verb "to deify." For as the nous acts to comprehend God, it is directly acted upon by God. As a result, the process of noeticization becomes the process wherein the nous is made holy, made in fact divine. In this sense, both the noun and the verb are at once the cause and the effect of each other. That is, the nous comes into existence only because noeticization is occurring, while noeticizing can occur only because the nous exists to make it happen. Each is wholly distinct from—yet perfectly fitting into—the other.[123]

From this perspective, then, we can understand a crucial aspect of poetic technique in the Akathist. Here is the opening twelve-line stanza of the poem, first in transliterated Greek, then in a very literal English translation:

Chaire, thi'es i chara eklampsei,
Chaire, thi'es i ara ekleipsei.

Chaire, tou pesantos Adam i anaklesis,
Chaire, ton daryon tes Evas i lytrosis.

Chaire, hypsos thysanavaton anthropinis logismis,
Chaire, vathos thystheoreton ke angelon opthalmis.

Chaire, hoti hyparcheis vasileos kathedra,
Chaire, hoti vastazeis ton vastazonta panta.

Chaire, aster emphaivon ton helion,
Chaire, gaster entheou sarkoseos.

Chaire, thi'es neourgeite i ktisis,
Chaire, thi'es brephourgeite ho Ktistes.

Rejoice! You through whom joy will shine forth,
Rejoice! You through whom the curse will vanish.

Rejoice! the recalling of the fallen Adam,
Rejoice! the redeeming of Eve's tears.

Rejoice! O Height beyond human thoughts,
Rejoice! O Depth invisible even to angelic eyes.

Rejoice! for You are the King's throne,
Rejoice! for You bear Him who is bearing all things.

Rejoice! O Star revealing the Sun,
Rejoice! O Womb of divine incarnation.

Rejoice! You through whom creation is refashioned,
Rejoice! You through whom the Creator is born a baby.

This first stanza exhibits all four organizing strategies we earlier noted. The first couplet has both early and ending rhyme as well as having these rhymes (*chara/ara; eklámpses/ekleípsei*) show vivid semantic contrast. The second couplet rhymes the unstressed final syllables (*-sis*) while contrasting the sounds of the stressed syllables (*anák-/lytro-*) and having the two words share similar meanings (recalling/redeeming). The third couplet rhymes early, middle, and late, with a contrast in meaning at the end. The fourth couplet begins with a light, unstressed midline rhyme, then progresses into directly repeating the same word, first as a main verb (*vastázeis*) and finally as a participle (*vastázonta*). The fifth couplet rhymes the second word in each line while sharply contrasting both sound and sense in the final words. The sixth, and last, couplet repeats or rhymes every word—and nearly every syllable—while contrasting the meanings of the two main subjects and the two main verbs. Thus, the four organizing strategies are beautifully and subtly varied in the stanza.

ANTINOMY IN THE *AKATHIST*

Now, these poetic strategies—and all their many hundreds of variations in the *Akathist*—can perhaps be best understood as exhibiting the phenomenon called *antinomy*.[124] In 1914, Fr. Pavel Florensky, Russian Orthodox priest and religious philosopher, published *The Pillar and Ground of the Truth*, in which he explored Eastern Orthodox theology, liturgy, and ascetic discipline in the powerful light of Kantian antinomy: the richest, fullest exploration of the term yet created. An example may help illustrate something of Florensky's rich fullness. Central to Christian understanding is the assertion that Christ Jesus is fully divine—one hundred percent God—and, simultaneously, fully human, one hundred percent: and He is, in sum, no more than one hundred percent. How is this so? How can He be simultaneously fully human *and* fully divine? Here is radical antinomy, here is the difficult, challenging, jarring contradiction that lies at—indeed *is*—the very foundation of Christendom. Using this example (along with several others), Florensky holds that an antinomy exhibits four fundamental qualities:

1. an antinomy cannot be resolved simply by merging one of its terms into the other; the contradictory elements must always remain sharply distinct (Christ's humanity cannot be merged into His divinity, nor vice versa);

2. an antinomy therefore disrupts (if not shatters) merely logical processes so thoroughly that rationality itself must be at least circumscribed if not entirely set aside;

3. though logically irresolvable, an antinomy must be resolved so that one can know and experience the coherence of unified truth (Christ is one person, not two); and

4. an antinomy finds its right and true resolution only along lines that keep distinct the two terms and yet cohere their contradiction; and these lines, Florensky holds, are the Orthodox path of ascetic discipline, a path characterized by an always deepening love and a forever widening humility.

Given these four qualities, the antinomy of Christ's nature thus finds resolution in the way in which our deepening love for Him and our consequently widening humility before all His creation come to fit exactly and fully His humble love for us. So seen, these four qualities can be understood as steps on the way wherein one moves from the darkness of unresolvability into the brightness of illumined love.

Let us now return to the poetic strategies of the first stanza of the Akathist. Each of the six couplets exhibits a tension that can be properly termed *antinomic*. In the first couplet, for example, *chara* (joy) and *ara* (curse) are an antinomy that is resolved through the unified presence of "You," the Mother of God, through whom—in an untranslatably exact Greek rhyme—the joy shines forth (*eklámpsei*) and the curse vanishes (*ekleípsei*). The *chara* (joy) and the *ara* (curse) cannot be resolved by merging one term into the other; they remain distinct. Yet their respective verbs overcome their contradiction in the exactness of their rhyme—while sustaining the differences. Similarly, in the second couplet, Adam's recalling (*anáklesis*) and Eve's redemption (*lytrosis*) are at once kept distinct in sound, yet resolved in sense.

In the third couplet, the antinomy of height (*hypsos*) and depth (*váthos*) is simultaneously sustained in meaning and yet resolved as a close "rhyme." The fourth couplet begins with a light, unstressed midline rhyme (*-eis* final), then progresses into a strong repetition of *vastázeis* and *vastázonta* ("bears" and "bearing"). And, similarly, in the final two couplets, the antinomic plays of sound and sense simultaneously sustain and resolve a series of contradictions. And the *way* that these contradictions are always resolved—in every couplet in this stanza, and in every stanza of the whole poem—is the way wherein we are called by the poem to enter directly into her vast love and her deep humility. And every fear vanishes.

In this light, then, the astonishing phrase from the third couplet of stanza 19—"en-noeticizing the nous" (translated in my source as "gave guidance to the thoughtless")—can be seen as exhibiting the same antinomical movement.

> Rejoice, Pillar of virginity.
>
> Rejoice, Gate of salvation.
>
> Rejoice, Leader of noetic refashioning.
>
> Rejoice, Bestower of divine goodness.
>
> Rejoice, for you regenerated those conceived in shame.
>
> Rejoice, for you en-noeticized the nous.
>
> Rejoice, you who abolished the corrupter of hearts.
>
> Rejoice, you who gave birth to the Sower of chastity.
>
> Rejoice, bridal Chamber of a seedless marriage.
>
> Rejoice, you who joined the faithful to the Lord.
>
> Rejoice, fair Nursing-mother of virgins.
>
> Rejoice, bridal Escort of holy souls.
>
> Rejoice, O Bride Ever-Virgin.

The second couplet of stanza 19 calls the Holy Mother *archeyé noetís anapláseos,* "Leader of noetic refashioning." This phrase in the second couplet illumines "en-noeticizing the nous" in the third. That is, as you attentively engage the poem, the Holy Mother is reshaping the nous in such a way that it is becoming "more noetic"—that is, swifter, richer and more comprehensive in seeing and knowing "God or the inner essences . . . of created things by means of direct apprehension or spiritual perception." And in so becoming increasingly noeticized, the nous (as St. Diadochos beauti-fully quotes from Psalm 44:15) "shall enter into the King's palace," and once there, the nous becomes entirely beautiful—so beautiful, the Psalm says, that God Himself "shall greatly desire your beauty" (44:11). And your noetic beauty, the Psalm continues, arises solely from your truly seeing and fully knowing that God the King "is Himself thy Lord."

Psalm 44

Here is the whole of Psalm 44 in my published translation:

1 My heart has overflowed with a good word, I myself say my works to the king, my tongue is the pen of a swift-writing scribe.

2 Thou art fairer than the sons of men, grace has been poured on thy lips, therefore God has blessed thee forever.

3 Gird thy sword upon thy thigh, O mighty one, in thy splendor and thy beauty.

4 And string thy bow, prosper and reign because of truth, gentleness and righteousness, and wondrously shall thy right hand guide thee.

5 Thine arrows are sharp, O mighty one, in the heart of the king's enemies; the peoples shall fall under thee.

6 Thy throne, O God, is for ever and ever, thy royal scepter is a scepter of uprightness.

7 Thou hast loved righteousness and hated iniquity; therefore God, thy God, has anointed thee with the oil of gladness more than thy companions.

8 Myrrh and aloes and cassia exhale from thy garments, and from the ivory palaces they have gladdened thee,

9 These daughters of kings in thine honor. At thy right hand stood the queen dressed in gold-woven raiment richly embroidered.

10 Listen, O daughter, behold and incline thine ear: forget thine own people and thy father's house.

11 For the king shall greatly desire thy beauty, for he is himself thy Lord.

12 And the daughters of Tyre shall worship him with gifts, the rich among the people shall entreat thy countenance.

13 The king's daughter is all glorious within, her clothing is woven with gold.

14 The virgins who follow after her shall be brought to the king, those near her shall be brought to thee.

15 They shall be brought with gladness and rejoicing, they shall enter into the king's palace.

16 In place of thy fathers are sons born to thee, whom thou shalt make princes over all the earth.

17 I will make thy name to be remembered from generation to generation; all peoples shall give praise to thee unto ages of ages, forever.

Here is a central psalmic antinomy in the Akathist: your becoming noetically beautiful is solely the consequence of a widening humility and a deepening love in you: humility before God and before all things, and love for all things and for God. And the antinomy is such that *the moment you shift your attention from God's beauty to your own, you instantly lose both.* Conversely, if you sustain your attention on divine beauty, you yourself increase in noetic beauty.

And such achievement of noetic beauty is what stanza 19 signifies in its final couplet. Here, the Holy Mother is called not only the Leader of noetic refashioning but also the Bestower of divine beneficence. St. Gregory of Nyssa makes a crucial point about this phrase: as the Holy Mother bestows her gifts upon us, we, the beneficiaries of her *agathótes,* become identical with the divine giver of them. This couplet rhymes the two nouns *archeyé* (leader) and *choreyé* (bestower) as well as the two adjectives *noetés* (noetic) and *theikes* (divine). The couplet thus creates and resolves an antinomy that simultaneously connects and distinguishes the beauty of the human *nous* and the divine Giver of that beauty. In this sense, then, *earthly antinomy is the way that divine beauty takes root in us.*

Thus, we can see how the Akathist heals the beholder's mind of terror. As the attentive listener is made noetically beautiful by the poem, he is thereby becoming free from terror's disfiguring attack on the noetic faculty itself. In 626 AD, when Patriarch Sergius led the procession with the icon of the Mother of God, the terror gripping the entire city was thickly palpable and darkly alive.

Florensky's *Iconostasis*

In the autumn of 1922 in Russia, Fr. Pavel Florensky wrote his final theological work, *Iconostasis,* in circumstances not unlike the seventh-century siege of Constantinople. In October of 1917, the Bolsheviks had seized power, and during the next several years, they succeeded in installing a brutal new reality everywhere in Russia: "in homes and schools and churches and offices and farms and barracks," a reality characterized everywhere by the terrifying actuality or threat of the newly created Soviet gulags. For nearly seventeen years, from 1917 to 1933, Fr. Pavel existed in the palpable darkness of Soviet sadism and systematic violence. This period ends with his arrest on February 25, 1933, as an enemy of the Soviet state, and his entry into the gulags on June 27, 1933. And on December 8, 1937, he was executed. Until his execution, Fr. Pavel endured the demonic agonies of the camp by focusing all his mind on the technical work that prison authorities compelled him to do—and by concentrating all his heart on caring for and loving his wracked and dying fellow prisoners. An extraordinary final image comes down to us from a survivor. On December 8, as Fr. Pavel's body was being carried through the camp to the prison gates, hundreds of prisoners risked the rage of their captors to kneel as their spiritual father passed by.[125]

His 1922 work, *Iconostasis,* on the theory and practice of iconography, may be usefully compared to Patriarch Sergius's procession of the icon around the terrified city: it is the arrival of divine reality into the midst of earthly terror. While Russia would not be freed of the terror until nearly the end of the twentieth century, Florensky's *Iconostasis* resembles the seventh-century Akathist in everywhere affirming the iconic aliveness of the Mother of God, an illumined aliveness that heals the mind of every terror.

FACE AND COUNTENANCE

About a third of the way into the work, Fr. Pavel distinguishes between two words that, in Russian, have the same root: face (*litzo*) and countenance (*lik*). He says this: "By *face (litzo),* we mean that which we see in ordinary daylight consciousness, that which we see as the recognizable appearance of the real world; and we can speak . . . of all natural things and creations with whom we are in conscious relation as having a face: as, for example, we speak of the face of nature" (*Iconostasis,* 50–51). The face of another person, then, is a boundary between our subjective preoccupations and its objective presence. In being so, the face absorbs our consciousness and is thereby "subconsciously forming in us the basis for a further process of knowing" (51). In other words, as we look at another's face, that face gathers our gazing into itself in such a way that we can never be entirely certain whether we are seeing the completely *objective* face or a face also carrying our own subjectivities. The face is, in this sense, always unstable. If we were artists and if we were to sketch the other's face, our sketch would reveal, says Florensky, "at least as much if not more . . . [our] own cognitive organization, as it does the ontological reality of the face itself" (51). We are thus encountering the reality of antinomy. We ceaselessly project onto the other's face our own needs, desires, and preoccupations; and yet the other's face is also and always objectively present.

Entirely otherwise is the other's *countenance* (in Russian, *lik*—which is the root of *litzo,* or face). Florensky continues, "the *countenance (lik)* of a thing manifests its ontological reality."

> In *Genesis, the image of God* is differentiated from *the likeness of God*; and long ago, the Holy Tradition of the Church explained that the *image of God* must be understood as the ontologically actual gift of God, as the spiritual ground of each created person; whereas the *likeness of God* must be understood as the potentiality to attain spiritual perfection; that is, to construct the *likeness of God* in ourselves from that totality of our empirical personalities called the *image of God*, to incarnate in the flesh of our personality the hidden inheritance of our sacred likeness to God: and to reveal this incarnation in our *face (litzo)*. (*Iconostasis*, 51-52)

When we do, says Florensky, "our *face (litzo)* becomes a *countenance (lik)*." He concludes: "We are beholding a countenance, then, whenever we have before us a face that has fully realized within itself its likeness to God: and then we rightly say, Here is the image of God, meaning: Here is depicted the prototype of Him" (52).

Florensky's understanding is, I submit, extraordinary. Our *face,* he holds, has the potential to become our *countenance* in the same way that the *image of God* we are born with can become a genuine *likeness of God.* In other words, when your face has become a genuine countenance, we can say you look precisely the way that God wants you to look. Your face has become *essentialized.* Florensky puts it this way: "Everything accidental, everything caused by things external to this essence— that is, everything in our face which is not the face itself—is swept away by an energy like a strong fountain of water breaking through a thick material husk. . . ." A moment later, Florensky calls this energy "the supreme heavenly beauty of a precise reality . . . the ray from the source of all images" (52).

And this last phrase of Florensky's in turn connects directly to a phrase in the Akathist, one that describes the Holy Mother as the "Ray of the Noetic Sun" (stanza 21). To attend deeply to the Akathist is therefore to behold the noetic beauty of the face—better: the *countenance*—of the Holy Mother: and it is thus for one's face to become a noetically beautiful countenance in the "Ray of the Noetic Sun." This "supreme heavenly beauty," says Florensky, is "a precise reality," a reality with exact and living actuality. And the reality of this beauty acts in such a way that both the beholder and the beheld remain at once distinct from, and yet related to, each other. Here is the antinomy of noetic beauty.

The Icon and the Iconic Poem

From this perspective, we can now understand how the Akathist is an *iconic poem*. In stanza 1, the Holy Mother is called "Height beyond human thought" and "Depth invisible even to angelic eyes." She is therefore at once entirely invisible and fully visible in precisely the same way every living person is always, at the same moment, entirely hidden from, yet fully revealed to, our eyes. This antinomy of hidden openness runs so sharp and deep and wide that whenever we become aware of it in any of our significant relationships we are stunned, awed—and often not a little frightened. At every moment in the Akathist, the Holy Mother exhibits this antinomy of hiddenness and revelation—and resolves it at every moment in the perfective humility and love of noetic beauty. In stanza 15, we find this crucial line:

> Chaire, e tanantía eis tautó agagousa.
>
> Rejoice! You who conduct opposites into unity.

The poem here bestows upon her a title we can translate accurately as: the One Who Resolves All Antinomies. And she resolves all antinomies by both being herself noetically beautiful and bestowing that beauty on others. Thus, the Akathist is iconic because the actions of its beauty heal the mind of every terror by bringing the mind down into the heart, en-noeticizing the *nous*. And her face becomes, at every moment in the poem, pure countenance.

On January 6, 2004, I was in Greece, in a small town called Paramythia, located in the northern mountains, up near the Albanian border. Along with my younger son, Benedict (age 24), an Orthodox seminarian, and also with my American Orthodox friend Mark Montague, a theology student at that time living in Greece, I had come to this village to visit the ecclesiastical home of the Orthodox saint whose name I bear, Saint Donatos, a fourth-century bishop. It was mid-afternoon and the sun was brilliant on the snow-capped mountains when we arrived in the town in a rental car and went straight to the church of St. Donatos. Entering, I saw for the first time an icon of my saint.

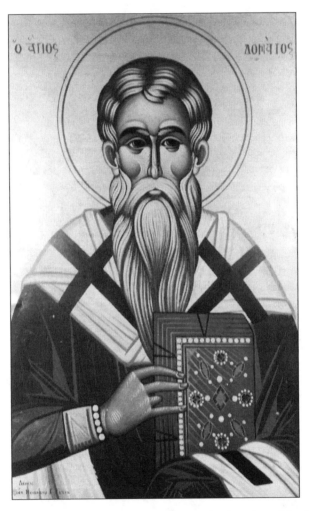

St. Donatos of Euroea. Icon given to Don in 2004 by the priest of the Church of St. Donatos in Paramythia, Greece. Photo by Brett Nolte.

I had been Orthodox for twenty years, and I had been seeking to discover something of my saint, having been given his name by my first father in

Orthodoxy, Fr. Vladimir Sovyrda. Now I stood before him, awed by his beauty and clarity.

The next morning, after Liturgy at St. Donatos's church, we phoned a Father Methodios of Gerimeriou Monastery, some forty kilometers away. We had been given his name and phone number by the deputy abbot of a monastery on Mount Athos, where we had visited the previous week (along with my older son, David). We had told the deputy abbot where we were going next and why, and he was delighted because he had been born and raised in Paramythia and had a brother named Donatos. Fr. Methodios warmly invited us to visit that very day, and after a drive on narrow switch-back mountain roads, we arrived at Gerimeriou in the brilliant sunlight of a winter mountain afternoon. Fr. Methodios was young, warmly welcoming, and beautifully *measured* in the way of Orthodox monks.

Over tea and a light monastic lunch, Fr. Methodios explained the history and meaning of Gerimeriou Monastery. He also told us much of the history and significance of St. Donatos in that region of Greece. He explained: "While St. Donatos is barely known outside northern Greece—not even in the cathedrals of Athens and Thessaloniki—he is known and loved in this region." And those long centuries of love explain why, in September of 2000, when the relics of St. Donatos were returned to Paramythia after having been taken to Italy by twelfth-century crusaders—"those long centuries of undying love," Father explained, "from the end of the fourth century to this present moment, explain why, in September 2000, over ten thousand people, nearly every family in the region, came to welcome the saint home. Donatos loved his people!" he exclaimed, "and he was our true teacher in loving the way Christ loved. We will never forget him."

Father then took us around the monastery, showing us the ancient and holy beauty of its many sacred possessions. As we finished our tour and came outside the main church, Father paused, suddenly subdued and somber in tone as he pointed to the twelfth-century iconic frescoes on the white stuccoed church walls. "Here are scenes from the life of Christ," he said, "please look at the faces." We were all deeply shocked. The faces in the icons were all deliberately mutilated as if to obliterate them. Father said, "Muslim invaders did this." These mutilated faces deeply chilled our hearts.

Months later, in mid-June, I saw the Byzantine icon exhibit at the Metropolitan Museum in New York. I stood before a large icon of the Crucifixion, and once again the face of Christ had been entirely obliterated by iconoclasts. I was seeing an attack not merely on noetic beauty but on the very noetic faculty itself.

The final paragraph of Florensky's *Iconostasis* illumines the dreadful meaning of these iconic mutilations:

> For no matter where on earth the saint's remains are, and no
> matter what their physical condition, his resurrected and deified
> body lives in eternity, and the icon that shows him forth does not
> merely *depict* the holy witness but *is* the very witness himself. It
> is not the icon that, as a monument of art, deserves our atten-
> tive study; rather, it is the saint himself who, through the icon,
> is teaching us. And if in that moment when, through the tini-
> est gap or break, the icon ontologically separates itself from the
> saint, then the saint hides himself from us in the unapproachable
> sphere, and the icon becomes in that moment merely one more
> thing among the world's other things. In this terrible moment,
> a vital connection between earth and heaven disintegrates into
> a cancerous spot that kills that area of life in us where the saint
> once lived; and then there arises in us the dreadful fear that this
> cancerous separation will spread. (*Iconostasis*, 165)

This "cancerous separation" of icon from saint is precisely what the knife
of the terrorist mutilator is seeking to bring about, producing in us "the
dreadful fear that this cancerous separation will spread." For the icon—
and the iconic poem—"does not," in Florensky's words, "merely *depict* the
holy witness but *is* the very witness himself"—or, as is the case with the
Akathist, the very witness herself. And it is the very saint herself who,
"through the icon" (as Florensky says)—or through, as we have seen, the
iconic poem—"is teaching us" directly and fully.

In this way, then, Florensky's final paragraph also speaks directly into
the seventh-century circumstances of the Akathist to the Holy Mother.
The terror filling the besieged city of Constantinople in 626 AD was precisely the "dreadful fear" Florensky here speaks about. And this terror was
healed by the icon of the Holy Mother, an icon that (like any truly Orthodox icon) did not, in Florensky's words, "merely *depict* the holy witness but
[*was*] the very witness" herself. For the mutilated faces of the Gerimeriou
icons were—and *are*—terrifying in precisely the same way the surrounding invaders in 626 AD were terrifying: the terror that living presence
might become one more dead thing among the world's other dead things.
And then, as now, all such terror is healed in the same way: by the direct
action of iconic art, verbal or visual, upon the beholder.

UNIQUE RESOLVER OF ALL ANTINOMIES

Each stanza of the Akathist ends with the same refrain line: "Chaire, nymphe anymphete"—a sharply antinomic line whose Greek rhyme is entirely

untranslatable: the usual "Rejoice! O Bride Unwedded" cannot reflect the rhyme *nymphe/anymphete*. But the antinomic *meaning* fully translates: childbearing and chastity. So acute is the antinomic *connection* in the Holy Mother between these two terms that, in relation to her, we may say that this antinomy is *Who She Is*. Florensky, in his 1914 book *The Pillar and Ground of the Truth*, says, so strongly interconnected are these two terms that if one takes hold of *one* of the two, then the *other* term will become established in a power "directly proportional to the religious elevation of the ascetic"; that is, the depth of one's spiritual intensity (218). Florensky continues: "only true virginity is capable of understanding the whole significance of marriage." "On the other hand," he says, "only a pure marriage, only a conjugal consciousness full of grace makes it possible to understand the significance of virginity." Thus, both marriage and monasticism are *ontological,* not institutional: that is, both have to do with unceasing aliveness and living actuality. And in its refrain line, *nymphe anymphete,* the Akathist says that this antinomy is resolvable only—and yet fully—in the iconic presence of the Holy Mother. For only she, who is herself the Resolver of All Antinomies, can bestow upon us that noetic beauty that heals the mind of all its experience of contradiction and terror.

The iconic poem, then, embraces antinomy in such a way that (in Florensky's words) "the pretensions of the rational mind are tamed" (7), and, consequently, noetic beauty can begin to flourish. Florensky also says: "The closer one is to God, the more distinct are the contradictions," adding: "What is important is the experience of antinomicalness" (117–18). The iconic poem is precisely this experience of antinomicalness, the experience in which the jarring contradictions are held and affirmed. The poetic strategies of the Akathist are therefore ones which all good poems employ. And, assuredly, seventh-century Byzantium did not invent but, rather, inherited the poetics of antinomy from earlier Hebrew and classical Greek literary cultures. But unique to the Akathist is, I think, the way in which its antinomies are simultaneously affirmed in their contradictory sharpness and resolved in our experience of them: that is, in our experience of antinomy as the very essence of the Holy Mother's love for us, and of ours—in the experience of this poem—for her.

During those weeks in the spring of 1987, the icon I was working on was John the Baptist. Very slowly the thick darkness of the board began to become the brightness of St. John's iconic countenance. But this brightness became fully and all at once *realized* only in the final moments when my teacher, Vladislav Andrejev, very gently and lovingly took my inexpert brush into his own hand for a brief, miraculous minute. He applied countless quick, very fine and perfect lines to the iconic face: and all at once the living countenance of the saint was fully before us. And I knew at that moment what I know to this day. In all iconic art, one's own hand must know exactly when the hand of the greater artist needs to hold firmly and beautifully one's own brush. When Vladislav's hand bestowed noetic beauty on the icon, and the saint's face became his countenance, my own hand became connected to my heart. Here is the resolution of antinomy. Here is the action of noetic beauty.

Robert Frost and Home

A Conjunction of Darkness and Grace

We dance round in a ring and suppose,
But the Secret sits in the middle and knows.

—R. Frost (1942)[126]

In "The Death of the Hired Man" Robert Frost wrote what is perhaps one of the most wryly funny definitions in American literature of home:[127]

"Home is the place where, when you have to go there,
They have to take you in."[128]

What's funny, of course, is the conjunction of opposites: the gritting-your-teeth *obligations* of home conjoined with the almost universal associations of the word *home* with love and warmth and grace and sympathy and acceptance. "You have to go there"—"they have to take you in": here is no love, no warmth, no grace, no sympathy, no acceptance—and yet we smile at this: a knowing, wry smile—but still a smile.

What's not so famous—in fact, what comes every time as a real surprise—is the immediate response this famous definition provokes in the other main character in the poem. Warren pronounces his famous witticism; then his wife, Mary, says immediately:

"I should have called it
Something you somehow haven't to deserve."

Against Warren's wit stands Mary's definition of home as pure grace: as, that is, something you don't ever have to struggle to earn, but something purely given, as pure grace, pure gift. Between these two definitions occur, in the work of Robert Frost, some of the most interesting images of home (and the absence of home) in our literature.

I want to begin by repeating something I heard William Cook of Dartmouth say in a lecture at The Frost Place in Franconia: "Robert Frost is *not*—I repeat, *not*—a nature poet." Cook was saying what I think is quite true: Frost's interest in the natural world—in the flowers, the trees, the stone walls and fields—is in its power to help us see *our* lives, *our* homes, and *their* possibilities. And what interests him about our homes and their possibilities for darkness or for grace (or more often for both darkness and grace together) is, I believe, the way our homes depend so deeply on *our words*: on, that is, the things we say to each other and the way we say them. Here, I think, is Frost's great subject as a poet.

Consider "An Old Man's Winter Night."[129] This is a home where all relations are gone; hence, the walls are very thin: "A light he was to no one but himself." "He consigned to the moon," says Frost, charge over his roof and wall and their icicles and snow, and he sleeps: he turns wholly inward. He shifts once in response to the log shifting in the stove, his heavy breathing eases a moment—then back inward, into depths of sleep. This is no home—it is age, it is night, it is winter—and it is absolute inwardness. Note the last lines:

> One aged man—one man—can't keep a house,
> A farm, a countryside, or if he can,
> It's thus he does it of a winter night.[130]

If a house is kept, then a farm is kept and a countryside is kept: a widening zone of homesteadiness. The old man's zone of home is contracted into one tiny point—a point known only in the absolute privacy of his sleeping: and that point *may* (Frost says) be enough.

Some of the great texts of Frost's poetry of home are too long to quote or to analyze, but I want at least to give their titles:

"Death of the Hired Man"

"Home Burial"—a text where, as the couple grieve their dead child, they bury their marriage and their home

"The Hill Wife"—a sequence of five lyrics

"In the Home Stretch"

"West-Running Brook"—perhaps Frost's most complex and beautiful poem about home: about how home is when it is fully right, fully home.

"A Servant to Servant"

In all these poems—and in the hundreds of wonderful poems in his collected work—the natural world is experienced through, or in terms of, the human world of home. And since many of these poems are dark or ironic, we naturally ask: What was Frost's own home like, the one he grew up in and the one he made as an adult?

To ask this question is to place ourselves squarely before Lawrence Thompson's three-volume (almost two thousand page) biography of Frost. Now, it is many years since Thompson published the first volume (in 1966)—certainly time enough to absorb the initial shock it made. This shock was, of course, the collapse of an illusion about Robert Frost—the illusion that he *in himself*, and *apart from the poems*, embodied something like practical wisdom: a shrewd, clear, compassionate wisdom that can grace a person's old age. We read Thompson and saw something else: anxiety, anger, obsession, violence, meanness, furtiveness, cringing helplessness, an insatiable need for approval, and an endless will to control others. It was a devastating picture—painstakingly constructed in massive detail. Our illusion certainly collapsed; how could it have survived such an assault?

And yet: what exactly has Thompson told us? William Pritchard has asked the question: Why have we come to trust so completely and so uncritically a writer such as Thompson who writes so *badly*?[131] This is surely worth considering; for the flat, pedestrian prose of Thompson's pages most assuredly contributes to the general *dispiritedness* of the Frost he presents to us. But I think it's worse than dull prose; the deeper problem in Thompson's work is a profound failure of perception. For as we look *through* Thompson's prose and into, say, Frost's parents and early childhood, we can see something disturbed and disturbing, yes, but at the same time something at once violent and graceful—an alcoholic father (who was also kind and generous when sober) and a spiritual mother who loved poetry and singing (but whose spiritual escapes carried also for young Robby a disorienting element of fear).

Robert's father, William Prescott Frost, Jr.—son of a Lawrence, Massachusetts, cotton mill foreman—was a complex, driven man. An 1872 Harvard graduate, he became the principal of a small private school in Pennsylvania, where he and Isabelle Moodie met. She was graceful, aristocratic, and cultured. Her father, a sea captain, had drowned at sea. Her mother (according to Thompson) was a "hussy who ran away from the

arduous duties of motherhood." Isabelle's paternal grandparents, decent
Scots-Presbyterians, raised her. On the night of her grandfather's death,
she sees a vision of bright angels circling to welcome him.[132] Isabelle grew
up believing strongly in her psychic abilities, her "second sight." Later, she
would join the Church of the New Jerusalem, based on the writings of Emmanuel Swedenborg—an extraordinary man, brilliant in many areas, who
never saw materialist explanations as satisfactory.[133] It is Swedenborg that
Robert hears about in detail all through his childhood.

After William and Isabelle marry, they move West to San Francisco,
where William, already deep into alcoholic behavior patterns, works as
a newspaperman and is swept with delighted excitement into the gold-
rush aftermath of greed and violence. In these first months of Robert's
life, Thompson tells us that William "smashed furniture in a rage" if his
wife expressed the slightest apprehension or protest. Having experienced
her own infancy in a smashed home and finding herself as a mother once
again in a violent and dangerous home, she would escape with the baby
and go into the streets at night. Thus, as a father, William Frost was a
stern and harsh disciplinarian and an abusive alcoholic—and yet, as I have
said, he was also kind and generous when sober. He took young Robby on
walks in the city while gathering news stories—"bars and backrooms were
my education," Robert said.

At bedtime, his mother would read to him and tell him about the
worlds beyond this world, of "second sight" and the angels. She read him
the Bible, especially the prophets and their accounts of hearing God's
Voice. And so the boy, too, began to have second sight and to hear voices—
sometimes mocking ones; and he was *very* scared. His mother eased his
fear, taught him that such experiences were openings to God's love and
God's wisdom—while one dreams. Young Robby wrote a story at age ten,
from a dream: of a secret valley inhabited by Indians who had escaped
from their enemies, where they now led a serene life—and who welcomed
the dreamer as a hero and as one of them. At night he would tell himself
this story, over and over, adding episodes.

His father (meanwhile) kept drinking, and then decided to run for
public office. The campaign was grueling; besides the alcoholism, he now
had another affliction: TB. William lost the election. Robby watched his
father die—slowly. He coughed blood continuously; he drank. On the night
of his death, he calls Robby in—eleven years old. The boy is frightened and
recalls nothing later except this one admonition: "Don't hang about street
corners after dark." By morning William Frost was dead, leaving a total es-
tate, after funeral expenses, of eight dollars cash.

Certainly we may say this: the walls of home for young Robby Frost were very thin—and they opened into quite literal experiences of Heaven and Hell. Equally, when he married Elinor Miriam White on December 19, 1895, and became himself a husband, then father of four children, he carried something of this home of his childhood into his own making of a home (as of course we all do). Robert and Elinor were married in his mother's Swedenborgian meeting house. Swedenborg said that married love endures *far* into eternity. "The actual reason," Rob later wrote, "is that in a marriage of truly conjugal love each becomes a more and more *interior* person. For this love opens the interiors of their minds. . . ." Robert and Elinor's marriage was so; and therefore it brought up for both of them the total content of each of their inner lives. There is no hiding in a marriage; no pose can be long held; no inwardness that is not manifested.

Thus, in Robert's marriage to Elinor, there was also his father's rationalism when sober, and tremendous rage and vast fear when he wasn't, with his mother's depths of serenity and spiritual gift (not, for her son, entirely free of another sort of fear). And in Elinor's marriage to Robert, there was *her* father, who had abandoned his Unitarian ministry when he found he didn't believe in God any longer and then turned a hobby—cabinet making and fine carpentry—into a quite profitable business. Thus he adapted his outer circumstances to his inward life, while his wife was embarrassed, resentful, and disapproving—and his daughter, Elinor, admiring and delighted.

Poem after poem in Robert Frost's nearly half-century of publishing reflect the theme of home: home, that is, as a place where *safety* and *danger* meet; where the *active relation* between those in the home *defines* that home; where secrets may be either the saving realm of interior life or the destructive arena of violence and threat of violence—or both; and where something far within, some tiny part of light, yet seems to hold—seems never to break, never to be extinguished entirely.

Fyodor Dostoevsky writes at the closing of his *Brothers Karamazov*:

> You must know that there is nothing higher, or stronger, or sounder, or more useful afterwards in life, than some good memory, especially a memory from childhood, from the parental home. . . . If a man stores up many such memories to take into life, then he is saved for his whole life. And even if one good memory remains with us in our hearts, that alone may serve some day for our salvation.[134]

I want to end by having us read and discuss a single poem of Robert Frost's: "The Thatch."

"The Thatch," a Chiasmus of Home, *by Xenia Sheehan*

The author's notes end here. As editor, I approach the poem in a manner Don would surely have recognized as appropriate, especially after he began to study *chiasmus* closely. The pattern is so striking in this poem. The line indents and numbering are my additions so as to better reveal the chiastic form:

THE THATCH, BY ROBERT FROST[135]

A   1. Out alone in the winter rain,

2. Intent on giving and taking pain.

B   3. But never was I far out of sight

4. Of a certain upper-window light.

C   5. The light was what it was all about:

6. I would not go in till the light went out;

7. It would not go out till I came in.

D   8. Well, we should see which one would win,

9. We should see which one would be first
to yield.

E   10. The world was a black invisible field.'

11. The rain by rights was snow for cold.

12. The wind was another layer of mold.

F   13. But the strangest thing: in the
thick old thatch,

14. Where summer birds had been
given hatch,

15. Had fed in chorus, and lived
to fledge,

16. Some still were living in hermitage.

G   17. And as I passed along the eaves,

18. So low I brushed the straw
with my sleeves,

19. I flushed birds out of hole
after hole,

                    20. Into the darkness. It grieved
                        my soul,

F'   21. It started a grief within a grief,

                    22. To think their case was beyond relief

E'   23. They could not go flying about
                        in search

                    24. Of their nest again, nor find a perch.

                    25. They must brood where they fell in
                        mulch and mire,

D'   26. Trusting feathers and inward fire

                    27. Till daylight made it safe for a flyer.

C'   28. My greater grief was by so much reduced

                    29. As I thought of them without nest or roost.

                    30. That was how that grief started to melt.

B'   31. They tell me the cottage where we dwelt,

             32. Its wind-torn thatch goes now unmended;

             33. Its life of hundreds of years has ended

A'   34. By letting the rain I knew outdoors

        35. In on to the upper chamber floors.

Give the pattern a loose attentiveness. Trust it to yield meaning, but never force it. I doubt anyone writes good chiasmus exactly, sometimes not even deliberately—I keep finding gorgeous chiastic passages in Don's prose writing, which I'm sure were not deliberate. He had an ear for chiasmus. But a whole 35-line poem? Surely Frost knew exactly what he was doing.

Having no notes for this discussion, I informally assembled (though not together) a surrogate "class" to fill in for the missing discussion.[136]

HARD SAYIN', NOT KNOWIN'

I begin with Sydney Lea, who kindly sent me an essay entitled "Fact, Dream, and Labor: Robert Frost and the New England Attitude." Originally presented at The Frost Place, the lecture then became a chapter in his book *A Hundred Himalayas*. It makes a good starting point for looking at this poem, as the Frost he writes of is surely the one we see in the poem—a "true Yankee provincial" who "refuses to hang a hat on a single peg." Lea elaborates:

"*Hard sayin', not knowin',* as my older neighbors often put it. Not knowing, I nonetheless suspect that Frost was like any great man or woman—or like any man or woman, period. He could be almost monstrous and he could be almost extremely tender."[137]

"Anything more than the truth would have seemed too weak," Lea quotes from Frost's sonnet "Mowing," then asks, "But what would be more than truth? What would it weaken, and how? Frost tellingly appears to dismiss the notion of the revelatory, let alone the apocalyptic, which, after all, might have wrongly entered the eager reader's consciousness when that reader beheld a lone figure with a scythe." "Yet, even if he claims to discard them, these supra-mundane associations are the ones that immediately leap to his mind as he mows." "Fact and dream, the physical and the speculative," Lea writes,

> perpetually coexist in Frost's own seekings, and he urges us to
> see that coexistence not merely as a hallmark of his work but
> also as a condition of human life. We too must ponder the rela-
> tions of the rational and the supra-rational, the practical and the
> emotional; we must likewise understand the perils of becoming
> schematic in our ponderings on apparent opposites. . . . But it
> is precisely the *effort* at understanding that Frost summons us
> to. Religious or otherwise, such effort to make the world cohere
> by way of our own impositions will be relentless and, doubtless,
> inconclusive this side of the grave.

Such a coexistence of layers of reality and their often secret interrelations—though I hesitate to say which layer is fact here and which is dream—is exactly at the heart of the poem we are looking at: that is, the secret community of creatures living symbiotically within the thatch of the narrator's house. The existence and exposure of this layer is the poem's heart, from which its life and meaning flow, or fail to. What a wonderful employment for the chiasmus, which can say without knowing, can say first one thing and then its opposite, and can get to a whole thing from different directions without ruling out one or the other. Among other things, I take this as permission not to rule out the range of speculation, religious and otherwise, that the poem seems both to invite and reject as it works its way, soaked in winter rain from beginning to end, from an entrenched warfare within and between two people (generally thought to be man and wife, even Robert and Elinor, who did choose for a time to live "under thatch"), by way of different griefs, one old, the other new, to a quietly resigned and self-knowing compassion for those, including themselves, who have suffered for the couple's failure to make a home and protect its secret inner life.

Bear in mind Don's definition of home as a place where *safety* and *danger* meet; where secrets may be either the saving realm of interior life, holding a family together, or the destructive arena of violence and threat of violence; or both. The poem focuses on the secrets kept in the thatch, unknown even to their keepers. Was there treasure or value in the thatch that in fact kept the home, or could have done if the home's in-dwellers had recognized their role as its protectors? If, that is, they'd been able to move beyond their own centrifugal contentions that would end by breaking the home apart?

Apart from its secrets, home is also, Don says, a place where something far within, some tiny part of light, seems to hold—seems never to break, never to be extinguished entirely. Or is it in fact extinguished here? Was it only an idea? The narrator, even after he has moved on, does not seem to have extinguished his memory of home. In the poem, an inextinguishable light such as this is the very point of contention. It's a light the narrator won't go in to. Is it a saving thing, someone's love for him? His wife hoping to light his way back from depression? Christ's light, as once taught to the poet by his mother—calling him to yield, to come in out of the wet and cold? Is it too possessive a love? Is it entrapping? Is there even another person at all in that upper room refusing to extinguish the light? Or is it simply a light signifying whatever holds its own against the narrator's darkness?

To move the circle of unknowns still further out, is it a decision he's making in the present to leave this home, or is it a long-ago departure being remembered? Or something such as a memory or hunger for home that keeps the light of "home" burning as idea or memory when it's time to move on? Or is the light the whole realm of interior life (which seems at this point in time or memory committed to anger or at least to intransigence and darkness)? What threat or secret is hidden there? Or what door has closed in him that makes it no longer home? And does it matter? He's obviously toughened himself to endure the world's dark and cold, and survivors seldom like to have their armor threatened by yielding to such things as love.

One reader asks if we might be seeing a prodigal son making his initial exit. Another sees his resemblance to Lear at the end when he finally *sees* outside himself and has pity on the "poor naked wretches wheresoe'er they be," which raises the question of Lear's blindness at this stage. Does the light under the thatch have to do with seeing and failing to see? Is that the source of contention? Does the one inside insist that he *see*? Does the speaker not want to see? He has after all quite firmly chosen a chilling darkness.

The reader who sees Lear's likeness in the speaker offers a darker view of the poem than most, suggesting it's a tragedy in which pity came too late, as it did for Lear. Beginning in a self-imposed abandonment by the person in the lighted room (or of her by him), it goes on to the birds, expelled from safety, captive now in the cold and darkness, mulch and mire; and then to the narrator's final turn away from his solipsism, brought about by pity and grief; like Lear in the storm.

This reader sees the speaker as both repelled by the light in the upper chamber, and at the same time tethered to it. The speaker, she suggests, sees that the birds' refusal to follow the dictates of natural migration has led to their misery, but for some—those who can hold on to the inner fire and the protection of feathers—there may be redemption with the morning's light. Does the poem's speaker see this clearly enough to return to the upper chamber while the light remains lit? Or does he "win," and, by so doing, actually lose the light altogether? Hard knowin', but it seems in this view that the poem may end with a "sadder but wiser" melancholy self-recognition.

Whatever the answer, it's the light that drew his attention initially: "The light was what it was all about"; it's the problem requiring resolution. And it looks as if the resolution involves making some kind of peace with whatever that home has meant to him, with himself and his behaviors and expectations and regrets, and finally with the ordinary, crumbling, daylight and rained-on reality of a home that's no longer a home for anyone. Certainly the rain on the upper chamber floor (presumably that same room the light was in) implies that a more general and impersonal light of day is reaching into the room by the end, though it has no power to light the dark, and the home is a ruin. Whatever its secrets, it's all exposed now to the daylight and rain. (I remember feeling that way once when I returned to my childhood home to find there'd been an electrical fire on the third floor where my room had been, and the cubby walls—behind which my childish wolves had lived in threatening secrecy, known only to me—were all gone. To see the daylight in those once-dark places was a great relief!)

Another reader has focused more on God's presence in the poem. She asks, What is hell? and maintains that it is the suffering of being unable to love. She sees the relation to the poem of this quotation from Fr. Alexander Schmemann's *For the Life of the World*: "God acted so that man might understand who he really was and where his hunger had been driving him. The light God sent was his Son: the same light that had been shining unextinguished in the world's darkness all along, seen now in full brightness."[138]

Another, herself a mother, sees in it a young man experiencing the grief of a conflict with his parent(s?) that makes his house no longer home. In his anger and pain he does some destructive thing, and in doing it he comes to identify with both the birds and his parent and in time to realize and own that one's pain often causes hurt to others (in a deliberate yet unintended way). This marks the beginning of compassion towards his parent and a point of hope for healing and return. He grieves seeing the birds (himself now?) evicted into the dark wet outside. Unable to fly or form a new nest on the spot, they must wait out the darkness of the night experiencing in innocence the pain of a separation from their home that they weren't prepared for. The speaker offers no solution besides waiting out the darkness and looking towards the building of a different home. To go in while the light is on would be to acknowledge it as the home it no longer is.

To this reader the light seems that of a parent waiting up for him, grieved by whatever they've done to drive him out, hoping for a chance to resolve the conflict (perhaps a recurring one) which the young man is not willing to go inside to hear. The damage to the relationship, like the thatch, is never repaired, and thus the rain (expressing the pain of being outside of home) gets in and makes the house unlivable, no longer a home. He moves on in life but later hears how the rain destroyed the house, perhaps learning from it the consequences of broken relationship(s) on a person. Maybe he's told how it affected his parent specifically. A sad reading.

Before looking at the specific chiastic structure of the poem, I want to add one more small piece to the puzzle. I had an opportunity to speak on the phone with Jay Parini at Middlebury College, who has written a biography of Frost. He pointed out, as Don has also suggested, the conflict for Frost created by his father's rationalism and his mother's mysticism, and I thought of the antinomy this could form in a person's life, even granted that Frost's father died when he was ten. This made me think about the man out in the winter-wet-night as torn between the two parents (his own antinomy now, which goes on living within him). He has hardened his mind against his mother's mystical solutions, needs to have that light put out, finds it won't go out, and since his mother had loved and protected him in his childhood, he finds his resistance to her a grief. Possibly such an inner conflict has even carried forward, if only in his own imagining, to create a fault line in his adult home, or the sense of "home" he carries within him. For all our inner brokennesses affect our ability to make an adult home. And I considered how this might manifest in a poem such as this as the narrator's thoughtless breaking of the thatch community, innocent victims of his own broken carelessness. Hence his compassion, self-knowing, and grief for them, even for himself, also apparently homeless here. For our inner breaks, like geologic fault lines, reveal themselves as brokenness—earthquakes even— around and about us. But as we meet them with grieving compassion and become aware of how we've inflicted our brokenness on others, and repent and grieve for that, there can follow some level of healing or peace. Though in this case, there can be no restoration, only greater wisdom in which the past can be put to rest and cease to haunt us.

Reading the Chiasmus

Looking now at the poem's actual antinomies, we become aware of the opposing forces pulling the home apart. The marriage (if that's what it is) is contentious from the start:

A. The narrator (whether husband or son) is out alone in the winter rain (lines 1–2), "intent on giving and taking pain." By the end of the poem (lines 34–35), he and the rain are indoors and "the rain I knew outdoors" is in the past. The emotional intensity of the narrator's younger self has opposed the mature one (as active memory?) but seems to have become quieter now.

B. He is never "far out of sight of a certain upper-window light" (ll. 3–4). I've mentioned some different suggestions about what that light might be or who (if anyone) is keeping it lit. Or could it represent his own intensities, resentments, yearnings, and perhaps nostalgia about the very idea of home? "The light was what it was all about" (l. 5). Does the light somehow give proof of the home's *life*, which he would prefer to relegate to the dead? Perhaps "home" (or its failure) is some kind of light (or absence of light) for each of us. The antinomy here (in ll. 31–33) is that his dwelling in the cottage has become wholly a thing of the past, and he hears from others that the cottage itself is now dead. From that perspective, there seems no emotion left but a sort of quiet or resigned acceptance. How did he get there?

C. The light was what it was all about in ll. 5–7, but in ll. 28–30 the focus has changed and his greater and older grief is starting to melt in his newfound grief for the life that had inhabited the thatch. He is now beginning to think of other lives than his own and to recognize his responsibility in carelessly driving them from their homes.

D. Where at first (ll. 8–9) he was immobilized in fierce contention, in ll. 26–27 he is wholly released from himself in his concern for the birds who have only "feathers and inward fire" to trust in for their safety.

E. In ll. 10–12, he is more immediately, viscerally, aware of the blackness, rain, cold, wind, and mold of the world, but not now for his own sake; for in ll. 23–25 he is seeing in detail the difficulties of the birds' situation, knowing that he can go elsewhere, but they cannot and "must brood where they fell in mulch and mire."

F. Approaching the center, he has opened now to awareness of the other life of the birds and their long history in what he thought was *his* home (13–16), and this has released his grief to become "a grief within a grief, / To think their case was beyond relief."

G. He is released from himself at last into full awareness of his complicity in flushing the birds out into the darkness. And his soul can grieve, for both his own blindness and the birds' plight. Their lives are now part of his in a way they never were when they simply lived in secret in his roof. These relations can almost be said to be those of a home, a functioning home. And he is able to leave this home behind in compassionate regret, knowing and caring about his own part in its failure, rather than disconnecting from it in angry grief. Both have yielded in their frozen contention: the speaker and the offending light. He can go forward more wisely now, with his past integrated rather than simply left behind, the bright light of pain yielding over time to the world's everyday light.

What has been gained by approaching this chiastically? Could the story have been told as well in straight narration? For one thing, straight narration begins to seem artificial the more I get used to thinking chiastically. I don't think memory and revelation work straightforwardly. It also seems to me that, without chiasmus, we tend to get locked in oppositional stances that don't move—like the hard contention of lines 6 and 7 in this poem. Relationship fails to happen, secrets are kept secret, awareness of our context and our part in it fails so develop. One must even ask: Has the narrator's newfound compassion, engendered by understanding the destruction of home he has brought upon the thatch residents, become now a kind of light in him? Certainly he seems quietly brighter and even a bit richer of spirit at the end. If we follow Don's point about carrying all our family history inwardly from home to home, from parents to parenting, the gift in this poem of compassionate grief is the kind of grace that allows memories to soften into good ones that "may serve some day for our salvation." So my conclusion is that this is not a dark poem but it is a sad one, richly supporting Lea's claim that, for Frost, any "effort to make the world cohere by way of our own impositions will be relentless and, doubtless, inconclusive this side of the grave."

I would take a further and possibly outrageous step and bring St. Maximus back into the equation. He says that, to fulfill our role as humans, we are called to bring into unity in our own person those things which by nature are far distant from each other. In this poem, I think we can see that this speaker has, in the end, taken a first step in that direction. He has not failed; he has allowed grace (conspicuously absent in the beginning) to work its way into his darkness. Perhaps it could be said that in the end he has repented of his intransigent anger and, in his compassion for the birds, has accepted into himself something of the light he "would not go in" to before, turning it into a light that illumines rather than challenges. And thus he has received a grace from the very darkness of his home. Perhaps to accept that light at the beginning would have been a lie. But now it's not.

Hard sayin', not knowin'. Darkness and grace. An antinomy. A home.

Lyricized by God

Transfiguring Violence through Psalmic Technique

The Mind of David and the Mind of Christ

MY EXPERIENCE IN PRAYING the Psalms for over two decades has given me a tiny, fleeting glimpse of a vast and very great subject.[139] I can put the subject this way: the Psalms disclose the mind of David in the process of becoming the mind of Christ. The fundamental question, therefore, is, how do the Psalms accomplish this transformative process?

The phrase "the mind of Christ" is of course St. Paul's, when, in First Corinthians, he writes this astonishing sentence: "We have the mind of Christ" (2:16). St. Paul's point in this chapter of the epistle is that we possess in ourselves the mind of Christ *solely because* God has given us this mind in order that we may know—in St. Paul's own words—"the things freely given us by God." Itself a gift, the mind of Christ in us is thus the mode wherein we know God's gifts.[140] For St. Paul, then, the essence of our mental life can best be expressed as human gratitude for divine self-giving.

To help understand the ways wherein St. Paul's immense insight can illumine the Psalms, I begin by considering two crucial chapters—the sixteenth and seventeenth—in the Davidic narratives in First Samuel.[141] In these chapters, we can distinguish three moments—or dimensions of Davidic experience—which, taken together, beautifully reveal what I am calling the mind of David.

The First Moment: Formed in Humility

The first moment occurs when the prophet Samuel comes to the house of Jesse to choose a new king to replace Saul, the first king of Israel. David is the eighth, and youngest, son of Jesse. Now, his humble status in his father's house, akin to that of a servant, is made plain when Jesse brings each of his eldest seven sons to Samuel in order of age, hoping each time that Samuel will choose *this* son as king. But Samuel, at first attracted by Eliab's outward appearance (for which the Lord tells him to "have no regard"), follows God, who "sees into the heart" (1 Sam 16:7), in refusing all seven sons. He says of each, "The Lord has not chosen this one" (l. 10). Samuel then turns to Jesse, "Are these all the sons you have?" (l. 11). For God had made plain to Samuel that in this house was, indeed, the second (but first true) king. Jesse responds, "There is still the youngest. He is tending the sheep." "Send for him," says Samuel. When the youth is brought in, Samuel sees David's beautiful face as inwardly God says to him, "Arise, anoint him: this is the one" (1. 12). "And the Spirit of the Lord came upon David from that day forward."

I want to focus for a moment on a single aspect of this narrative: the status David holds in his father's house. It is plain that he is something of an afterthought, as Jesse, apparently, quite simply forgets him when Samuel—a figure of vast religious prestige in Israel—shows up to anoint a new king and parades his noble sons before him. We are invited by the narrative to imagine Jesse's moment of surprise, if not slight shock, when Samuel asks, "Are these all the sons you have?" Oh, yes, yes, there *is* another one (but really, you know . . .). My point is this: In the very midst of his family's disregard for this youngest son who tends the sheep, God, who "sees into the heart," works salvation by raising David up, through Samuel, into kingship. All through Scripture, this same reality holds: the stone that was rejected becomes the cornerstone; the barren woman gives birth to the blessed child; the suffering servant heals the whole nation. Humble in external ways, the mind of David is revealed as possessing immense value.

The Second Moment: Made Coherent in Music

The second moment immediately follows. When King Saul hears from his servants that Jesse has a son, David, skilled in playing the lyre, he calls the boy to his court. Now, Saul has been afflicted with a psychic derangement so profound that his closest servants had suggested the one solution that could reconstitute the wholeness of the king's psyche: let a man play the lyre when the psychosis is upon the king, and then he "shall be well" (1

Sam 16:16). David is brought before the king, and (just as Samuel did) Saul looks upon the face of David and immediately loves him so much that he grants him a great courtly honor: he makes David his armor-bearer, a role somewhat akin to that of personal secretary to a modern president. Saul then sends word to Jesse, asking the father that the son be permitted to come to the court not simply to take a prestigious job but, more deeply, to enter into a genuine relationship with the king: "And Saul sent to Jesse, saying, Let David, I beg you, stand before me: for he has found favor in my sight" (16:22). Then, within this relationship, one akin to that of an adopted son to his adoptive father, David takes up the lyre when the king's derangement erupts in a psychotic episode: "David took the lyre and played [it] with his hand, so that Saul was refreshed and made well, and the evil spirit departed from him" (16:23).

The essential thing to note here is that this narrative explicitly connects psychological health and musical pattern. David's music *causes* Saul's healing because the music itself is (the narrator tells us) "with the Lord" (16:18). David's music is therefore *not* self-performance. Rather, it is filled with a heavenly power to *ensoul* the listener. The verb used in line 23—"Saul was refreshed"—carries in Hebrew the meaning of entering into a spacious openness, a place where one can now freely breathe. When, in the second century BC, this verb was translated into Greek, the translators chose *anapsycho*, a lovely verb that means "to ascend up into one's soul." Saul regains his soul because David's music has this power to bring the listener up into that spacious place where one's soul can breathe freely and fully. Here, then, is what I am calling the second moment in the formation of David's mind: he actively practices the heavenly music wherein we become psychologically coherent. Thus ends the sixteenth chapter of First Samuel.

Chiastic Pattern in First Samuel. These first two moments of the Davidic mind—the revelation of worthiness in one who is discounted, and the creation of psychological coherence through music—may now be seen as themselves constituting an harmonic sequence. That is, the humble insignificance and the heavenly music are as distinct from one another as any two notes in a musical sequence can be. Yet the sixteenth chapter establishes between them a finely persuasive harmony. The way the chapter does this is through the literary pattern termed *chiasmus*.

Now, every student of biblical poetics owes a great debt to Fr. John Breck's magnificent book, *The Shape of Biblical Language*.[142] This work elucidates *chiastic* structures in biblical texts in ways both richly significant and immediately comprehensible. Chiasmus, says Breck, is that pattern which trains us "to read from the center outward and from the extremities toward the center." So deep and widespread is the use of this pattern in all ancient literary cultures, Breck continues, that "writers in antiquity drew upon it almost instinctively" (29, 34). In this pattern, the first and the final lines of a given biblical passage connect to one another; then the second line connects to the next-to-last line; the third to the third-to-last; and so on, until an exact midpoint is reached. Now, the *kind* of connection between each pair of lines varies immensely. Sometimes, the connection is direct repetition or simple parallelism; at other times, it is direct opposition. More often, the connection is one of intensification, with the second line in the chiastic pair in some way deepening the first, making it sharper and more drastic; and the intensification derives from, happens as a result of, emerges out of, the line at the center. Thus the pattern's midpoint provides a kind of pivot, one upon which the passage's entire significance may be seen to turn. Everything first flows toward this pivot; then everything flows out from it, changed in some way—transformed, indeed transfigured, without being at all "transcendentalized."

Chapter 16 of First Samuel possesses such a pattern. The first line mourns for Saul's psychic derangement; the final line (16:23) exhibits Saul's psychic repatterning through David's music—the connection is straight opposition. The second line (16:2) has Samuel fearfully telling God that Saul will discover the anointing of a new king at Jesse's house and then has God telling Samuel to use a sacrificial ritual to cover up the anointing from Saul. The second-to-last line (16:22) has Saul sending a message to Jesse and asking him to give up—indeed to sacrifice—his son David for the court's and the king's sake. Here, the connection between this pair of lines is richly intensifying. That is, Samuel's cover-up in line 2 succeeds so completely that Saul in line 22 begs Jesse to send him the very person he would otherwise actively hate (as his usurper)—and Saul begs in the voice of the one love that could (and, for a time, actually *will*) heal him, the love he has for David. In so doing, the latter line (22) simultaneously parallels and reverses, and thereby intensifies, the former (l. 2). Thus, this connection makes manifest that *operation* which underlies all the Davidic narratives (indeed, all of Scripture): that invisible action wherein human persons freely choose what God—wholly unbeknownst to them—is willing for their redemption.

In this way, the chiastic pattern progresses through the whole sixteenth chapter, each verse sounding its own distinct note, yet each at the same time harmonically connecting to another. And as the narrative continues and the pattern unfolds, the contradictions grow ever sharper: David is disregarded by his family, David is raised by his king; Saul is broken by psychosis, Saul is made well by music. What resolves the chapter's whole pattern is the single verse at the midpoint: "Arise, anoint him: this is the one" (l. 12). At this point, David is brought out from the darkness of his lowly status in his family to be anointed by God to become the light for all Israel. Then, from this point, David is made present to Saul as the bringer of musical light into the king's psychic darkness. Everything flows to this midpoint; and then everything flows from it. Its significance could not be clearer. All our sufferings and humiliations are healed and reconciled in those actions wherein God gives Himself to us in the midst of our brokenness. Through David's music, Saul finds in the darkness of his psychotic depression a way back to God. Similarly, in the very midst of his outward disregard, David is anointed by Samuel to be king through God's direct command and is given music for the divine healing of the broken world.

THE THIRD MOMENT: PERFECTED IN STILLNESS

But in the next chapter (the seventeenth) of First Samuel, the mind of David achieves its third and perfective dimension: stillness. In his book *Leap Over a Wall*, Eugene H. Peterson beautifully describes the scene in the seventeenth chapter when David faces the Philistine giant, Goliath. At first, David follows Saul's urging to put on Saul's own armor. But then he sets aside the armor, saying, "I cannot use these, I have not tested them" (1 Sam 17:39). Then David steps over to the brook to choose the stones for his sling. Peterson writes:

> My attention is caught and held by this wonderful but improbable scene: David on his knees at the brook; David kneeling and selecting five smooth stones, feeling each one, testing it for balance and size; David out in the middle of the valley of Elah—in full view of two armies, Philistine and Israelite, gathered on each side of the valley—kneeling at the brook, exposed and vulnerable. He's such a slight figure, this young shepherd. He's so unprotected. The air is heavy with hostility. There isn't a man on either side of the valley who isn't hefting a spear, sharpening a sword, getting ready to kill. The valley of Elah is a cauldron in which fear and hate and arrogance have been stirred and cooked for weeks into what's now a volatile and lethal brew. And David, seemingly oblivious to the danger, ignoring the spiked forest of spears and the glint of swords, kneels at the brook.[143]

Peterson has here supremely seen this astonishing moment. I want to emphasize what I call the *iconic* dimension in this scene: as David gazes down into the brook, he enters into what St. Isaac the Syrian calls *hesychia*, or *stillness*. In his magnificent *Ascetical Homilies*, that greatest of Orthodox books on the teaching of prayer, St. Isaac defines stillness as "silence to all things," a word that in Syriac also means "quietness, calmness, quiescence."[144] Amidst all the self-assertive yet terrified noise of all the violent restlessness, David simply, and entirely, *sets aside* the whole imminent catastrophe, choosing instead to enter into this moment of silence and stillness. "It is ridiculous," says St. Isaac, "for us to speak of achieving stillness if we do not abandon all things and separate ourselves from every care."[145] As Peterson perceptively notes, David sets aside Saul's armor, "traveling light, delivered from an immense clutter" (42)—words that almost could come from a homily of St. Isaac's. And the mind's spins of anxiety are surely part of this clutter, for anxiety is the borrowed armor that the mind takes on in its desperate attempt to protect itself. As David kneels at the brook, Peterson imagines how the rippling water catches the sunlight and illumines David's breathtakingly beautiful face, now wholly concentrated in perfect stillness.

What expression do we see in David's face at this moment? I think we are to see every possible human expression, with every conceivable human emotion, all of them equally vividly present. That is, David's face is here perfectly *iconic* in just the same way Christ's face is in every true Orthodox icon. For what David's face, in this moment, beautifully holds is precisely what moves Saul to great love when he first sees David: the beauty of comprehensive stillness.

That is, stillness *is* every human expression all at once and perfectly, in the same way that white is the presence of all color. Stillness is therefore what an entire life can come to express when a person learns to set aside (as David does here) every possible armor and to choose, instead, to love God. What we see here in David, then, is the understanding that stillness is a discipline. St. Isaac says: "learn what is the life of stillness, what is its work, what mysteries are concealed in this discipline" (*Homilies* 65:319). This discipline is something as strong as a bronze spear and as light as a lyric poem—and strong partly because it is lyrical, and light partly because it is bronzen. In this way, the discipline of stillness can embrace and hold every conceivable aspect of the Davidic mind in the same way it can express every conceivable expression of the Davidic face.

In this way, the mind of David—ennobled in his family's disregard and strengthened in the graces of music—now gains its perfective purposiveness in stillness. Only as he kneels at the brook, in stillness, can David reconcile Jesse's dismissive indifference and Saul's prestigious elevation of him. But such reconciliation can never be achieved as mere cognitive process; it can only be achieved as an *actual practice actually lived.*

The mind of David may thus be understood as that long discipline of stillness wherein the ruining oppositions of actual experience are held within the musical disciplines of lyric art: held, until God Himself can be seen in the very ruins themselves: seen, and felt, and overwhelmingly and gratefully loved. This overwhelming and grateful love is the mind of David.[146]

The Spiritual Significances of Psalmic Technique

Thus, a great question opens before us. If the mind of David is formed in humility, made coherent in music, and perfected in stillness, then what is the spiritual significance of psalmic technique? Or—to put the same question in the form we first asked it—how does the mind of David become in the Psalms the mind of Christ?

There are three dimensions to the spiritual significance of psalmic technique. What I am seeking in my work is the theology of Orthodox poetic form. For the theology of Orthodox poetics is one with the theology of Orthodox worship. And to the extent that the greatest of Orthodox poetic forms is the Divine Liturgy, then to that extent the theology of Orthodox poetics is one with the poetics of the Psalms: for the Liturgy is deeply psalmic in both shape and substance.

Perhaps Breck's greatest insight into biblical chiastic pattern is his discussion of the pattern's double movement: (1) the movement from the passage's midpoint forward and back to its two extremities (that is, its first and final lines), combined with (2) the movement from the passage's narrative start to its narrative conclusion. When these two movements are combined, the result is a situation wherein the forward narrative movement constantly *doubles back* to earlier points—but always at a higher, more intense and more comprehensive point. Yet each *doubling-back* is necessarily *moving away* from the passage's midpoint; hence, each *doubling-back* can be seen to "ascend" from this midpoint. Equally, and at the same time, the movement toward this midpoint can be seen to "descend" toward it. These two distinct movements thus interlock and cohere.[147]

Let us examine Psalm 66 to establish our bearings. Here is the text, arranged to emphasize the chiastic pattern:

A God be merciful unto us, and bless us and cause his face to shine upon us;

  B that thy way may be known upon earth, thy saving health among all nations.

C Let the people praise thee, O God; let all the people praise thee.

    D O let the nations be glad and sing for joy: for thou hast judged the people righteously, and shalt govern the nations upon earth.

C' Let the people praise thee, O God; let all the people praise thee.

B' Then indeed the earth yields her increase; and God, our own God, indeed blesses us.

A' God does bless us, and all the ends of the earth do fear him.

The forward narrative movement in this lyric is quite plain to see: it begins with imploring God's blessing and ends with the fullest reality of that blessing having been received on earth. Equally plain is the psalm's midpoint center of significance: the lyricizing of our political life occurs when we let God govern the whole of our earthly life. Immediately around this midpoint is a pair of exactly repeating lines. But because the repeat line (C') occurs *after* the midpoint, the line gains an added intensity from it. Hence, this repeat line may be said to *ascend upward* from the center—while at the same moment it intersects with the *descending movement* of line C. These two movements thus interlock and cohere.

In the next pair of lines out from the center (ll. B and B'), the same interlocking occurs. The "salvation" that, in line B, God is implored to give becomes, in B', the earth's agricultural bountifulness. Thus, the way of the heavenly God may be seen to descend upon the earth (in the psalm's first half) as the way (in the second half) of an actual fruitfulness of the fields. The result of such fruitfulness is that we can behold the very face of God shining upon us *in and through* our very awe and reverence of Him as He directly acts within the nation's political life. The significance of the psalm's double movement is therefore clear: as God descends into our actual life on earth, we ascend into actually beholding His face. The psalm catches and holds these two opposed movements in and as one clear lyric form.

The First Dimension: The Experience of Antinomy

Here, then, is the first dimension of psalmic technique. Chiastic patterning at once shapes and is shaped by the *experience of antinomy*. Now, this term *antinomy* seems first to have been used in classical Roman law to describe the circumstance of every jury trial: one side completely prosecutes while the other side entirely defends. According to all legal assumption, the truth can arise *only* through such jarring antinomical interaction. The philosophic use of the term begins with Immanuel Kant's *Critique of Pure Reason* (1781); and from Kant's work forward, the word exhibits a powerful and complex life. In his magnificent 1914 book, *The Pillar and Ground of the Truth*, Pavel Florensky explores major areas of Eastern Orthodox theology in the light of this term, *antinomy*. In so doing, Florensky's explorations become, I believe, very useful to understanding chiastic patterning in the Psalms.

Antinomy does *not* say, Florensky notes, "Either one or the other is false." "It also does not say," Florensky continues, "'Neither the one nor the other is true.' It only says, 'Both the one and the other are true, but each in its own way. Reconciliation and unity are higher than rationality.'"[148] Antinomicalness is therefore, above everything else, an *experience*. It is the experience of disjunction, the experience wherein human discursive rationality breaks helplessly apart in the face of—better, *in the teeth of*—harsh, dissonant realities. Such realities are the very ground of all biblical (indeed, all *human*) experience. The agony of forced exile is, at the same moment, the way of redemptive joy; the created world is simultaneously completely good, completely fallen, and completely redeemed; Christ is at once fully human and fully divine. There is no direct way wherein merely (that is, untransformed) human rationality can reconcile the disjunctive elements in these realities; equally, there is no way whereby any element can be eliminated without radically destroying that reality. Thus, mere rationality simply breaks down when it directly confronts such antinomies as these. And chiastic pattern in the Psalms is thus the literary structure that most perfectly fits the experience of antinomy. For the contrastive structure not only identifies just what the antinomies are, but firmly and directly *holds* all of their jarring contradictions.

But psalmic antinomy has a deeper significance: it contains its own reconciliations. Florensky puts it this way: "this [Davidic] mind itself is the healing organ of the world" (*Pillar and Ground*, 118). The mind of David is continually broken on the reefs of all the world's most dreadful antinomies. Psalm 86:16 (LXX) says: "Thy furies have swept through me, thy terrors have utterly unmade me." That is, I am overwhelmed with terror and fury, yet I am blessed because God is Himself steering the agony. What merely human rationality could even survive, let alone master, such fierce antinomy? The rational mind thus breaks. Yet once so broken—and it is broken in the action of every psalm—the mind of David can then be *lyricized by God*. Why does Saul not know this boy whose singing has already healed him? Nevertheless, such redemptive lyricism cannot be rationally comprehended. The salvific mind of David can teach, praise, and love God, but it cannot (as will the mind of Christ in the Gospels) finally *comprehend* God. Yet the line in the Psalms between genuinely loving and fully knowing God is the thinnest and finest line imaginable. So thin and so fine is it that here, at this line, we may see how the mind of David begins, through the chiastic art of lyric antinomy, to become indeed the mind of Christ. The Davidic mind becomes so open to God that it draws near to becoming divinized in the very intimacy.

Here, then, is the first dimension of psalmic technique. Through the chiastic patterning of antinomical experience, the mind of David draws close to God in deepest love.

The Second Dimension: Blessedness

The second dimension of significance to psalmic technique arises from the first: the dimension of *blessedness*. The first word in the entire Psalter is *blessed*: "Blessed is the man who walks not in the counsel of the ungodly." The word then occurs some thirty times throughout the Psalms. Now, in his *Pillar and Ground of the Truth*, Florensky explores the roots of the Greek word used by the Septuagint to translate the Hebrew: the Greek word is *ma-karios*. The roots of this word, Florensky notes, are *ma-kar*: "do not devour yourself" (140). Self-devouring always and everywhere occurs, Florensky explains, *when the self seeks to isolate itself from God and from other persons and to establish itself as the triumphant king of its own self-generated world.* Blessedness begins to arrive when the self ceases to sustain the ferocity of such self-isolation—and thereby the self-devouring also begins to cease. "Makarios," Florensky says, "essentially expresses the idea that the dizzily whirling heart has found rest, that the heart's soaring passions have been fully calmed . . . [and that] the heart ceases to devour itself."[149]

In this understanding of psalmic blessedness, we can see the significance of the *double movement* in Psalms. That is, "the dizzily whirling heart" is seeking, through the chiastic pattern's antinomical movements, to find its point of rest and stillness in God. In this sense, blessedness is not simply the negation of self-devouring but (in Florensky's words) "the eternal conversion of devouring [and] the stepping on the head of [isolated] selfhood" (*Pillar and Ground*, 139). This conversion of self-devouring into blessedness is given, in psalm after psalm, as the actual experience that the chiastic pattern is perfectly registering. And as each psalm enacts this conversion, "the dizzily whirling heart" finds stillness and peace at each psalm's center. In so doing, the mind of David begins to approach the mind of Christ. Such is the action of psalmic blessedness.

Moreover, as the whole Psalter proceeds, each successive occurrence of blessedness—each entry we make into the peace that lies outside our isolation from God and others within a self-generated and self-enclosed reality—gathers in all the prior experiences, deepening and intensifying the entire significance of blessedness. For the whole Psalter unfolds in the very same fashion every psalm does: in antinomical movements within chiastic patterns. And as it does, the antinomies grow always sharper and more dire as the mind of David continues to grow correspondingly more illumined in blessedness. Thus, the second dimension of significance to psalmic technique registers fully this experience of blessedness.

THE THIRD DIMENSION: MEMORY ETERNAL

The third dimension of psalmic technique gathers in the first two and becomes their shared ground. For as the mind of David draws near to God, first in love and then in blessedness, psalmic technique then reveals its most perfective dimension: the dimension of *memory*. Again, Florensky beautifully defines the significance of psalmic memory when he refers to the wise thief who asks on the cross: "Lord, remember me when you come in your kingdom," to which Christ responds: "Truly, I say to you, this day you shall be with me in paradise" (Luke 23:42–43). Florensky explains:

> In other words, "to be remembered" by the Lord is the same thing as "to be in paradise." "To be in paradise" is to be in eternal memory and, consequently, to have eternal existence and therefore an eternal memory of God. Without remembrance of God we die, but our very remembrance of God is possible through God's remembrance of us. (*Pillar and* Ground, 144)

Here is an astonishing insight. Florensky is saying that our remembering of God and His remembering of us directly converge at a place beyond death, the place of eternal memory. In its antinomical movements throughout the Psalter, the mind of David *remembers* and *is remembered by* the active presence of God. Yet this deepening of memory is never, in the Psalms, a simple straight line. For now, in Psalm 17, David sees God face to face; then, in Psalm 87, he grieves God's total abandonment of him. Yet such intimacies and abandonments are both grounded in the rocksolid depths of ineradicable memory. Thus, psalmic memory exhibits a *double movement*: (1) we remember and forget God in a kind of inescapable eddying into and out of each psalm's center; and (2) we are remembered by Him in an irreversible movement running straight from our birth and into our death and then beyond. Thus, the fulfillment of all desires in the Psalms occurs always as perfect memory: "I shall never forget thy statutes, / In them thou hast quickened me to life" (118:93)—a line that is the chiastic center of the longest psalm. The essential connection is here plain: to *not forget God* is to *be quickened by Him*; that is, to be given actual life, as the baby in the womb is "quickened," is the direct function of psalmic memory. In this way, memory may be best understood as the generative, or creative, principle of all psalmic thought.[150]

Such are some of the spiritual significances of psalmic technique. And thus such are the movements whereby the mind of David draws near to the mind of Christ.

Reverse Restoration and Kenosis

We may now discern a significant set of connections. David's rejection by Jesse in First Samuel plainly marks his entry into the difficulties of antinomical experience. That is, when Jesse overlooks his youngest son, David enters into that experience wherein his father is both the one who most directly hurts him and the one whom he loves and honors. Such experience cannot be rationally contained, for it is the experience of antinomy. Similarly, David's healing of Saul manifests his entry into the experience of blessedness. Finally, David's moment of profound stillness while kneeling at the brook discloses his remembering of—and being remembered by—God. Thus, the connections emerge: the three dimensions of chiastic patterning in the Psalms are perfectly congruent with the three dimensions of the Davidic mind as portrayed in First Samuel: his formation in humility, his healing through music, his perfection in stillness.

The mind of David is thus *always becoming* the mind of Christ. Such a generative process of transformation in the Psalms has this essential property: the mind of Christ *fulfills* the mind of David, but it never overwhelms it, never uses it up or casts it aside. In other words, Christ as Messiah does not employ the Davidic mind as instrument. Instead, the mind of Christ unceasingly *remembers* the Davidic mind, thereby holding David in eternal memory in the fullness of his personhood. Thus, the relation of Christ to David is, in Psalms, a *kenotic*, self-emptying, relationship. Kenosis is the action wherein the mind of David becomes the mind of Christ.

One crucial aspect of kenotic action in David (and in us) is what Florensky terms *reverse restoration*: as the I empties itself in love for the other, "there occurs a reverse restoration of the I in the norm of being proper to it" (*Pillar and Ground*, 67). The isolated I, self-willful and therefore self-hating, tries to operate in a mode of existence entirely foreign to its actual nature. The kenotic I, self-emptying in love of the other, finds itself restored to its proper mode. This mode, says Florensky, has "universal and eternal significance" (67–68), a significance that *ascends* solely through the *descent* into complete kenosis. In Christ's death and resurrection, we see revealed the full significance of every other act of kenosis. Thus, Christ *restores* the mind of David, now redeemed and glorified in that action of eternal memory we call His death and resurrection. It is this understanding of kenosis that most directly informs St. Paul's powerful understanding, in First Corinthians, of the mind of Christ.

The Kenosis Continues in Translation

In the penultimate chapter of Second Samuel, we are given the final words of David as he is dying. His last words are a tiny psalm, the first line of which is: "The spirit of the Lord has spoken by me, and His word was on my tongue." The Hebrew for this line is (as biblical Hebrew always is) extremely beautiful—transliterated, the line looks and sounds approximately like this:

> Ru - ah Adonai dibar - bi v'milato al - l'shoni

These five words (actually, word-clusters) themselves form a tiny chiastic pattern, with the verb *dibar-bi* ("he has spoken") providing the center:

> Ru-ah
>
>   Adonai
>
>   dibar-bi
>
>   v'milato
>
> al-l'shoni

The spirit of God (*ru-ah Adonai*) powerfully descends into the center of His having spoken. Then out from the center there arises the comparably strong incarnation of God's word on David's tongue. Now, the rhythmic movement of the Hebrew line is slow, and dense, and inexorable, like tidal movements onto an ocean beach. Syllabic echoes serve to punctuate this rhythm: the *-bi* at the center is rhymed with the *-ni* at the end; the vowel sound in the *-ah* that ends the first word is echoed in the *al-* that begins the last word. Such echoings help to sculpt the rhythm into its densely comprehensible shape. The final effect is indeed oceanic: the wave's long, slow surge onto the beach followed by its comparably powerful and deliberate withdrawal back into the ocean. This is the characteristic rhythm of much biblical Hebrew poetry.

When the second-century BC Greek translators rendered this line in the magnificent translation of the Hebrew Scripture called the Septuagint, they did so this way:

Pnévma Kyríou elálisen en eme, ke o lógos avtoú epí glossis mou.

What is most interesting in this Greek is its extreme literalness. So extreme is it, in fact, that it here disarrays ordinary Greek syntax in order to reflect a key feature of Hebrew: that is, the phrase *en eme* is placed *after* the verb so as to catch something of the suffixing so characteristic of Hebrew verbs. Here, and almost everywhere, Septuagint Greek will go to great lengths to sustain the accuracy of its mapping.

But the rhythmic movement of the Greek line could not be more unlike Hebrew. Where the Hebrew moves oceanically, the Greek moves balletically. Thus, rather than being carried on slow, strong tidal movements, we are instead brought into a quick, bright, and intricate dance as it is being perfectly executed. And so assured is the line's rhythmic movement that it can even execute a Hebrew "gesture" and never lose its perfect balance: such is everywhere the genius of Septuagint Psalmic Greek. In this way, the final effect of the Greek rhythm may best be seen as one of balletic perfection. Thus, while being vastly different, the Greek rhythm is nevertheless an admirable *counter-response* to the Hebrew: a response, that is, that fully matches but never anywhere attempts to rival the Hebrew reality it is responding to.

In this sense, then, Septuagint Greek gives itself in love to the Hebrew original, in an act of kenosis. For on every single page, almost in every sentence and phrase, we can witness how the Greek language is *dying to itself* so that the Hebrew may live. It dies the death of its own syntactic coherence, over and over, a coherence fully and beautifully established in Homer and brought to a luminous magnificence in Pindar, Sophocles, and Plato. Yet each time it so dies, the Greek is restored to its own true mode of being. For each time Septuagint Greek willingly dies in love for biblical Hebrew, it enters into that perfective stillness we call eternal memory. And here, in this realm of eternal memory, Septuagint Greek achieves its immense significance: it becomes *zo-ópios*, "life-giving." For here Septuagint Greek remembers and is remembered by the God of Abraham, Isaac, and Jacob at the very same moment it foresees this central fact of the Gospels: that when, two centuries hence, Our Lord will quote Scripture, He will do so, sometimes via an Aramaic version, in Septuagint Greek. Such are the life-giving actions of eternal memory.

PSALMIC INTIMACY AS AN EXPERIENCE OF ANTINOMY

In the sixth century AD, Cassiodorus composed in Latin his magnificent commentary on the entire Psalter. In his preface, he quotes a passage from St. Athanasius about (says Cassiodorus) "the peculiar nature of the Psalter":

> Whoever recites the words of a psalm seems to be repeating his own words, to be singing in solitude words of a psalm composed by himself; it does not seem to be another speaking or explaining what he takes up and reads. It is as though he were speaking from his own person, such is the nature of the words he utters. He seems to be expressing the kind of language used as if spoken from the heart. He seems to offer words to God.[151]

St. Athanasius here perfectly expresses the experience of probably every attentive reader of Psalms: the experience of intimacy. As experience, every act of intimacy is, at first, an experience of *shock*. At one moment, a person is far from you; the next instant, that person is immensely close, and vivid, and actual. Systemic shock is one's entry into real intimacy. St. Athanasius is saying that the systemic shock of the Psalms is so great that their words actually become, for every one of us, our own most intimate words.

But genuine intimacy must never be taken as a form of self-aggrandizement. That is, in the experience of intimacy, the other sustains "otherness" at the very same time (and to the very same depth) that the other becomes wholly identified with the I. The Psalms are one's own words at the very moment they remain fully David's and then fully Christ's. In other words, in the same way that the mind of Christ restores the Davidic mind, so, too, the Psalms restore us to ourselves in "the mode of being proper" to us: in the mode, that is, wherein we remember God and are remembered by Him. The shock of psalmic intimacy is an operation of eternal memory.

These dynamics of psalmic intimacy are beautifully recognized by St. Athanasius. When he says that the reader of Psalms experiences the words "as though he were speaking from his own person," Athanasius is perfectly registering the essential "as-if" quality of psalmic intimacy. We are *fully in* the other and yet, in the very same instant, the other remains *fully operative on* us. In this way, psalmic intimacy is fundamentally an experience of antinomy, an experience wherein every psalm seems to declare the words of Christ Himself when He says to the Father: "I in them, and Thou in Me, that they may be made perfect in one" (John 17:23). The effects of psalmic intimacy are therefore vast beyond all our reckonings.

The First Day

A Composer's Introduction
to *Vespers*

BENEDICT SHEEHAN

Editor's Note: I conclude Part Two of the book with Benedict's essay for several reasons: It addresses lyric art in the finest and most exact sense. It is much about the music and shape of Psalms. It represents a legacy of Don Sheehan's teachings about chiasmus and antinomy as they have found their way not only into his son's music but into his very process of composition—to discover, in both, his own unique meanings. And it beautifully illustrates Don's point in chapter 10 about how one person's patient, prayerful work may bear unforeseeable, even miraculous, fruit under the masterful hands of another.

Don, unlike Benedict, was no musician. Yet he was deeply aware of the music in things; he knew how to hear it, listened to it, understood its movements; he heard the music of other languages, and he wrote it in his own. Eventually, as he says at the end of chapter 4, the music he heard, its contours and rhythms, became actual for him in the chant voice of the Church in prayer. It was the same voice, he says, that had spoken the ancient prayer in his heart and led him to the Church as he struggled to reconcile the oppositions that had governed his own life: his Night and his Day.

For me, listening for three joyous days to the rehearsals that preceded the recording of this piece was the experience of a lifetime, rivaled only by the celebratory fireworks that lit up the night following its completion—courtesy of its sponsor, St Tikhon's Monastery (and of course the date, July 4). I was also blessed to be present at the concert premier a year later. As Don might say: it was almost enough. I can only hope that he also was present to it.

Benedict Sheehan conducting the St. Tikhon Choir.

In the beginning God created the heaven and the earth.

And the earth was without form, and void; and darkness was upon the face of the deep. And the Spirit of God moved upon the face of the waters.

And God said, Let there be light: and there was light.

And God saw the light, that it was good; and God divided the light from the darkness.

And God called the light Day, and the darkness he called Night. And the evening and the morning were the first day. (Gen 1:1–5 KJV)

"Like Rachmaninoff"?

The story of *Vespers*—a choral setting of the evening office of the Orthodox Church—begins about six years ago with a simple proposal from Fr.
Sergius, abbot of St. Tikhon's Monastery and my longtime friend and em-
ployer: that I write a Vespers based on traditional Russian chant. "Like
Rachmaninoff," he said.

I actually first found my way into the serious study of music as a
teenager in no small part through Robert Shaw's landmark recording
of Rachmaninoff's 1915 masterwork, so the idea of trying my hand at a
Rachmaninoff-esque Vespers of my own had immediate appeal for me.
The austerely simple and well-worn Russian church melodies used in
the piece coupled with Rachmaninoff's gorgeous quasi-orchestral late-
Romantic choral writing has always been for me—and for audiences all
over the world—a truly magical combination. I've been captivated by it
ever since I first heard it, and it continues to inspire me today. I knew I
couldn't just mimic Rachmaninoff's style and approach, though, so where
would my own piece come from? Where to begin?

In many ways, I see Rachmaninoff's *Vespers* as standing at the crest of
the whole wave of Russian ecclesiastical art and culture before the Russian
Revolution, encompassing all the profound and complex beauty and mass
of contradictions that is Russian Orthodoxy.[152] His piece was arguably the
crowning achievement of the work of the Moscow Synodal School, which
was itself a product of nationalist movements in Russian music and culture at the end of the nineteenth century, actively engaged in parsing out a
uniquely Russian voice from the myriad influences represented in the Slavic
tradition as a whole—Scandinavian, Central Asian, Bulgarian, Byzantine
Greek, Ukrainian, Polish, Italian, Austro-Hungarian, French, German, and
others besides. No easy task, to be sure. To my mind, the work of the Synodal School, and of Rachmaninoff in particular, was immensely successful,
but only insofar as it attempted to *synthesize* rather than to *purify*, to accept inherited cultural complexity as a body of riches upon which to draw
rather than as a disordered mess to be regulated and purged of alien elements. Certainly many, if not most, nationalist movements in the twentieth
century chose purity over synthesis (as did some in the Synodal School),
so it's remarkable to me that Rachmaninoff and his colleagues—especially
Gretchaninoff, Chesnokov, and Kastalsky—largely chose a different path.
The choice between purity and synthesis is perhaps the most important cultural decision facing us today with nationalism seemingly on the rise once
again. In the twentieth century the thirst for purity in the political sphere
resulted in the tragic loss of tens of millions of lives by century's end, so with

that in mind I think Rachmaninoff's vision of an artistic synthesis between East and West—and between old and new—is more relevant now than ever.

Synthesis

Synthesis, then, was my starting point. My *Vespers* is, first and foremost, a synthesis of chant with my own background and musical inheritance, a piece at once arising from the Orthodox tradition and solidly within the currents of my own life. As a son of Anglo-Irish-Scottish-French-Dutch-American converts to Eastern Orthodoxy, I'm no stranger to the notion of synthesis. At least as it exists in this country, Orthodoxy is itself a product of synthesis, a panoply of ethnic traditions and ecclesiastical cultures that have been forced into contact with one another—and with countless other religious traditions besides—here in North America. Russian, Greek, Syrian, Lebanese, Romanian, Albanian, Ukrainian, Georgian (the list goes on), all are united primarily by a common creed and a shared (though richly varied) set of liturgical rites. The music in American Orthodox parishes naturally reflects this diversity, especially in the English-speaking congregations in which I grew up and in which I still work today. My piece, therefore, can be seen as an attempt to honor and legitimize this diversity within American Orthodoxy, as well as to create an artistic vision of unity that can be expanded upon, both in my own work and through the work of others.

The work of synthesis is difficult, though, both culturally and musically. Diversity is inherently complicated and can often represent a frustrating obstacle to efficiently achieving goals. However, I find that struggling for unity in a way that leaves inherent complexity intact ultimately renders much more satisfying solutions than holding to an abstract notion of unity under whose sway all complexity must either conform or be eliminated. This has become for me a governing philosophy. One of the specific ways this philosophy manifests itself musically in my *Vespers* is the frequent use of irregular-meter chant melodies. For me, finding a chant that refused to fit into either regular time-signatures or symmetrical phrase lengths was an exciting challenge and nearly always generated interesting and unexpected musical results. Thus were born *The Opening Psalm, Blessed Is the Man, Rejoice, O Virgin,* and *The Closing Psalm,* all of which are based on rhythmically knotty Russian chants from the medieval monastic tradition and none of which, to my knowledge, had ever been arranged before. If a melody wouldn't fit into a box, I let the melody create its own uniquely-shaped container.

Arising out of this, I also took as paradigmatic the inherent rhythmic irregularity of the liturgical texts. Given that every word in *Vespers* (at least as presented here in English translation) is essentially blank verse or prose, rigid metrical treatment of the text seemed to me to be out of place. This is especially evident in the soloist parts in *The Opening Psalm*, *Great Litany*, and *The Trisagion Prayers*—where I went about as far as I could towards notating the actual rhythms of speech—as well as in the trio sections of *Blessed Is the Man* and the semi-choruses of *The Lamp-Lighting Psalms*. Maybe it's because I'm a lifelong stutterer, and thus acutely aware of both the immense complexity and elusive beauty of speech rhythms, that I find the rhythmic patterns of the spoken word so endlessly fascinating. My love affair with rap, the poetry of Gerard Manley Hopkins, and Carnatic Indian Konnakol (which I discovered only recently) may also have something to do with it. Whatever the reason, I chose in my *Vespers* to treat the inherent rhythmic complexity of the text as a body of musical riches to be synthesized within a larger rhythmic structure rather than as a thing to be purified of inconsistencies and forced into regular barlines and periods. This is not to say anything against texts that are neatly metered to begin with—I love those too and will happily set them to music—but rather to say that my approach is largely one of accepting things as I find them and then seeing what arises.

Psalmody and Chiastic Structure

The core of Vespers, as of all the daily offices, is the singing of psalms. The cycle of psalms sung at appointed hours of the day establishes the fundamental rhythm of monastic services going back at least to the third century of the Christian era. Psalms are often called the "backbone" of Orthodox services. Like an actual backbone, however, they are frequently ignored in common practice, being either chanted on a monotone by a solo reader or extensively abbreviated or even omitted altogether in favor of changeable hymnography. Thus, one of my conscious goals in composing *Vespers* was to place a renewed emphasis on the singing of psalms.

Using my late father's wonderful translations, I delved into the Vespers psalms, and in particular into the psalms' chiastic structure. Chiastic structure is an ancient poetic device named for the Greek letter *chi* (X) and employed throughout the psalms as well as in many books of the Bible.[153] Loosely defined, it functions a little like a palindrome where the first line of a section is mirrored by the last, the second by the second to last, and so on towards a center-point.[154] According to my father, who studied and wrote about chiastic structure extensively, the center-point may not be the exact numerical middle of a psalm—he explained to me once that it is frequently offset a little towards the end (which starts sounding suspiciously like the Golden Mean to me [0.618])—but that every psalm has a line somewhere near the middle, or a little past it, that casts light both forward and backward in the psalm. For a composer, a large-scale structural concept like this offers irresistible insights, both into the formal organization of a text as well as into its layers of meaning. (Bach and Brahms, incidentally, were also famously interested in chiastic structure.) I used a chiastic approach to a significant extent in organizing the two longest movements of Vespers, *The Opening Psalm* and *The Closing Psalm*.[155]

Once I began thinking chiastically, though, it was hard to stop, and so it gradually became evident to me that *Vespers* itself could be organized along chiastic lines. Thus *The Opening Psalm* and the musically related *Closing Psalm* emerged to form the bookends of the piece, with *The Lamp-Lighting Psalms/Stikhira of the Resurrection* and *The Lord Is King* surrounding the (off-center) center-point of *O Gladsome Light*. Though not a psalm itself, *O Gladsome Light (Φῶς Ἱλαρόν, Lumen Hilare)*—which proclaims Jesus to be the "Gladsome Light of the holy glory of the immortal Father"—is the earliest known Christian hymn still in common use and has effectively been the "theme-song" of Vespers for the entire history of Christianity. Realizing that *O Gladsome Light* was also the chiastic heart of Vespers—something I think I had sensed intuitively from long years in church—I saw that *light*, and in particular, *light from darkness*, was somehow thematic of Vespers as a whole.

Light from Darkness

Vespers is, significantly, the beginning of the liturgical day in Orthodoxy, not the end of it.[156] Just as the world emerged—or rather, say the particle physicists that I've been reading about lately, continually *emerges*—out of the darkness of non-being, so the Christian liturgical day begins each evening with the setting of the sun. At the risk of waxing philosophical, allow me to observe here that what perhaps seems at first glance to be an accident of liturgical scheduling becomes upon closer inspection a powerful existential symbol, and one, moreover, that sends out threads of connection deep into the realms of cosmology, biology, quantum mechanics, and human psychology. Almost on a daily basis I ask myself, *Where does this infinite universe and all its matter come from? Where do I come from, and why do I exist at all? Where do my thoughts come from, and why are they so often irrational?* Underneath such questions, at least for me, lies a veritable ocean of darkness and my own tiny lights almost always seem comically incapable of illuminating any of it. And yet at the same time within these unsettled depths there also seems to me to be something, or perhaps some*one*—a presence, a mind, a voice—that says gently, but with tireless insistence, "Let there be light." And behold, for no apparent reason, there *is* light—there is meaning, there is form, there is personhood, there is consciousness—and not only *is* it, but it is *good*.

For me as a composer these are not merely philosophical or metaphysical musings. These questions are inextricably tied to the actual daily experience of composition. Every artist knows the terrifying and crippling power of The Blank Page. *How can I possibly bring something out of nothing?* And then, as every artist also knows, once you've made the monumental effort to produce that *something*, you inevitably ask yourself, *how do I know whether or not it's good?* This is a very real and often very bitter struggle for me, and I know it is for others as well. For myself, I've discovered that the way forward is actually encapsulated in some way in the very first words of Genesis. The first task is just to put something—*anything*—on the page, so that it's not blank anymore. *And God said, Let there be light.* Then, whatever I've put there, whether it's my own idea or someone else's, I accept it as it is and work with it—I don't change it or criticize it, at least not at first, but I rather allow it to suggest its own emergent forms and patterns. *And God saw the light, that it was good: and God divided the light from the darkness.* After discovering and rejoicing in the unique qualities of whatever I have to work with, I then gently start organizing it into clearer and clearer shapes and more and more meaningful forms. *And God called the light Day, and the darkness he called Night.* And finally, I have to decide to stop and move on to the next thing. *And the evening and morning were the first day.*

I said at the beginning that Fr. Sergius had initially planted the idea for my *Vespers* about six years ago. This seems, at first glance, like rather a long time to write a sixty-minute choral piece. The truth is that for the first few years I kept putting *Vespers* off as other projects—including writing my *Liturgy*—demanded more immediate attention. I did take a few stabs at three movements, composing a first, much shorter, version of *The Opening Psalm* based on Valaam Chant, which I performed as a standalone piece in 2016; an entirely different *Blessed Is the Man*, also based on Valaam Chant, which I premiered in Kansas City in 2018; and an *O Gladsome Light* which I eventually finished in 2020, but that has yet to see the light of day. In the summer of 2019 I started over again on *The Opening Psalm*, this time with an eye towards setting the entire thirty-five verses of the text, and managed to write the movement in its current form. I felt I had finally made a good beginning, though I wasn't sure where to go from there.

Then, in March of 2020, the COVID-19 pandemic swept the globe and sent the world into months of lockdown. Projects were canceled and the music world came to a veritable standstill. Suddenly, with no choirs to conduct or events to organize, I had lots of time to compose. So, in the spirit of accepting things as I found them (what else could I have done?), I decided it was time to write *Vespers* in earnest. Beginning that March, and building on the foundation I had laid down the summer before with *The Opening Psalm*, I worked steadily, finishing the rest of the piece almost exactly a year later, in March of 2021. During this same period I also managed to finish *A Christmas Carol*, write *Liturgy No. 2* from start to finish, and make a solid beginning on *Akathist*, a forthcoming oratorio for chorus and orchestra. It was an intensely productive time for me. In the midst of one of the darkest periods that many of us have ever experienced, I found that there was light.

So perhaps this is the message of *Vespers*, this setting of the ancient evening office that begins each new day: from the descent into darkness comes a mysterious and gladsome light. This has certainly been my own experience over this past year and a half, with all its unresolvable complexities and knotty irregular rhythms: something new and bright and *good* is being created. I pray that my piece, whatever its flaws and inconsistencies, will bring some light to you as well.

August 20, 2021

PART THREE

Envy and The Mystery of Freedom

ENVY, THAT GREAT UNMAKER of every music, disorders our capacity to resolve antinomies—to enter, that is, into our *harmonia* and become persons.
The essays in Part Three begin with René Girard's theories about envy and
violence, especially as they are borne out in three of Shakespeare's plays.
Two Orthodox saints—Isaac the Syrian in the seventh century, and Pavel
Florensky in the twentieth—have given us comparable language to describe
the pathway of spiritual growth that leads to personhood. It is a pathway
that begins in the ways we are entrapped, and the strategies we use to survive, within a world of antinomic realities.

Part Three continues in chapter 16 with an essay on the unmaking of
music through the workings of envy within a choir. It then takes us into the
struggle to embrace our particular cross as we faithfully, ascetically, work
to receive its teaching and comprehend in our hearts the fullness that holds
conflicts in union, a process Don thought of as re-musicalization.

In the penultimate chapter, Don tells us how the Orthodox understanding of human relational nature—as articulated in the fourth century
by the Cappadocian Fathers, artificers of the doctrine of the Trinity—is
enacted in the Orthodox Liturgy. There, in the Liturgy itself, the envy-
driven sacrificial mechanism is dismantled and the pathway to genuine
personhood—the ascent into blessedness—is restored in the joy of humility, the descent into repentance.

The book concludes in chapter 18 with Don's journaled reflections on St. Isaac the Syrian's *Ascetical Homilies*, the aim of which is precisely the ascetic dissolution of one's ego, personality, and temperament. He leads us through ascetic *praxis* to the final stage of the journey to personhood, wherein, guided by the Holy Spirit, we may find we "have received the Spirit of adoption in the mystery of freedom" and become able to "soar on wings in the realms of the bodiless" and "gaze upon the entire world with the full comprehension of God's perfective presence in it" (*Ascetical Homilies*, 52).

Pavel Florensky views the journey to glory from the other direction: as it is mirrored in the gazing face itself. Inherently "unstable," the human face first masks itself in reactive mediation of the various inner and outer realities calling for its response. But then, through spiritual practice, it may grow to become a genuine countenance.

The beauty of such an achieved countenance is described by C. S. Lewis with joyful reverence in his novel *Perelandra*:

> And how shall I—I who have not seen him—tell you what he was like? It was hard even for Ransom to tell me of the King's face. But we dare not withhold the truth. It was that face which no man can say he does not know. You might ask how it was possible to look upon it and not to commit idolatry, not to mistake it for that of which it was the likeness. For the resemblance was, in its own fashion, infinite, so that almost you could wonder at finding no sorrows in his brow and no wounds in his hands and feet. . . . Plaster images of the Holy One may before now have drawn to themselves the adoration they were meant to arouse for the reality. But here, where His live image, like Him within and without, made by His own bare hands out of the depth of divine artistry, His masterpiece of self-portraiture coming forth from His workshop to delight all worlds, walked and spoke before Ransom's eyes, it could never be taken for more than an image. Nay, the very beauty of it lay in the certainty that it was a copy, like and not the same, an echo, a rhyme, an exquisite reverberation of the uncreated music prolonged in a created medium.[157]

—*Xenia Sheehan*

14

Envy and Self-Emptying Love in Shakespeare

ca. 1999

Courtney Cook on Rewriting Violence

PROFESSOR DON SHEEHAN KICKS off his two-term freshman composition course at Dartmouth in a most unusual way.[158] He asks students to remember violence—to dredge up their memories of bullies and bullying, of beatings inflicted or experienced, of anger, of isolation, of rape. He does this, in spite of their reticence and obvious discomfort, because he believes violence is our most common denominator, that it is a concept to which almost any academic discussion will inevitably return, and—disturbingly—that students just starting at Dartmouth have already encountered more violence, emotional and physical, than any other human experience. Sheehan's call to remember violence is not only a means of dispelling one of the most basic myths about violence—that violent behavior happens only to other people; he sees it also as the most direct way to the introspection and self-understanding that are critical to clear thinking and writing.

Sheehan believes students can't become writers and thinkers until they've discovered what he calls their "personhood."[159] He feels that students must think far more deeply and bravely to write well. "Every part of your being is involved in writing—there have to be changes on all levels," he says. To foster this, Sheehan requires students to work at that inquiry in daily journals. In early entries, students fill their notebooks with outpourings

about violence—fights with fathers, bouts with bulimia and anorexia, difficult breakups, cruel teammates. By the end of the course students are writing more formal, researched compositions.

Along the way they are guided by Sheehan's deliberate, if idiosyncratic,
choices of readings.[160] Even the foundation text for the course is a bit un-
orthodox. It isn't about composition or literature. It's an anthropological
book, *Violence Unveiled*, by Gil Bailie.[161] Taking up French anthropologist
René Girard's theory that scapegoating underscores much of violence, Bailie
contends that human beings actually thrive on their habit of blaming others
for their suffering. He argues that most of the world's cultures ritualize scapegoating, endowing violence toward an other with moral fervor to achieve cultural order. By perfectly describing the one-upmanship that has defined, for
example, the Cold War or the conflicts in Bosnia or Kosovo, Bailie articulates
the unifying effects of the practice of revenge. It is, he says, a "mechanism for
preserving culture that is as old as culture itself."

Sheehan then helps his students apply this view of the pervasiveness
of violence to a sweeping range of literature. The class reads Ursula Hegi's
novel of the Holocaust, *Stones from the River*, which explores the sufferings of a young dwarf in Nazi Germany, and the journalist Peter Maas's
collection of essays *Love Thy Neighbor: A Story of War*, which chronicles
his observations of war-torn Bosnia. Sheehan also introduces several of
Shakespeare's sonnets, which he believes "uniquely reveal what is perhaps
one of our most serious relational afflictions: erotic envy." In the sonnets,
he says, we can see the ubiquity—and personal familiarity—of this "affliction," as well as the emotionally violent behavior it engenders. Sheehan
also exposes his students to a biblical perspective on violence: the *Gospel
of Mark*, the story of how Jesus tried to counteract violence by offering
love rather than revenge toward oppressors.

During the second term of the course, the students continue to ex-
plore violence—and possible solutions to it. They receive a truly epic dose
when they read Fyodor Dostoevsky's *The Brothers Karamazov*. The characters Father Zosima and Alyosha Karamazov offer what Sheehan calls
"kenotic," or self-emptying, love to the suffering and angry people around
them. Through them, Dostoevsky holds out the delirious possibility of
a life free from violent influence. The novel offers lessons both literary
and personal, says Sheehan. Dostoevsky suggests that solving the world's
addiction to violence isn't about retribution or logic, but that it is about
offering love—unabashed love—in spite of it. . . .

Ultimately, the success of the course depends on the students' ability
to see the connection between searching introspection—painful though it
may be—and literate expression. By the last day of the class, it is the hopeful

and peaceful words of Alyosha Karamazov that are its fitting epitaph: "Let us never forget how good we once felt here, all together, united by such good and kind feelings as made us . . . perhaps better than we actually are."

—*Courtney Cook*

Shakespeare's Insight into the Turmoil of Envy

TROILUS AND CRESSIDA

One of the deepest diagnoses of envy's mimetic turmoil is Shakespeare's play *Troilus and Cressida*. In this play, Shakespeare attempts to think through in dramatic terms all the ways wherein envious desire actually—and terribly— works. At one crucial point, the character Ulysses says this:

> . . . no man is lord of anything,
> Though in and of him there is much consisting,
> Till he communicates his parts to others;
> Nor doth he of himself know them for aught
> Till he behold them forméd in th' applause
> Where they're extended; who like an arch reverb'rate
> The voice again; or, like a gate of steel
> Fronting the sun, receives and renders back
> His figure and his heat. (III:3, 115–23)

This is an astonishing insight into envy. Envy says that we do not know our- selves until we are applauded by others. Our own voice is made clear to us only in the reverberations coming back to us in others' applause. Then Ulysses uses a powerful image: the sun itself can know its shape and strength only where the steel gate gives "his figure and his heat" dazzlingly back to it.

In his book on Shakespeare, *A Theatre of Envy*, René Girard says that in *Troilus and Cressida* we see described a media-crazed world precisely like our own, a world wherein "the value of human beings is measured primarily by something we call their 'visibility.'"[162] To be visible is, in this sense, to be the object of every envious gaze. If the envious gaze of others is withdrawn— "if," says Girard, "the desires of these others are not riveted on him" (145) —then he becomes invisible even to himself. In such a case, the person may well fall into a kind of self-hate, swept suddenly into a heartsick depression wherein (at least for a time) he cannot "see" himself as being himself.

The scene between Ulysses and Achilles where the speech occurs has further insights. The plot of the play, drawn from Homer, is surely familiar.

Achilles, the greatest Greek warrior at the siege of Troy, has withdrawn from the fighting in envious anger at the Greek commander, Agamemnon, and consequently the Greeks begin to lose ground to the Trojans—such is the familiar starting point of the plot. Agamemnon calls together all his commanders (including, of course, Ulysses, the canniest strategist among the Greeks) to assess the situation. Shakespeare then invents a new plotline to fit perfectly his dramatization of envy in this play: he has Ulysses conceive a plan to deflect adulation away from Achilles and onto another (and far inferior) Greek warrior, Ajax. The point of Ulysses' plan is to make Achilles once more crave the envious gaze of others by depriving him of it, a craving that can be fed only—so Ulysses schemes—by Achilles returning to the battle and leading the Greeks to victory over Troy.

At least initially, the plan works precisely as Ulysses conceives it. In a stunning scene, he has the Greek commanders—all of whom have been, up to now, Achilles' envious admirers—deliberately snub Achilles with a finely dismissive contempt. And the very instant the adulation all at once ceases, Achilles becomes depressed. "What," he says to Ulysses, "are all my deeds forgot?" Shakespeare's point is plain: such strategic intelligence as Ulysses' resides solely in the capacity to read aright the dynamics of mimetic envy.

Then Ulysses responds to Achilles—and the speech is one of Shakespeare's masterpieces. Ulysses explains that in a world driven by envious resentments, no one and nothing can long hold any admiring gaze. For this is a world where, in Girard's words, "the pace of fashion accelerates; idols are erected and toppled at a faster and faster rate" (*Theatre of Envy*, 148). Here are the first lines of Ulysses' great speech:

> Time hath, my lord, a wallet at his back,
> Wherein he puts alms for oblivion,
> A great-sized monster of ingratitudes:
> Those scraps are good deeds past, which are devoured
> As fast as they are made, forgot as soon
> As done. (III:3, 145–50)

"This is an intensely historical world, a world where history is 'hot,'" says Girard (148). Such heat is the direct result of envy's action, the intensities of which consume every good action of every good person the instant such actions occur. The present is therefore experienced as grounded in resentment, or ingratitude; it becomes the arena—or carnival—wherein we ceaselessly consume and instantly forget and endlessly crave gain. In other words, the world of *Troilus and Cressida* is precisely our media-driven world of mimetic spins of desire.

At midpoint in his speech to Achilles, Ulysses says this:

No.
But something may be done that we will not;
And sometimes we are devils to ourselves,
When we will tempt the frailty of our powers,
Presuming on their changeful potency. (IV:4, 92–96)

Mimetic desire is in us a vastly stronger power than our will; and if we attempt to pit mere will against such desire, then we wind up becoming our own worst devils. Will power, says Troilus, is "changeful," its strength utterly unreliable against what he calls (a moment before) a "dumb-discoursive devil," that is, one that communicates perfectly without speaking a single word. Troilus is here trying to teach Cressida how to maneuver in the teeth of mimetic desire, how to beat the demons of her own envious hungers. But the fate of the two lovers is exactly what happens in the battlefield to Achilles: violent rending. Thus, Shakespeare's point in connecting the love affair and the war is to show (in Girard's fine phrase) that all mimetic strategy "is nothing but a complicated form of self-delusion" (139). Mimetic maneuvering produces only mimetic escalation and finally something like dismemberment: such is Shakespeare's diagnosis of the turmoil of envy.

At play's conclusion, Pandarus, who has steered and manipulated the mimetic process of the disastrous love affair, steps stage-front to speak an epilogue to us, the audience. In the closing couplet of the entire play, he tells us that he will die about two months hence of venereal disease, and that, because we watched this play, we will be the direct heirs of his sickness.

Till then I'll sweat, and seek about for eases.
And at that time bequeath you my diseases. (V:10, 57–58)

Shakespeare's significance could not be plainer. Envy's effects are fatally contagious in the same way that sexual diseases are. Once infected, you can only "sweat" and try to ease the pain (presumably by maneuvering to win every mimetic competition). But, in this bleakest of Shakespeare's plays, you assuredly cannot be cured of the illness called envy. You can only infect everyone around you as you inevitably die of this relational disease.

THE WINTER'S TALE

In his late play *The Winter's Tale*, Shakespeare manifests in his final scene what is perhaps his most miraculous insight. The situation in the play is this. In Act I, King Leontes becomes consumed with violent envy against his beloved wife, Hermione, and his dearest friend, Polixenes, for their supposed adultery. This charge of adultery is completely baseless; there is not the slightest shred of evidence of anything even remotely amiss between Hermione and Polixenes; and there is every evidence that Leontes is simply—and violently—sick with the mimetic contagion of envy: and with no cause for the envy arising from the others whom he envies. Leontes' vicious accusation brings about his wife's death. And at the moment of her death, Leontes suddenly understands that she has been all along entirely innocent while he throughout has been dreadfully sick. With this understanding, Leontes then begins a penitential process under the direction of Paulina, his deceased wife's confidante and loyal friend.

By the play's final scene, when some sixteen years have passed in repentance, Leontes is led by Paulina to view a newly completed statue of his deceased wife. As he gazes at the statue, Leontes is again awestruck by her immense beauty and is humbled again by his great crimes:

> O, thus she stood,
> Even with such life of majesty—warm life,
> As now it coldly stands—when first I wooed her.
> I am ashamed: does not the stone rebuke me,
> For being more stone than it? (V:3, 34–38)

The whole of Leontes' penitential process is here focused in this single and terrible awareness: I am more stone than this statue. Such implacable, indeed ruthless, clarity strips from Leontes every last shred and least rag of self-justifying self-pity. "My evils," Leontes says in the next line, are "conjured to remembrance." That is, all his crimes are now called back into that present dimension of eternal memory where one imaginatively comprehends the full spiritual catastrophe one's own sins have caused. "Grant me to see my own transgressions," says the Orthodox prayer of Great Lent. Such fullness of sight is here given to Leontes. And his heart becomes stone.

Then an astonishing shift begins to happen. From the depths of total penitential self-awareness, Leontes looks once more at the statue of Hermione. And as if for the first time, he sees her as she is, apart from all the violence of his desirings. And all at once he moves to kiss the statue's lips. But Paulina stops him, saying that the paint is still wet and he will smear it. The point is plain. Leontes must not take the image of a person for the reality of personhood. Yet Leontes' heart—stone cold a moment before—has begun to awaken.

Paulina then says, "If you can behold it, / I'll make the statue move indeed, descend / And take you by the hand" (V:3, 87–89). All at once, a miracle is impending, and Leontes (awestruck) nods consent. Paulina then speaks these extraordinary lines:

> Music, awake her; strike.
> 'Tis time; descend; be stone no more; approach;
> Strike all that look upon with marvel; come;
> I'll fill your grave up. Stir; nay, come away;
> Bequeath to death your numbness; for from him
> Dear Life redeems you. (V:3, 124–29)

Hermione steps down from the pedestal, stone no more but fully alive. Then it is revealed: she had not died sixteen years before but had been hidden away by Paulina. And now, with Leontes fully repentant, Hermione can stand forth again. As in a chiastic pattern, Leontes' descent into penitential depths has triggered both her and his reawakening into life. From the passional death accomplished through freely chosen repentance, Leontes' real life has been resurrected. This moment of resurrection speaks back across a decade of Shakespeare's plays—a decade that includes *Othello*, *King Lear*, and *Macbeth*—to that terrible conclusion of *Troilus and Cressida* when we inherit the fatal mimetic and sexual contagion from Pandarus. Now we inherit the redemption of "Dear life." The whole scene is a tiny but perfect icon of the resurrection.

In Dying, One Begins Truly to Live

With this (attractively improbable) tale of a statue coming to life, Shakespeare achieves his magnificent insight. In disengaging oneself from the dealing of mimetic violence to those one actually loves, one dies (as St. Isaac the Syrian would say) to the whole "onward flow" of the envy-driven world.[163] And in this dying, one begins truly to live.

Shakespeare's meaning here is magnificent. Repentance is an ontological shift, a change at (and of) the depths of one's being. In the action of repentance, one fully disengages from one's violent dealing of death to others—disengages, so as to shift completely into the kenotic giving of one's love to those others. The action of repentance is therefore a chiastic action, one wherein our descent into penitential depths becomes the way of our ascent into blessedness. And just as Leontes does not know when he stands before the statue that his wife actually lives—we cannot truly repent in order to feel better. The chiasmus of true repentance is always necessarily a blind descent: into a darkness we cannot see through. We let go of our violence not because we already have a good grip on love. We let go because we have come to experience, at the very depths of our being, that all our holding on is very death.

Hence, every real penitential action is necessarily an action of faith. The very moment before she awakens the statue of Hermione, Paulina says to Leontes: "It is required / You do awake your faith." Faith is the force that drives repentance, transforming the corrosive actions of self-devouring into the lyrical movements of blessedness. Psalm 10:5 says: "he who loves violence hates his own soul." The converse also holds: he who truly loves another ceases to devour himself. Such is the action of penitential faith.

WE STAND BEFORE PSALMS

We stand before Psalms in the very way that Leontes stands before the statue. We are often moved by psalmic beauty, but too often the Psalms are like stone to us. In order for the Psalms to awaken in us, something petrified, something like stone in us, must be moved from our hearts, something we cling to as if for dear life, something we see as the very rocksolid strength of our life. But God always stands in an antinomical relation to us, casting us down in our supposed strengths so as to raise us up in our real weaknesses. Thus, the chiastic pattern of each psalm is, in itself, an icon of God's relation to us. Similarly, each psalm's movements of descent and ascent perfectly reflect our ceaseless turnings away from and toward Him. This, indeed, is the message at the chiastic heart of the entire Psalter, the midpoint of Psalm 77[78]:

> 34. When he slew them they sought him and repented and rose up early in their prayers to God.
>
> 35. They remembered that God is their helper, the Most High God their redeemer.
>
> 36. So they loved him with their mouths but were lying to him with their tongues,
>
> 37. For their hearts were not straight with him, they were unfaithful to his covenant.
>
> 38. But he is compassionate and will be gracious to their sins and will not destroy them, again and again foregoing his wrath, never kindling all his anger.

Thus, as we awaken to our own hearts' stoniness, we can come to see in Psalms how the mind of David is always becoming the mind of Christ—and, therefore, we see how we can begin to acquire through the Psalms this very mind of Christ. Each time we open the Psalter, we say, "Music, awake us; strike!" And each time it does. Deeper, and deeper still.

To Be Free of Envy!

For twenty summers now [1978–98], I have directed a week-long writers' conference for poets called the Festival of Poetry at The Frost Place in Franconia, New Hampshire. For the past several years, I have begun each conference by saying to the fifty or so participants: You are here at this conference to make—not your own art—but the art of at least one other person here better and fuller and richer. You are here to fall so much in love with another person's poems that you would give all your art over to them—freely, deeply, unhesitatingly—so that these poems, and their poet, can become more beautifully and movingly true.

Here is the astounding thing. I need only to say this, and a conference of fifty participants and ten faculty members will attempt to do exactly that—not all, of course, but many, if not most. Some will achieve it with breathtaking lucidity and grace. What such attempts to love can accomplish is an "unmaking of envy" and, thus, the possibility of genuine human contact.

This spring, a woman who participated in the 1997 festival wrote me a beautiful letter:

> . . . Your advice about falling in love with someone else's work really steered me during the conference and after. Ann and I have been writing and calling back and forth, and she and her sons are coming east this summer and staying with my family during a family reunion. Three of us from the festival get together about every six weeks or so to work on our poems . . . to be free of envy! All those poets are so strong and talented!

The point couldn't be clearer: as our envy diminishes, we often experience the arrival of what may well be our first real friendships since early childhood, friendships within which—and through which—our own art grows richer and fuller. As the woman from last summer says in her letter: "I wrote a great deal at the festival and continued once home. After a three-year hiatus, I actually sent poems out and two journals have taken some poems of mine."

A single sentence from the Gospel of St. John speaks deeply to these points: It is a sentence so comprehensive that Dostoevsky used it to explain all of his vast and great final novel, *The Brothers Karamazov*: "Verily,

verily, I say unto you, except a grain of wheat fall into the ground and die, it abideth alone; but if it die, it bringeth forth much fruit" (John 12:24).[164] If all artists were to let their artwork deliberately go into that cold darkness where all prestige dies—and to do so in deepest love for another's art—then an immense fruitfulness would begin.

15

From the Mask of Contempt to the Unveiled Countenance

Shakespeare, St. Isaac, and Florensky

ALMOST EXACTLY MIDPOINT IN Shakespeare's disturbing play *Troilus and Cressida,* the character Ulysses calls it "strange" that one knows oneself only when one is applauded by others. Achilles responds by saying:

This is not strange, Ulysses.
The beauty that is borne here in the face
The bearer knows not, but commends itself
To others' eyes; nor doth the eye itself,
That most pure spirit of sense, behold itself,
Not going from itself, but eye to eye opposed
Salutes each other with each other's form.
For speculation turns not to itself
Till it hath travelled, and is mirrored there
Where it may see itself. This is not strange at all. (III:3, 103–12)

My interest here is not this extraordinary play and its many startling consequences (for which see chapter 14), but rather what this passage helps us understand about the way we see each other's faces. The plain meaning here is fairly straightforward: You can see your own face's beauty only when you engage another's admiring gaze. The point I want to make is this: the perceptual activity that Achilles here describes is simultaneously true and false. But the only way to seeing its great truth lies in first com-prehending the depths of its falsity.

St. Isaac's Three Modes of Knowledge

St. Isaac the Syrian's great *Ascetical Homilies* can, I think, help us here. In Homily 52, St. Isaac discusses his justly famous three degrees of knowl-edge. His discussion is rich and comprehensive; hence, the best summary is his own:

> The first degree of knowledge renders the soul cold to works that go in pursuit of God. The second makes her fervent in the swift course on the level of faith. But the third is rest from la-bour, which is the type of the age to come, for the soul takes delight solely in the mind's meditation upon the mysteries of the good things to come. (*Homilies*, 52:261–62)

THE FIRST MODE

The action of Shakespeare's *Troilus and Cressida* occurs entirely within St. Isaac's first degree of knowledge. So psychically chilling is this play that *all* the characters in it are entirely corrupt. And the play's final lines reveal that we, the audience, have also been made incurably sick *solely by our watching this play.* The first degree of knowledge is therefore the gaze that regards all things in the coldest contempt. Here, then, is the root of the falsity in Achilles' speech. By determining who you are *solely from the gaze of the other,* you are committing two wrongs at once: you are depriving the other of any objectively real personhood; and you are condemning yourself to an endlessly unstable reality. Such is the spiritual action of contempt.

THE MIDDLE MODE

But Achilles' speech has implications that reach beyond the play's im-mediate context. Achilles calls the eye "that most pure spirit" of the five senses. In St. Isaac's second degree of knowledge, the eye loses its icy contempt and becomes "fervent" as the perceiver enters into (as he says earlier in Homily 52) a life of "fasting, prayer, mercy, reading of the di-vine Scripture, the modes of virtue, battle with the passions, and the rest" (260). When one undertakes such a life, then one learns to see the way wherein the Holy Spirit is using such means as fasting, prayer, and mercy to bring one along "the swift course" called faith in God. And—this is the crucial point—the realm wherein one's eye beholds this sacred operation is never in the gaze of another but is always and only within one's own soul. That is, true and right Orthodox ascetic life is never something we compel another to do; rather, it is only and always something we do to and in our own person. The goal of all ascetic life, says St. Isaac, is to make "straight the pathways in the heart" (52:260). Such straightening can occur when we cease hungrily gazing at the other's face and turn our gaze instead toward the face of God Himself. Thus, the ascetic life of St. Isaac's middle mode of knowledge can be understood as a *disentangling* of one's gaze from the other's face so as to untwist the pathways in one's own heart. Achilles' beautiful phrase about "that most pure spirit" of one's gaze points toward but never reaches this wondrous second degree.

The Third Mode

But nothing in all of Shakespeare's work—except for a few fleeting glimpses in the final three plays—touches St. Isaac's third degree of knowledge. Here, in this highest mode, knowledge begins (says St. Isaac) "to gain experience in inward matters which are hidden from the eyes," for now "the inner senses awaken for spiritual doing" in what he calls the resurrection of the mind. If the ascetic practice of the middle mode arises from our own spiritual labors, then the resurrection of our mind is a gift of the Holy Spirit—the gift (he says) of "adoption in the mystery of freedom." Now, he continues, the soul "can soar on wings in the realms of the bodiless and touch the depths of the unfathomable sea, musing upon the wondrous and divine workings of God's governance" of all the creation (52:261). One now gazes upon the entire world with the full comprehension of God's perfective presence in it. One now beholds Him everywhere, seeing His face in everyone and everything.

Thus, in comparing Achilles' speech and St. Isaac's Homily 52, we can see two quite distinct models of perceptual travel. In Shakespeare, the gaze goes outward to attempt to meet, in the eyes of another, something of the reality of oneself. In St. Isaac, the gaze goes inward to behold, in the realm of one's own soul, something of the reality of the Holy Spirit. In the first arc of travel the gaze almost always fails to attain its object: the perception of oneself in another. In the second, it always learns to surrender, through ascetic practice, all its own willfulness so as to reach its beautifully desired end: the perception of the Holy Spirit in oneself and in all creation—in (one can say) the face of everyone and everything.

St. Isaac then clearly notes that, since our nature "is not yet completely elevated above the state of mortality," we cannot now unceasingly dwell in the third degree of knowledge but we must always return (as he says) to "the second, middle degree, working virtue that is inherent in her [the soul's] nature by means natural to the body" (52:262). Hence, one must (as he says in Homily 37:186) "remain in the squalor of [one's] ascetic discipline"—in, that is, the unglamorous, imperfect, broken yet true practice of prayer, fasting, and mercy to all and to everything.

Here, then, is the Isaacian key to seeing every human face (including one's own) aright: you are seeing rightly, he says, "when, after thoroughly examining yourself, you find that you are full of mercy for all mankind, and that your heart is afflicted by the intensity of your pity for men and burns as it were with fire, without your making distinctions between persons." You can *know* this, says St. Isaac, and still not *do* this; and then you come to resemble, he says, "the man who carries under his arm a lyre adorned and furnished with strong strings, but his fingers do not know, being untrained, how to play them" (*Homilies*, Appendix A, 392). The requisite training is, plainly, the ascetic practice of the second, or middle, mode of knowledge. *And the goal of all such ascetic practice is not—decidedly not—self-purification or self-beautification but is, rather, this self-emptying love for all and in all. Only in this way does the face of another come into true focus.* Thus, St. Isaac perfectly connects for us the necessity to sustain even badly done ascetic discipline with the reality of perfect self-emptying love.

Fleeing Shakespeare's World of Cold Contempt

It is in this light, then, that we can begin to see something of what our Lord is saying when He prays to the Father about the disciples: "I pray not that Thou shouldest take them out of the world, but that Thou shouldest keep them from the evil [one]" (John 17:15). To be in the world and *not* be so protected means to have one's gaze caught in the arc of cold and merciless contempt for everything. Such contempt is foundational in that—like the swiftest of poisons—it unmakes all of the creation by an irreversible degradation of every act of creation. In *Troilus and Cressida*, the character Thersites perfectly embodies this spirit of destructive contempt; and in so doing, he expresses exactly St. Isaac's first mode of knowledge. Late in the play, Thersites boasts, "I am bastard begot, bastard instructed, bastard in mind, bastard in valour, in everything illegitimate" (V:8, 8). Then in the next scene, Shakespeare has Achilles and his gang surround the unarmed and pleading Hector and ruthlessly murder him—a scene that so degrades the epic glories of Homer's *Iliad* (Shakespeare's source for his play) as to make these Homeric glories—and every other conceivable glory—seem irremediably fraudulent. In other words, to be both *in* and *of* the world means to make (as Thersites says) "everything illegitimate." At such a point, all faces—including one's own—become opaque masks in that they become seething cauldrons of contempt. Except, of course, the victim's face, which is another story.

It is against this dark Shakespearean background that we can, I think, rightly understand St. Isaac's constant injunction in the *Ascetical Homilies* to abandon every association with all other people—as, for example, in Homily 44:219 where he tells us that "God commands us to flee from all men and thus to love stillness." If we flee all association with every person, then how are we simply to obey—let alone fulfill—Christ's commandment to love every person? The answer, I believe, is that to "flee all association" means to abandon all one's cold contempt of others. "Do you wish," asks St. Isaac, "to acquire in your soul the love of your neighbor according to the commandment of the Gospel?" And then he answers, "Separate yourself from him, and then the heat and flame and love of him will burn in you and you will rejoice over the sight of his countenance as though you beheld an angel of light." In your abandoning of your contemptuous gaze at your neighbor's face, your own face becomes "a hundredfold more resplendent than the brilliance of the sun itself" by the operation of the Holy Spirit within your soul—and then your neighbor's face comes into accurate focus (44:219). In Psalm 20:12, the psalmist sings to God: "Thou shalt make ready their countenance." Because our faces are created by God, you can see the face of another only when you have so fully surrendered your poisonous contempt that you "rejoice over the sight of his countenance as though you beheld an angel of light" (44:220). Plainly, such seeing is a phenomenon *in* but not *of* the world. To achieve it, we must entirely fell the first mode of knowledge.

Florensky's Mask, Face, and Countenance

We may, I think, rightly connect Fr. Pavel Florensky's distinction of mask, face, and countenance (see also chapter 10) to St. Isaac's three modes of knowledge. The Florenskian mask (*lichina*), which he calls the "absolute opposite of *countenance (lik)*," represents the first mode in the sense that the poisonous spirit of contempt degrades the world in the same way that the mask darkens the face (*litzo*). The mask not only gives no hint whatever of God's image, but it also actively *lies*, "falsely pointing," Florensky says, "to non-essential things" (*Iconostasis*, 53). The first verse of the first psalm says: "Blessed is the man who walks not in the counsel of the ungodly, nor takes the way of the sinful, nor sits in the seat of the scornful," for at the very root of psalmic blessedness is this understanding of contempt's destructiveness.

ISAAC'S MIDDLE MODE AND FLORENSKY'S "FACE" SHARE INSTABILITY

St. Isaac's middle mode of knowledge thus describes the Florenskian face. One interesting point of connection between these two discussions is the notion of *instability*. The face, says Florensky, is "one of many possible sketches," the details of which "are, at the moment, still unfinished" (*Iconostasis*, 51). As a result, the face reveals at least as much if not more of the person's self-willed and consciously chosen organization as it does of the full reality of that person in God. That is, we can (and do) *arrange* our faces to elicit from others the response we demand; and such deliberate arrangements move us away from countenance and toward mask. Thus, the face—unlike the countenance—exhibits instability. It is always, Florensky believed, moving toward becoming either a countenance or a mask. Similarly, St. Isaac notes that the second mode of knowledge is "still corporeal and composite" (*Homilies*, 52:260); and in being so, this mode is inherently an unfinished portrait. In this light, then, we may say that one looks at a Renaissance portrait to see a *face* but looks at an Orthodox icon to see a *countenance*.

THE HIGHEST MODE: THE COUNTENANCE

Thus, St. Isaac's highest mode of knowledge becomes manifest in us when our face is transfigured into a countenance. The beautiful final line of Psalm 16[17] has the psalmist proclaim to God: "As for me, in righteousness I shall behold thy countenance, I shall be satisfied in beholding thy glory." That is, when I act in the righteousness of ascetic practice (St. Isaac's middle mode), then I will see the face of God. But when I awaken fully and finally from the darkness of my contempt, then I will be filled with His manifest glory: with, that is, the fullness of His unveiled countenance. In this way, then, this moment when one's face becomes countenance repeats the moment when Moses receives the commandments on Mt. Sinai as well as the moment when Jesus is transfigured on Mt. Tabor: for in all three moments, the face becomes purest light.

Human Contempt in the Place of Loving God

We are now finally at a place where we may see what is true about Achilles' speech. The relational disaster he describes can be understood as a transplantation of our right relation to God. We can know nothing whatever about our own face (better: our *countenance*, using Florensky's distinction) until we disengage our gaze from the face of the other and instead look into the face of God. Then we are overwhelmed by the splendor of His gaze, and we are swept up into the fullest love imaginable. And at that moment of supreme aliveness in love, God Himself "makes ready our countenance" (Ps 20:12), He bestows upon us our unique and perfective face. Then, an instant later, we turn our gaze back to the face of the other to see—in St. Isaac's words—"his countenance as though . . . [it belonged to] an angel of light" (*Homilies* 44:220).

What Achilles does is to transplant this true way of loving God into the false ground of human contempt; and St. Isaac's third mode of knowledge thus descends into the first. In such a descent, the ascetic straightening of one's heart is replaced by the violent acting out of one's passions. But what remains intact in Achilles' speech is the *shape* of relational truth. And this intact shape gives the speech its dimension of truth. Interestingly, when Ulysses responds to Achilles' speech, he uses a metaphor that underscores this point. Ulysses says that the applause of other people "receives and renders back" to us who we actually are "like a gate of steel / Fronting the sun" (III:3). If we changed Ulysses' sun from signifying the applause of others and understood it as the loving face of God, then we would restore true relational content to the metaphor's true shape; one's life would open to its truth rather than be halted before a steel gate. Such restoration reverses—indeed, *untwists*—Achilles' false transplantation.

The Human Face Seen in Christ

One final point. At the very start of his play *Timon of Athens,* Shakespeare has a poet gazing at a newly painted portrait of Lord Timon himself. In rapt wonder, the poet says, "what a mental power / This eye shoots forth!" (I:1, 42). The remark is casual; no one responds to it; it has no further significance in the play. Yet, all by itself, the remark is immensely significant for our understanding here. For—and this is the great point—the portrait is not at all a dead thing; it is, rather, something directly connected to a living face. Florensky articulates the point in this way: We would not, he says, describe to someone the portrait of a friend or father by saying it was merely a painted object. Instead, "we would say, placing it in their hands, 'This is my father, this is my friend.' Manifestly, for the religious consciousness, the painting . . . is not apart from or opposed to the human face; it is understood as being *together with* the face. . ." (*Iconostasis*, 164).

Shakespeare's poet knows this Florenskian fact about the portrait of a face, because the painting acts *in the present moment* to manifest to the beholder Lord Timon's intense aliveness. Thus, the *presentness* of the portrait, like the action of the Orthodox icon, touches what is at once the deepest mystery and the simplest fact about the human face seen in Christ: its aliveness so far exceeds everything we mean by life that even death itself is no end to it. And the one right response to this endless aliveness is therefore that beautiful Greek outcry that shapes the stanzas in the Orthodox prayer service of the Akathist to the Mother of God: *Chaire,* meaning "Rejoice!" or "Glory!" or "Hail!" Here, in this single perfective word, is the end of every contempt and the fullness of every countenance.

16

Music, Awake Us; Strike!

The Choral Experience of Envy

Cleansed of all envy, we become musicalized.

—D. S.

IN THE BIBLICAL NARRATIVE of the Garden and the Fall (Genesis 3), we see a situation wherein the serpent—as René Girard's perceptive associate Gil Bailie explains—"tells Eve that the fruit will make her *like* God," pointing out that even in circumstances "as unconducive to envy, covetousness, and resentment as the Garden of Eden, the serpent's gaudy desire is all that it takes to unhinge the human race and shove it on its grasping and violent 'career.'"[165] If the choir conductor is Leontes of Shakespeare's *Winter's Tale*, standing before the (apparently) stone statue of his wife, Hermione, then the choir resembles Eve in the Garden when the beguiling call into mimetic envy begins to sound.[166] At such a moment (and it is almost every moment), the singer can either begin her "violent 'career'" of mimetic turmoil called musical prestige or she can choose the other path, the one wherein music can become that "constant prayer" called by St. Isaac *katharótes*, or *limpid purity*. On this path—opening in every choral moment, both rehearsal and performance—the singer *self-emptyingly gives all her art* to every other singer so that all of them—and *not* she, though she is included in the all—may be filled with the music's glory. Then the miracle occurs. Every other singer becomes, in voice and whole person, divinely and beautifully alive. And so does the music. And so does she.[167]

It is the same for the conductor. In order for musical life truly to begin, something petrified in him, something like stone in him, must die in
order for life to happen in his singers. The conductor's stony insensitivity is
rooted in his mimetic contagion and is fed by the envy born of his hunger for
prestige and the resentment arising from his exercise of power. And as the
conductor can begin to awaken to his own heart's stoniness, he can begin to
enter the miracle of stillness that all great music possesses. No technique in
the world, either musical or spiritual, can bring the conductor even one inch
closer to that miracle. Only in fully, penitentially, and self-emptyingly loving
the other—loving the singers and the composers, and above all loving the
God who is Himself the fullness of every other love and every beauty—can he
begin to draw near the miracle. Then, every time he stands before his chorus,
saying inwardly, "Music, awake us; strike!" so it does.

May this Glory Be My Share

Every choral singer knows the experience of envy. In the making of choral
art, the conductor inevitably seems to possess all the decisive power. The
singer's relation to that power (as the conductor's) is always complex and
sometimes disastrous. It is complex because the conductor is the center of
the attentive gaze of singers who look to her—with an intensity little short
of spellbound—to release their art. She literally holds their art in her hands
and therefore not only possesses a centrality—and an apparent glory—that
the singers do not, but actually has in her possession that which is their own.
Yet without her, the fullness of their art is forever unrealized, as, without
the singers, the conductor's art, too, is merely potential. So the relation is
complex and reciprocal. Each seems to hold (and often to withhold) the
glory of the other. Indeed, this is not peculiar to choruses; it is the human
condition. It brings to mind a line in a prayer: "May this Glory be my share."
And it recalls the tragedy of Genesis where glory, shared with humankind in
free abundance, yet appeared to be withheld and so was grasped. A share in
God's glory was not enough; humanity needed to be like God, to the extent of
taking His place. And so the disaster possible in all human relationships, and
especially in choruses, opens up. We want to be like the ones who seem to
possess the glory we feel is rightfully ours—and, even though we may admire
them intensely, we want them not to be like that, not to have the glory: that
is, we want to seize the glory and eliminate our rival.

In the choral experience, as in life, one singer's desire for musical
glory fuels the desire of every other—and thereby intensifies everyone's
desire. Such reciprocal intensification exhibits that definitive quality of

all desire termed by René Girard mimetic or imitative. Mimetic desire is therefore best understood as contagious. And, like a viral infection, the contagion of desire intensifies (rather than weakens) as it jumps swiftly, invisibly, and completely from one person to another. In a choir, the spiritual end result is exactly described by a choral singer who recently said of the choir, "I have an image of a crowd all scratching and scrambling across each other to get celebrity, mortally wounding each other in the process." Such are the dynamics of the mimetic disaster.

And here lies the conductor's most terrible power. The more she desires glory for herself, the more her singers will desire it for themselves, vying for her recognition and attention (as if to recapture from her the power they had initially bestowed upon her) and clawing each other for the prestige of solo parts, sometimes even searching for weaknesses in the conductor that might open a way for dethronement, or at least for contempt. Comparably, the conductor escalates the dynamics of envy by endlessly consuming her singers' hungry rivalry for the favors she can bestow and for the art she makes manifest in them. The result, for the conductor, is an insatiable appetite for her choir's envious gaze, an appetite properly seen as an addiction. There is, of course, an energy and intensity in all of this that will generate a certain musical excitement. But mimetic excitement will not finally make genuine music, for it is founded on a disintegrative and hence disharmonious process.

As we have seen, envy is, above all, a spiritual affliction. It is not a psychological condition—although it assuredly generates a storm of emotional effects in the afflicted. Nor is it an artistic activity—although it sustains an endless critique of other people's artistic practices and a ceaseless defense of one's own. Envy desires to have the beauty or power or talent that another possesses precisely because that other strongly and gracefully possesses it, and it desires this at the other's expense.

Like all spiritual affliction, the choral experience of envy almost always has a perfect cover-story: the singer is showing "respect" for the conductor's great skill, and the conductor is seeking a strong performance "for the audience," or "to honor the music." Such cover-stories camouflage and keep silent the operations of envy, for in such hushed hiddenness lies most of its power to persist in its disintegrative work.

THE LIE OF ENVY

Yet mimetic envy's fascination with the other is not in itself the catastrophe. The catastrophe is that envy is blind: it looks at the other and, like

Shakespeare's Achilles, sees only itself. If it were truly to see the other who holds its gaze, it would cease to be envy and turn to love. And the one who gazes would then experience fullness in place of the sharp pang of deprivation. For the neighbor whom we are commanded to love *as* ourself *is* ourself. That is, in self-emptyingly loving him, we *become* ourself. The lie of envy is that I must receive the other's envious gaze, or else tear him down, or even tear him apart (it is worth noting that Achilles, in his gruesome death scene in Shakespeare's *Troilus and Cressida*, is literally dismembered) in order to get from him a sense of my own worth. The truth of envy is that the other is indeed the key to my worth, for only in loving him do I possess the only value that is real: the likeness to God. "The Holy Spirit," writes Vladimir Lossky, "effaces Himself, as Person, before the created persons to whom He appropriates grace." Made in the divine image, we become like God—now truly like Him, without rivalry—when we, too, cease "to seek after what is personal; for the perfection of each person is fulfilled in total abandonment and in the renunciation of self. Every person who seeks his own self-assertion comes in the end only to the disintegration of his nature"[168] Thus, we decrease that the other may increase, and our art becomes grounded in harmony and truth rather than in conflict and lie.

Conducting as Spiritual Practice

It sometimes happens that a choral singer will sing under a conductor who accomplishes the relational miracle of loving simultaneously the whole choir—and every individual singer in it. The simultaneity is the miracle—and the key. For by doing both forms of loving at once—loving each singer actively and tirelessly at the very same moment he is also loving every other singer—the conductor unmakes mimetic desire. In this love, the conductor gives up his own hunger for prestige in order to achieve one immense end: to give all his art entirely to his singers. He empties himself of himself so as to bestow upon every single singer the fullness of each singer's personhood in this music. This is a genuinely real experience. And it is an experience that marks the end of mimetic envy.

A fine choral singer recently said of this experience, "When this happens, you feel as if you're one of maybe two or three other singers—even when there's really two or three hundred others." Such love is best understood as perfective, for as it moves toward its own luminous perfection, it brings about perfection in others. Here, then, is good mimesis, for it is likely that the singers will follow their conductor's lead and give their art also to him, and to one another.

Further, the experience of self-emptying love releases both conductor and choir from the always disintegrative search for the always illusory "ideal sound." Such a sound remains maddeningly just ahead of any sound the choir is actually making; and therefore it is sound that neither conductor nor choir can ever actually achieve. Human sound detached from the concrete, embodied reality of any given human person is therefore detached from love. The pursuit of such chimerical sound is fueled in both singer and conductor by envy of its "ideal beauty" and resentment against the living choral reality. Here, then, is full-blown mimetic contagion. Its first fruits are despair and anger; later ones include indifference and contempt. Only the conductor's actively self-emptying love of his singers, each singly and all together—and from thence reciprocally between every singer—can achieve any real release from these mimetic disintegrations.

In this way, choral conducting becomes a spiritual practice. And in being so, it can come to exhibit that spiritual reality wherein the conductor can begin through love to quiet down his own engagement in the mimetic turmoil all our lives exhibit. Such quieting down has long been known in the spiritual practices of Eastern Orthodox Christendom as the reality of stillness.

Becoming Musicalized: St. Isaac the Syrian

The single most essential book for any choral conductor is one that Russian novelist Fyodor Dostoevsky valued above every other book in the world, *The Ascetical Homilies of St. Isaac the Syrian*. Here is a passage from Homily 37, where St. Isaac first asks how we may know when a man has achieved stillness "in his manner of life," and then answers, "When a man is deemed worthy of constant prayer":

> When the Spirit dwells in a man, as the Apostle says, he never ceases to pray, since the Spirit Himself always prays [within him]. Then, whether he sleeps or wakes, prayer is never separated from his soul. If he eats, or drinks, or lies down, or does something, or even in slumber, the sweet fragrances and perfumes of prayer effortlessly exhale in his heart. He does not possess prayer in a limited way, but even though it should be outwardly still, at every moment it ministers within him secretly. For the silence of the limpidly pure is called prayer by one of the Christ-bearers, because their thoughts are divine motions. The movements of a pure heart and mind are meek

and gentle cries, whereby the pure chant in a hidden manner to
the Hidden God. (*Homilies* 37:182)

This passage can be seen to respond to Ulysses' speech in *Troilus
and Cressida*. The huge Shakespearean mimetic "monster of ingratitude"
devours all "good deeds" as "fast as they are made" because mimetic envy
immediately swallows up in hatred what it seizes in admiration. In other
words, nothing in mimetic envy abides, nothing holds, nothing stays still.
In sharp contrast, St. Isaac says that "constant prayer" in a man is never
"separated from his soul," that its fragrances always "effortlessly exhale
in his heart"—for that integrative gracefulness is what prayer's constancy
means. Where the turmoil of envy is ceaselessly destabilizing one's psyche,
or soul, constant prayer "at every moment" is stilling down one's soul by—a
beautiful word—*ministering* secretly within. In his speech, Ulysses also says
to Achilles, "The present eye praises the present object" (III:3, 180)—that
is, the mimetic gaze is constantly drawn by the latest mimetic lure—and
therefore "envious time" is always "calumniating time," at once outwardly
vicious and inwardly vacuous. Constant prayer, on the other hand, makes
all our inner processes into "divine motions," outwardly gentle and inwardly
musical. Such prayer signals the reality of stillness in us.

When our life moves toward stillness, we begin to enter into a spiritual
state that St. Isaac in his *Ascetical Homilies* beautifully terms *limpid purity*.
When this Isaacian term was translated from the original Syriac into Patristic Greek, *shapyutha* became *katharótes*, a Greek word that we know
as *cathartic*. The point is clear: stillness *cleanses* us of every aspect of that
relational affliction we call envy. The result, in St. Isaac, is a mental and
emotional purification "whereby [we] chant in a hidden manner to the Hidden God." In a word, by achieving stillness and being thereby cleansed of all
envy, we become *musicalized*: effortlessly and ceaselessly musicalized.

In Homily 4, St. Isaac says this:

> Consider yourself a stranger all the days of your life, wherever
> you may be, so that you may find deliverance from the injury
> which is born of familiarity. In every matter, consider your-
> self to be totally ignorant so as to escape the reproach which
> follows the suspicion that you wish to set aright other men's
> opinions. . . . If you begin to say something profitable, say it as
> though you yourself are still learning, and not with authority
> and shamelessness. (*Homilies* 4:33)

Understood as instructions to both the choral conductor and all his choral
singers, this passage strikes at the source of every mimetic infection. By being the ill-at-ease stranger, one is freed of the arrogance that always elicits

from others resentment and envy. When a conductor begins to speak to his chorus in such a way, he thereby frees both himself and his singers from what St. Isaac calls the "love of esteem, from which springs envy," and from the hunger for "human glory, which is the cause of resentment" (15). The very course of the world is fueled by these passions of envy and resentment. Hence to make these passions in any way abate or cease in our relational lives is to bring the world's terrible "onward flow" (in his phrase) to a complete standstill. Then the sweetness of genuine stillness can begin in all our relations. And in such sweetness is all music grounded.

17

On Behalf of All and For All

The ascetic fathers and mothers of the Holy Orthodox Tradition have long seen the operations of what René Girard terms *mimetic desire* as the definitive process of human sin and violence. One such essential teacher of Orthodoxy is the seventh-century Persian saint named Isaac of Syria. His seventy-seven *Ascetical Homilies* (beautifully translated and published by the Holy Transfiguration Monastery of Boston) are a profoundly rich comprehension of such sin and its penitential cure. For example, in Homily 51, St. Isaac writes: "If you love gentleness, be peaceful. If you are deemed worthy of peace, you will rejoice at all times. Seek understanding, not gold. Clothe yourself with humility, not fine linen. Gain peace, not a kingdom." Gold, fine linen, the prestige and power of a kingdom: here, in three brief images, is fully expressed the whole world of our mimetic desirings, a world characterized and driven by our ignorance, arrogance, and violence. What unmakes that entire world, St. Isaac says, is the deliberate clothing of oneself in humility, an action at once prompted by and leading to understanding and peace. And at the very heart of humility lies that which all our mimetic spins can never even begin to approach: joy.

St. Isaac continues: "No man has understanding if he is not humble, and he who lacks humility is devoid of understanding. No man is humble if he is not peaceful, and he who is not peaceful is not humble. And no man is peaceful without rejoicing." Joy unmakes the violence of mimetic desire because joy—in everything and everyone—unmakes the envy that drives all our desirings. And in unmaking mimetic desire, the joy of humility dismantles the whole sacrificial mechanism, bringing us to stand with Christ at the Cross rather than with His crucifying killers.

In all of this, St. Isaac speaks for the entire Orthodox ascetic tradition. After twenty centuries this tradition fully lives in every Orthodox believer's actual practices of (not mere ideas about) fasting, prayer, and confession. For, like the Cross of Christ, the practice of humility becomes the way of unceasing repentance, a way wherein *every believer comes to see the roots of the world's violence as planted entirely in himself,* a seeing that produces a joy in and love for everything and everyone in the world because *Christ Himself can therefore everywhere be seen.*

The Relational Nature of the Human Person

Western culture, almost wholly defined since Freud by its isolative psychologies, has shed very little light on the relational phenomena of human cultural reality. It has tended instead to isolate the human individual by defining him as a self-enclosed "bundle" of complexes or compulsions, seeing relationships as merely consequences of this compulsive "bundle." Just so, Western Christianity since the days of Martin Luther has spawned disintegrative ecclesiologies that define the Church primarily as a mere reflex of an individual's act of belief. Such a definition gives to the isolated individual all primacy in the realm of understanding and belief, thereby redefining the Church as merely an administrative superstructure. The historical result of such a redefinition could not be plainer: an ongoing fracturing of Christianity in the West.

The rise of isolative psychologies and the disintegration of Western ecclesiologies are historical phenomena that exhibit long and complex causations not easily explained, and certainly not in a brief essay. But their effects can be expressed by noting the direct link between them: If you fail to see the fundamentally relational nature of the human person (created in the image of the trinitarian God and sharing with all other persons a single human nature, just as the three Persons of God are yet one God, consubstantial and undivided)—if you fail to understand this you will also simultaneously fail to comprehend that the Church—spread through historical time (across ethnicities and languages) and in earthly space—is, in reality, the one Body of Christ.

Now, the Orthodox understanding of human relational nature was articulated in the fourth century by the Cappadocian Fathers, pre-eminently by St. Basil of Caesarea. Cappadocian thought has remained essential to sixteen centuries of Orthodox understanding, its insights and outlook as bright, rich, and useful today as when first struck, fired, and forged in the fourth century. In his essay "The Contribution of Cappadocia to Christian Thought," J. D. Zizioulas writes this:

> The person cannot exist in isolation. God is not alone; He is a communion [in the Trinity]. Love is not a feeling, a sentiment springing from nature like a flower from a tree. Love is a relationship, it is the free coming out of one's self, the breaking of one's will, a free submission to the will of another. It is the other and our relationship with him that gives us our identity, our otherness, making us "who we are"; that is, persons. . . . [169]

That is, we are, each of us, a person in and through our free acts of loving and being loved—and we are persons because, prior to and above our personhood, God is Himself three Persons: Father, Son, and Holy Spirit. "As a person," Bishop Zizioulas writes, "you exist as long as you love and are loved." As a person, therefore, you are fashioned in the Image of the God who died on the Cross in the supreme humility. Our fundamentally relational nature as persons thus flows from the fundamentally trinitarian nature of God as Three Persons in One; and, as Zizioulas says, "as is the case with God, so with us, too: personal identity emerges only from the exercise of love as freedom and of freedom as love." Just so, we become persons.

The Church Is the Living Body of the Person of Christ

Similarly, St. Basil's articulation of personhood discloses the Orthodox understanding of ecclesiology. In the Orthodox faith, the Church is not an administrative arrangement; it is not a dispensor of good deeds; it is not a public arena for private devotions; it is not a repository for twenty centuries of religious art and liturgical music. Rather, the Church can be these things solely because she is, primarily and essentially, the living Body of the Person of Christ. Consequently, the Church is the one and only space wherein human beings in their personhood can enter into loving communion with one another in Christ. And only in such communion are the negative mimetic entanglements of the violent collective loosed and undone and replaced with reciprocal, transpersonal kenosis, finding its fulfillment in love. The aim of the sacrificial mechanism described by Girard is the killing of the victim to yield social harmony. The aim of the Orthodox Liturgy is each person's free submission to Christ who, in dying in love for everyone, gives His undying life to us all. Such matters are not idle metaphors; they are living spiritual realities. In imitation of Christ's self-emptying gesture "on behalf of all and for all," the Christian becomes a participant in the Body of Christ, in the Life of the Church.

Simply put, Christ's recapitulation of human nature (putting on human nature, tasting death, and resurrecting the body, so that we "put on Christ" at Baptism and through all the Mysteries in the life of the Church), along with our imitation of Christ in the life of the Church, thrusts us into an ontological participatory relationship with Christ and those who make up the Body of Christ, His Church.[170] The sacrificial mechanism violently consumes all personhood; the Orthodox Liturgy alone bestows it. In the first we seize life for ourselves at another's expense; in the second, we are given life so that we may give it to others. And the life we are given is the Body of Christ, that is, the Church.

In light of the various breakdowns within institutional Christianity, René Girard himself offers a superb commentary on the profound need for genuine Orthodoxy:[171]

> In reality, no purely intellectual process and no experience of a purely philosophical nature can secure the individual the slightest victory over mimetic desire and its victimage delusions. Intellection can achieve only displacement and substitution, though these may give individuals the sense of having achieved such a victory. For there to be even the slightest degree of progress, the victimage delusion must be vanquished on the most intimate level of experience. . . .[172]

This necessary intimacy is precisely what the Orthodox life of "goodness, discipline and knowledge" (Ps 118:66)—a life conducted in full penitential joy and genuinely free obedience—seeks always to establish, sustain, and deepen: the actual intimacy of Christ's love.

Girard continues:

> . . . and this triumph, if it is not to remain a dead letter, must succeed in collapsing, or at the very least shaking to their foundations, all the things that are based upon our interdividual oppositions—consequently, everything that we can call our "ego," our "personality," our "temperament," and so on. Because of this, great works [of literature and knowledge] are few and far between.[173]

Many of these "great works" have been long held in Eastern Orthodox hands. One of them is St. Isaac's *Ascetical Homilies*, the aim of which is precisely the ascetic dissolution of one's ego, personality, and temperament; and another is a work by an author who himself read long and deeply in St. Isaac's *Homilies*: Dostoevsky's *Brothers Karamazov*. The voice of the spiritual model of the novel, Zosima, echoes throughout in imitation of Christ's active, kenotic love: "each of us is guilty in everything before everyone, and I most of all." All are called to imitate this injunction, to empty the ego and to be vulnerable to love, Eastern and Western churches alike, but its true teachers will be found in those preaching ascetical discipline, an emptying of self, a life lived in the virtues—in short, a full life lived in the Mysteries of the Church.

St. Isaac and the Unbusied Heart

THE MAN WHO IS pure in mind is not he who has no knowledge of evil, nor again he who never takes up human affairs—nor yet is purity of mind that we should not beseech men for any created thing. No, says Isaac, purity of mind is rather engaging these things without submitting to them; it is "to make a beginning to struggle with them."[174]

The mystery of Abba Isaac's *presence* in his words! To read St. Isaac the Syrian's *Homilies* is to engage directly a person who lives in Christ. As one reads the text of St. Isaac, one sees his words undergo three great transformations. First, the words become a *voice*, a real person's actual voice sounding right now. Every poet discovers this about his or her own poem. Every reader of St. Isaac makes exactly the same discovery. The difference is this: whereas the voice in any given poem is only lightly connected to the poet's actual voice (and therefore has qualities of performance), the voice of St. Isaac is profoundly related to his actual personhood. Thus, while the poem's voice is always bounded by the specific lyric techniques or purposes of that specific poem and once the poem is over the voice ceases, in St. Isaac, the voice endures beyond the given homily: endures and abides.

Second, in this way the words of St. Isaac become an actual *presence*. That is, the voice becomes incarnated in a tangible body and palpable soul. Because they are such a presence, St. Isaac's words enact memory: each word remembers all the other words, directly or invisibly becoming connected in such a way that, when any given word sounds, all the others echo and chime and resonate. And by enacting memory, the words of St. Isaac become flesh, a living person who does not die.

Finally, the person who *is* these words becomes the person of Christ Himself. This third transformation of St. Isaac's words is experienced by Isaac coming to know God; we experience it as his coming to be loved by God. Hence, this transformation opens the great mystery wherein we, as readers, enter into relation with St. Isaac *in and through the personhood of Christ Himself.* As St. Isaac seeks to know Christ, and as Christ beautifully manifests His love to St. Isaac, we—in Christ—come to know and love St. Isaac *in and through his knowing and loving Christ.*

St. Isaac the Syrian. Icon by Fr. Andrew Tregubov, Tregubov Studios, Claremont, New Hampshire. Used by permission.

The Unbusied Heart

In section 26 of Homily One, St. Isaac says: "Everything is wont to run to its kindred; and the soul that has a share of the Spirit, on hearing a phrase that has spiritual power hidden within, ardently draws out its content for herself." This running or flowing together of everything in kindredness has, as a member of this set, this noetic activity: the reader's soul ardently draws out from the written or spoken phrase the hidden power. The reader's flowingness in the Holy Spirit calls out the phrase's flowingness; the reader "rhymes" the phrase, where rhyming is the action, or operation, of the Holy Spirit.

Such an operation, says Abba Isaac, "has need of a heart unbusied with the earth and its converse." The unbusied heart! to be free of all longing for the spins and crazinesses of those things that most destroy us. In the immense noise and clatter of our ordinary lives, how *busy* our hearts are! "The man who craves esteem cannot be rid of the causes of grief" (1:5.13). Our hearts' incessant busyness is precisely driven by this craving.

Then this:

> When a man's thoughts are totally immersed in the delight of pursuing the wisdom treasured in the words of Scripture by means of the faculty that gains enlightenment from them, then he puts the world behind his back and forgets everything in it, and he blots out of his soul all memories that form images of the world. Often he does not even remember the employment of the habitual thoughts which visit human nature, and his soul remains in ecstasy by reason of those new encounters that arise from the sea of the Scripture's mysteries. (1:5.18)

This putting-away of the world is stillness as the mental (better, *noetic*) practice wherein the "images embodying the words" are blotted out *from the memory*. Such blotting-out means that we don't even remember how to *use* these images. Instead, psychic ecstasy occurs, the ecstasy in which the soul remains while she engages—*encounters*—the noetic mysteries that are arising from the depths of Scripture.

The *Philokalia*'s glossary tells us that the *nous* (adj. *noetic*) is "the highest faculty in man, through which—provided it is purified—he knows God or the inner essences or principles of created things by means of direct apprehension or spiritual perception." The key word is *direct*: the *nous* (or the noetic faculty in us) understands by immediate experience—fully, swiftly, beautifully understands.

Flattery and Self-Esteem

In Homily Two, St. Isaac writes:

> The lover of virtue is not he who does good with valiant struggle, but he who *accepts with joy the evils that attend virtue*. It is not so great a thing for me patiently to endure afflictions on behalf of virtue, as it is for the mind through the determination of its good volition to remain unconfused by the flattery of tantalizing pleasures. No kind of repentance that takes place after the removal of our free will will be a well-spring of joy, nor will it be reckoned for the reward of those who possess it.[175]

Isn't this *beautiful*? The "evils that attend virtue" are the feelings of self-congratulatory self-absorption that arise almost instantly after we do something even half-good. The mind can choose, of its own free will, not to engage such feelings; it can choose to remain "unconfused by the flattery of tantalizing pleasures." For joy, *alone*, possesses the power to still the spin of flattery: to still the mind. Hence, joy sustains our freedom by leading us out of our self-absorptions of self-flattery.

The addiction one develops for flattery removes one's free will; for it needs the flattering self-esteem that comes from others. As with all addictions, the addict soon loathes the substance he deeply craves; and therefore self-hate very soon becomes strongly a part of the addiction. And the false pleasure of self-hate charges still further the need for others' flattery—which of course charges still more the self-hate. The false repentance of self-hate therefore can never become, says Abba Isaac, "a well-spring of joy." And such false repentance "will [never] be reckoned for the reward of those who possess it." Hence, says the Abba, "the man who craves esteem cannot be rid of the causes of grief" (1:5.13). Here is the root of all depression, of all our inability to be rid of the causes of our grieving.

What, then, is one doing when one "accepts with joy the evils that attend virtue"? The evils that attend virtue—note well—are not *in* virtue; rather, they come along with it, like a swarm of poisonous gnats—these are the flatteries that flow from others to you. If you accept them with joy, you neither swallow them nor angrily bat them off: for to swallow them poisons you, while to bat at them is joyless: and both further the addiction. Acceptance with joy is hinted at most clearly in the next sentence: "Cover a man who stumbles, so long as you receive no harm from him, and give him encouragement; then your Master's loving-kindness will bear you up" (2:12).

Your flatterer is the "man who stumbles," and you are to encourage *him* without swallowing the poison he dispenses; and then Our Lord will bear

up—not him—but *you*. For every time the flattery comes toward you, you are
in great danger, you are very close to stumbling. But if you encourage *him*,
you will be upheld by Our Lord's mercy. St. Isaac adds this next: "Support
with a word the infirm and those who are grieved at heart," for the flatterer is
indeed sick and grieved. You are, he next says, to "commune with those who
are grieved at heart," to toil at your prayer in "the anguish of your heart"—and
then "the Source of mercy will be opened up to your petitions."

To encourage the flatterer therefore seems to mean to commune with
the heartsickness beneath the glittering words and then to pray for him (and
for yourself) to receive God's mercy. Such, at least in part, is what it seems to
mean to accept with joy the evils that attend virtue.

The Noetic Ray

A little further on, Abba Isaac tells us: "The beginning of the intellect's darkening (once a sign of it is visible in the soul) is to be seen, first of all, in sloth-
fulness with regard to the [church] services and [[private]] prayer."[176] He says
that if we *do* remain awake and alive in the church services and our rule of
prayer, we "cannot be led in the way of error." The noetic ray running in the
words of the Church and of our prayer—and our apprehension of it—saves
us, for it helps realign our minds and reconfigure our psyches to *fit* these
words, to *enter into* these words in their depth and power. For when we enter
their depth and power, then these words give "the heart a most sweet taste
through intuitions that awe the soul" (1:6.25). The noetic ray enables our
mind, Isaac says, "to distinguish" between depthlessness and sweetness.

St. Isaac is moved into God through the reading of Scripture. All the
words of Scripture are, for St. Isaac, charged with the noetic grandeur of
God.[177]

The World and the Passions

"*World*" in St. Isaac's usage "is a collective noun which is applied to the so-
called passions." Again, "When we wish to give a collective name to the passions, we call them *world*. And when we wish to designate them specifically
according to their names, we call them *passions*" (1:6.25). World = passions.
"The passions are the portions of the world's onward flow; and where the
passions cease, there the world's onward flow stands still" (2:15). The world
as passions; passions as the world. Where the passions fail and are rendered
inactive, "the world fails from its constitution and remains inactive."

The passions, says Abba Isaac, are these:

1. love of wealth

2. gathering objects of any kind

3. bodily pleasure, from which comes the passion of carnal intercourse

4. love of esteem, from which springs envy

5. the wielding of power

6. pride in the trappings of authority

7. stateliness and pomposity

8. human glory, which is the cause of resentment

9. fear for the body

In these nine passions are all of our lives. Especially fearful in their depths and massive in their effects are our love of esteem and our hunger for human glory, for from these spring all our envy and all our resentment: and envy and resentment drive all our violent destructiveness and sin. An immense subject then opens. How are we to unmake the world? how are we to become free of passion's fearful grip on us?

Taking Up the Cross through Praxis and Theoria

How are we to become free of passion's fearful grip on us? St. Isaac answers: take up the Cross. This is, he says, a twofold activity, "in conformity with the duality of our nature, which is divided into two parts" (1:13): *praxis* and *theoria*.

PRAXIS AND THE POWER OF ZEAL

Praxis is the patient endurance of "the tribulations of the flesh"—accomplished "by the activity of the soul's incensive part."[178] You actually *do* things; hence, *praxis* "is called *righteous activity*." The psychic power that works in *praxis* to purify the soul is "the power of zeal." To patiently endure the physical discomfort, hurt, distress arising from (for example) a rule of prayer: such endurance takes zeal.

Zeal, Isaac says, is "the force of the holy desire implanted naturally in the nature of the soul" (55:273). Set in motion by the soul's incensive faculty, zeal (1) *safeguards the boundaries of our psychic nature*—that's its first function; and (2) *sends forth the psyche's vehemence for the fulfilling of her desire for God*—that's the second function of zeal.

Function one. Since zeal can be (in Greek and Hebrew—and I think in Syriac) also translated as *jealousy*, zeal is an attribute of God before it is something in us. Florensky says that jealousy is the modern (that is, post-Enlightenment) world's most dreaded power; hence, it's the one that draws all our world's unceasing and fullest contempt and scorn and abuse, without the slightest reservation.

Yet zeal/jealousy does this: it safeguards the boundaries of our psyche (or soul). We are psychically extremely reckless; we smash through our own and others' psychic boundaries almost continuously, often enough in the name of doing good (we call it "loving"); that is, we are *deliberately* reckless now and then while being unconsciously reckless almost all the rest of the time. Such fearsome recklessness is the result of that psychic violation which arises from the absence of zeal/jealousy: that is, from the collapse of psychic safeguarding.

The probably apocryphal story about St. Isaac's one-day bishopric in Nineveh is, in fact, a story about a confrontation with psychic reckless-ness. On the day following his consecration, St. Isaac had two men, who were disputing about a loan, come to his residence. One insisted on being repaid (he was wealthy); the other begged for more time. St. Isaac brought up the Gospel teaching on not to take back what has been already given, asking for one day more for the debtor. The rich man answered, "Put aside the teachings of the Gospel!" St. Isaac said, "If the Gospel isn't present what am I doing here?" St. Isaac abdicated the bishopric.

The point of the story is plain. The rich lender crossed violently the psychic boundaries of both Isaac and the debtor at the very same moment. In this way, we can see what it means to violate psychic boundaries: it is to attack Christ, it is to crucify Him again. For in safeguarding the boundar-ies (as Bp. Isaac did with the debtor), zeal/jealousy leaves the realm of the crucifiers and becomes one with Him who is crucified. And as Christ Jesus safeguards every boundary everywhere, our zeal/jealousy will take us to the Cross, always and forever.

Function two. Zeal is the engine driving all our desire to be with God: it is the vehemence with which the psyche/soul goes to the Cross because she loves the One who is crucified. This intensity or vehemence drives every *praxis*, or righteous activity, of taking up the Cross.

THEORIA

The second part of the twofold activity of taking up the Cross is *theoria* (or divine vision). *Theoria*, says Isaac, is a cleansing—a purifying—of the noetic part of the soul, an action carried out by the appetitive, or desiring, or loving, part of the soul. If incensive *praxis* is creative, then appetitive *theoria* is receptive: it receives the pure grace of beholding God. One can (and *must*) do *praxis*; one cannot in any way whatever compel *theoria*; it is purely given. For this reason, says Abba Isaac, *theoria* lies at a point beyond the reach of prayer, a point *to* which prayer can lead but over which prayer has not the least power. *Theoria* has a distinct boundary. "But beyond this boundary," he says, "there is awestruck wonder and not prayer." He continues: "For what pertains to prayer has ceased, while a certain divine vision remains, and the mind does not pray a prayer" (23:116).

Dostoevsky perfectly depicts *theoria* in the "Cana of Galilee" chapter of *The Brothers Karamazov*, when Alyosha beholds his just-deceased Elder at the banquet feast in Cana when "the walls of the room" all at once open out:

> Yes, to him, to him, he came, the little wizened old man with fine wrinkles on his face, joyful and quietly laughing. Now there was no coffin anymore, and he was wearing the same clothes as the day before, when he sat with him and visitors gathered around them. His face was all uncovered and his eyes were radiant. Can it be that he, too, is at the banquet, that he, too, has been called to the marriage in Cana of Galilee . . . ?
>
> "I, too, my dear, I, too, have been called, called and chosen," the quiet voice spoke over him. "Why are you hiding here, out of sight . . . ? Come and join us."[179]

This is what *theoria* does: it calls us into the banquet where Christ Himself is. In this way, *praxis* and *theoria* work to one immensely glorious end: to be *in* Christ. Also, both *praxis* and *theoria* sustain the same boundary: *praxis*, from this side; *theoria*, from the other side, in the heavenly kingdom.[180]

THEORIA MAY NOT BE SOUGHT

St. Isaac is first of all, and most deeply and sustainedly, an *ascetic*; these *Homilies* are ascetical. Thus, in Homily Two, he gives us an understanding of *theoria* deeply embedded in ascetical warning: if you try to *seek theoria*, you find immense spiritual catastrophe, the wrath of God. You will, he says, be "put to silence by Divine punishment." *Praxis*, the patient endurance of

ST. ISAAC AND THE UNBUSIED HEART 231

ascetic affliction, never brings wrath; forced, will-driven *theoria* always does. "The things of God, they say, come of themselves, without one being aware of it. Yes, but only if the place is clean and not defiled" (2:13). Then he gives us a terrifying phrase: if you attempt to violate the boundary, you will "be cast aside in a lone region of the noetic world (which is the 'outer darkness,' outside God, a figure of Hell) like that man who shamelessly entered into the wedding feast with unclean garments" (2:14). That lone region, that outer darkness outside God: such horror attends us when we try to seize *theoria*. Only *praxis*, the unfailing consistency of prayer and every righteous action—small labors steadily undertaken in the humility of failure and in the fullness of confession: only *praxis* guides us aright.

Everything is given in Homily 2. Attend: "From exertions and watching there springs purity of thought. And out of purity of the thoughts, the light of the understanding dawns. From this the intellect is guided by grace into that wherein the senses have no power, either to teach, or to learn." *Praxis* purifies thought; from this purity arises light; by this light, grace guides the *nous* into that wondrous helplessness wherein all *theoria*—all insight into the divine mysteries hidden in all things—opens and opens. . . .

Separation from the World and the Soul's Great Stillness

This astonishing sentence occurs toward the end of Homily 2: "Observe also whether your mind remains unafflicted by hidden confrontations with the imprint of thoughts because of a mightier ardour for the Divine, which is wont to cut off vain recollections" (2:15). What happens in (and *to*) the mind when she invisibly confronts "the imprints of thoughts"? Such confrontations—such shocks of engagement—reveal that thoughts leave imprints, or scars; that thoughts are wounds;—or (better) that thoughts leave behind in their wake fine tracery lines that *in themselves* can reignite the mind in the same catastrophic fires. Only the "mightier ardour for the Divine" can put out these second-strike fires; only this stronger blaze can keep the mind steady ("unafflicted") when she comes upon those finely dangerous tracery lines left by "passing" thoughts like landmines still unexploded.

Abba Isaac ends Homily 2 by saying that these "few indications . . . will suffice a man for his enlightenment." Six pages, no more. Yet these six pages are enough. They suffice.

SEPARATION, STILLNESS, AND WONDER

Homily 3, nearly twelve pages long, begins: "When life's concerns do not incur into the soul from without, and she abides in her nature, then she does not require prolonged toil to penetrate into and understand the wisdom of God. For her separation from the world and her stillness naturally move her toward the understanding of God's creatures" (3:16). Here is St. Isaac's great and fearsome subject: separation from the world and the soul's great stillness. For it is only from the matrix of genuine stillness that there can arise the great experience of *wonder*. A trinity: separation; stillness; wonder—each being matrix for the next; the last—wonder—deepening the separation: "she is struck with wonder, and she remains with God." Plainly this trinity is, for Abba Isaac, first of all an actual *experience*—not just once, but many times.

FEAR

The single greatest psychic force in us that opposes this trinity is, says Isaac, *fear* (see Homily 73). Fear grips us whenever we draw near to the world's things (world understood as the collective name of our passionate spins about things). Is fear *natural* to the psyche? No, he says; the soul *by nature* is passionless. Thus even though the psyche is greatly *moved* by such passions as fear, she is herself translucent in her primordial stillness. The psyche "is moved to gladness by the body's gladness and she bears its afflictions" (3:17).

But fear has a divine significance when the soul fears God. Fear *for the soul* awakens zeal—and zeal (as we saw) guards the soul's boundaries when the soul is threatened, zeal keeps and saves the soul's zeal, *answers* the fearfulness, and (he says) "it is a good anxiety" (55:274). But when fearfulness is on behalf of something pertaining to the body, "it becomes satanic" (dark). Such fearfulness is like water seeping "into the foundation of the soul from without" (3:16): it rots the whole structure, and will, in time, bring it down with a fearsome crash.

PURITY OF MIND AND THE MOVEMENT OF THOUGHTS

In Homily 3, St. Isaac writes: "The man who is pure in mind is not he who has no knowledge of evil (for that is to be like a brute beast), nor he who is by nature on the level of infants [I gather: born retarded], nor again he who never takes up human affairs—nor yet is purity of mind that we should not beseech men for any created thing" (3:20). No, he says,

purity of mind is rather *engaging* these things *without submitting to them.*
Purity of mind is the struggle: the submission is impurity of mind. Purity
of mind is "to be rapt in things divine, and this comes about after a man
has practiced the virtues" (3:20). Such rapture is the wondrous fullness of
every conceivable stillness.

Against purity of mind is "movement of thoughts": that is, against
stillness is restlessness. The causes of the mind's restlessness are: the body's
willfulness; the imagination's endless replaying of things heard and seen;
the mind's "hardwiring" (that is, its habitual movements and predilec-
tions and long-acquired "tastes"); the psyche's momentary and/or long-
standing aberrations; and demonic attack via our passions. Through these
the mind's possible purity is always and steadily being undermined, being
corroded, being unmade.

Or rather: The mind is always and steadily engaged in vast warfare
against powerful enemies that are at once near, proximate, and distant:
throughout the day and the night equally the warfare continues. "Where-
fore," Isaac says, "every man must guard himself" (3:21). This unceasing violence against one's mind is coterminous with life itself: where one is, so is the
other. If even one of these causes of the mind's restlessness "could possibly be
done away with," then all the world's warfare would suddenly cease: "But it is
absurd to suppose any such thing," he goes on, because our nature needs the
(fallen) world's goods: our mind cannot disengage from the struggle. Hence,
the necessity of guarding oneself. Guarding means maintaining the divinely
given boundaries of all things, including one's own mind.

Purity of Heart in Separation from the World

But, says Abba Isaac, "Purity of mind is one thing, and purity of heart is
another." The major axis of difference is this: the mind is "quickly cleansed"
and "quickly soiled." But *the heart is purified only through long afflictions
patiently endured,* long "separation from fellowship with the world." And
once purified, the heart's "purity is not soiled by little things." Such a heart,
says Abba Isaac, can *digest* even the harshest, bitterest food. No "moderate
assault" can pose any real dangers (3:22).

"Long separation from all fellowship with the world"—here is St.
Isaac's great, sobering, and joyous teaching. Such a teaching is great because of its depth and breadth. Every single, last shred of passionate spinning about the world's ways: every last one is removed, unmade, its nerve
killed at the root. It is sobering because such an operation stills down all
of passion's intoxicating effects, all the exhilarative/depressive storms of

our emotional life simply dying fully out. We can scarcely even begin to imagine such an inner landscape so perfectly cleansed and so absolutely quieted. It is joyous because *Christ Himself stands in this new landscape fully revealed.* And He is revealed in ways at once deeply surprising and fully comprehended: as the supreme Other.

The Abba says in Homily 1: "In order to lay the foundation of virtue, nothing is better for a man than to contain himself by means of flight from the affairs of life, and to persevere in the illumined word of those straight and holy paths, even that word which in the Spirit the Psalmist named a lamp" (1:3). Christ Our Lord is that lamp; He is that noetic ray running amidst the lines of Scripture; He is the aim and fulfillment of every *praxis* and all *theoria.* "The man who cleanses his heart from the passions beholds the Lord at every moment" (15:84).

God's Fury

The removal, however—the cleansing—may not be a welcome process. The Psalms, two especially, LXX 87 and 89, can help us better to see what Isaac means when he says to flee all association. In Psalm 87 (16–18), God takes away from the psalmist all loved ones and friends—*furiously* takes away:

> Thy furies have swept through me, thy terrors have utterly unmade me,
>
> Swirling around me daily like waters, surrounding me from every side.
>
> Thou hast taken loved ones and friends far from me, even anyone who knew me, because of my misery.

And in Psalm 89 (7–11):

> For we were unmade by thy rage and rocked by thy wrath.
>
> Thou has set our iniquities before thee, our life in the light of thy countenance.
>
> For all our days have faded away, in thy rage we have been unmade. . . .
>
> Who could measure thine anger's strength? In our awe, how measure thy wrath?

This wrath is God's *exactness* in our lives, His deeply struck and immensely loving exactness, an exactness that cuts away all the thick and poisonous hazes of associational sickness in us.

Again, in Psalm 89:12 we read: "So make known thy right hand to us that our hearts be held fast in wisdom." God's right hand is His rage visited ascetically upon us, and because of this rage we can know the final line of Psalm 89: "And let our Lord's splendor be upon us; guide the works of our hands rightly for us, the works of our hands guide aright" (l. 17).

The Realms of Psyche and Body

Thus, central to Isaac's understanding is this: "The passions of the body have been implanted in it for its benefit and growth, and the same is true with respect to the passions of the soul" (3:19). His insight here is astonishing: whenever the psyche is compelled to follow the body, or the body the psyche, then the body is weakened and the psyche is tormented. "The flesh," says Isaac quoting Paul (Gal 5:17), "cannot lust after the spirit"—this is destruction for both. The principle seems to be this: the realms of psyche and body must remain each in their own proper boundaries. Whatever is *external* to either realm—that is, is boundary-violative—unmakes that realm. "For He has implanted in natures [that is, in both physical and psychic natures] that which causes each to grow."

But this is not mere static parallelism of realms. For the immediate question is: why is ascetic practice—wherein the soul chooses *for the body* the fasting and prayer that torments the body—why is such practice *good*? He answers that the soul is the body's caretaker and guide and (in a sense) parent. Even though the body's passions and motions are alien to the psyche's, still the soul can *take up* these motions and passions, nurturing them toward either life in God or death in the fallen world. Either way, the soul and the body become "partakers of one another" (3:20)—while still sustaining their unconfused separation.

The point is at once very fine and very powerful. "For," he says, "what is proper to the soul's nature is death to the body." The soul's nature inherently *loves* ascetic practice; if such love had no boundary (that is, if such love were *disincarnate*), then it would cause the body's death. Yet God's unfathomable wisdom has so arranged things that "by nature [that is, not merely accidentally, or now and then, but always and essentially and fully] the soul has been made sharer in the body's griefs, by reason of the union of her [the soul's] movement with the body's movement" (3:20).

THE MYSTERY OF THE HUMAN PERSON

This union of motions (physical and psychical) manifests God's vast wisdom, for it creates the essential mystery of the human person, that mystery wherein the soul's life shares in the body's life but without making such sharing become confusion: that is, sharing that sustains distinctness. And even (says dear Isaac) when the soul is raised up into the ocean of heavenly bliss (in *theoria*), "the body is permitted to retain a consciousness of what is proper to it" (3:20). The soul will never cast off the body, never discard it as useless or wrong. Yet even when the body is "found in sin," the soul still unceasingly retains the power to raise up its own "deliberations" (that is, its own ecstasy of insight).

ISRAEL IS THE BODY OF CHRIST

The way our soul is to our body, so Christ is to all the figures (for example, David) in Hebrew Scripture. Christ moves in the realms of heavenly *theoria* even here amidst earth's dark violence in such a way that He permits the incarnate Israel "to retain a consciousness of what is proper to it." For Israel is the body of Christ: the motions of Israel proper to her nature share in—participate in—the motions of Christ's psyche and mind.

And, in the same way, our body will beguile and mislead us, just as Israel betrays her Lord. But (here is the big point) Christ never casts off Israel: "since he is clad with a body, whether he wills it or not" (3:21), He is "vexed by thoughts and the assaults" of Israel—but He never discards her, never sets her aside; but always He loves her even as He knows she will finally crucify Him, committing that homicide that is their own final suicide. Yet He is never overcome by her because His "mind is caught away into good and divine recollections" (3:21).

From Psalm 147 (7–8): "He shall send his word and melt them, he shall breathe out his breath and the waters shall flow, declaring his word unto Jacob, his statutes and judgments to Israel." The two motions converge: the motion of water flowing, and the motion of the word being shown to Israel. This mysterious convergence ("his word shall run very swiftly"—three verses earlier) is the reason why *simultaneously* (1) the earth is breathtakingly beautiful, and (2) the earth can never equal the beauty of God's word and statutes and judgments. The convergence is never a co-mingling, a dissolution. The noetic ray between lines of Scripture bespeaks this convergence; for the ray calls us to see Him through the eyes of our faith.

Faith (*pistis*), that immense word! Homily 52, on the three degrees of knowledge, says that "Knowledge is perfected by faith," for "it is suitable that we should know only that the level of faith's activity is more lofty than knowledge" (52:257). Faith alone unmakes fearfulness.

Isaac says in Homily 37 that, "when the daybreak of the resurrection will dawn," then a man's "mind will turn to Scripture, which will instill in him faith in the resurrection and the end of all things in this world." The body breaks; Israel is cast down; Christ dies on the cross. Then the resurrection dawns and, "like a man who has encountered the light, he casts off the oppression of his sorrow and great joy stirs within him . . ." (37:166). Faith in the resurrection includes the raising up of the body of broken Israel; beyond all Hebraic fearfulness there is this joyous courage of the resurrection, that courage wherein all Israel becomes the Body of Christ Himself: *kata tas grafas*.[181]

Resurrecting Our Personhood from Passional Death

In Homily 4 Isaac writes: "Consider yourself a stranger all the days of your life, wherever you may be, so that you will find deliverance from the injury which is born of familiarity" (4:33). In the next sentence he says: "In every matter consider yourself to be totally ignorant so as to escape the reproach which follows the suspicion that you wish to set aright other men's passions." This injury arising from familiarity and this suspicion that you want to correct everyone's opinions: here is the root of that small but steady/deadly violence we do daily—hourly—minute by minute—in all our relations with everyone we meet. Be ill-at-ease, stranger; be foolishly uninformed and ignorant about everything: here is the one relational cure to all our relations' sicknesses. And even if (the Abba says) "you begin to say something profitable, say it as though you yourself are still learning, and not with authority and shamelessness."

This seems an impossible standard; but nothing else can accomplish the necessary work: to resurrect one's personhood from passional death— that is, from the psychic death wrought by those endless spins of the nine mimetic passions that beset and bedevil us. In Homily 37:179 the key question is put: How do you safeguard your mind when passions rise against it?

STUDY OF SCRIPTURE

Isaac's answer is central to all of his teaching: study of Scripture. This study "grows and abides" in Scriptures in our "seeking out their meanings." Such seeking becomes "sweetness of rumination," a sweetness that desert stillness *exalts.* In this exaltation, you are "continually struck by wonder" at God's active presence in Scriptures, a wonder that becomes "always drunken"—and this unceasing inebriation causes you to live *now* the "life after resurrection." *Reading Scriptures yields a way of life.*

Stillness aids this grace because, through stillness, your nous finds "a place to remain" within itself by means of the peace that the stillness endows. Furthermore: your nous is moved to memory—because now you set before your nous these two things: the glory of the age to come; and the hope that that glory effects in you these three things as perfect (and perfective) knowing:

1. that this glory *originated* in God's;

2. that this glory is now *being restored* by God;

3. that this glory's *origin* and *restoration* together cause you no longer to reflect upon nor to remember the (fallen) things of the (fallen) world.

As this glory (given by God) arrives and as (therefore) this hope in you arises—all by virtue of your having gone on reading Scriptures—then *theoria* happens: you see in the *same instant* that this current (fallen) world is nothing compared to the depths and heights of that wondrous world of glory.

A Final Journal Entry

A prayer: O Lord Jesus Christ, grant that I may love the writings of Abba St. Isaac in the grace with which You love them—and him; and, Abba St. Isaac, pray for me that I may love our Lord Jesus Christ in the grace with which you so immensely and beautifully love Him.

Abba says, "If you should beseech God for a thing and He is slow to hearken to you speedily, do not grieve, for you are not wiser than God. This happens to you either because you are not worthy to obtain your request, or because the pathways of your heart do not accord with your petitions (but rather the contrary), or because you have not yet reached the measure wherein you could receive the gift you ask for" (3:24).

The way this second sentence of Homily 3 opens is a tiny icon for all the Abba's openings of mind/nous. The first clause—we are not worthy of our prayers—is the ground base of all ascetic praxis: how could we ever possibly become worthy? Then the second clause: the petitions of our prayers must somehow be in accord with the pathways of our heart. This implies that such accord can indeed occur; and then our prayers and our hearts share a common syntax (or "pathways"). This common syntax comes about through our long, steady giving of our hearts *into* our prayers, a giving that in time reconfigures our heart's pathways into the prayers' syntax. Once we begin to accomplish even some part of this work, then we reach the measure (the Abba's third clause) wherein we could receive the gift we are seeking.

"We must not rush onward to great measures before the time" (so the Greek says; while the Syriac translates: "it is not right that great things should quickly fall into our hands" [3:24, n. 41]). Anything quickly gotten, he continues, is quickly lost; "whereas everything found with toil is also kept with careful watching."

The motion of the Abba's glorious mind in this sentence is from ascetic grounding through the heart's reconfiguring in prayer to the fullest measure of beholding God: a sudden motion made sober by ascetic praxis, made stable by watchfulness, and made glorious by—his next sentence:—"thirst for Christ, that He may make you drunk with His love."

Epilogue

XENIA SHEEHAN

DON WROTE A SENTENCE (well, truth be told, many) that I have drawn much sustenance and understanding from. One in particular belongs here, at the conclusion, as it is the first half of a chiasmus that spans two volumes of his work:

> Biblical meditation, rather than serving to bring the practitioner out of the dark swirl of history, plunges him or her directly *into* that fearful churning so as to reveal God as the *Presence-in-the-darkness*. (*Shield of Psalmic Prayer*, 48)

Just before the final journal entry in the final chapter of this volume, Don tells us (following St. Isaac) that, as the God-given glory (always remember, freely given, never to be sought after), if and as this glory arrives in us, hope arises—all by virtue of our having gone on reading Scriptures. And that is when *theoria* happens. Should we reach the end of that long journey, we would come to see *in the same instant* that this current, fallen, world is nothing compared to the depths and heights of that wondrous world of glory. For, viewed from Paradise in Dante's *Paradiso* 22, earth is but a "paltry semblance."

This is no denigration of earthly reality. The King Himself, who created it, took it as his own reality, chose to enter into its death, and thereby lifted it into His Glory. For this He created the world and us. Yet we must still understand it—both the world and our self—as nothing *in itself*. For in the chiasmus, as in Him, the world's nothing joins with God's revealed presence in response to . . . His Glory matched/accepted/received by virtue of our rising hope . . . and we see Him clearly. It is that match of His Glory with our hope—in C. S. Lewis's words, His sceptred with our kneeling love—that makes the union, and the Dance.

Chiastically, the two perspectives look like this:

Biblical meditation

Plunges us directly into the dark swirl
and fearful churning of history

To reveal God as the *Presence-in-the-darkness*

As the God-given glory arrives, and hope arises
in us, we see clearly

the God who reveals Himself as
the *Presence-in-the-darkness,*

Revealing the world as *nothing* compared to

The depths and heights of that wondrous glory

By virtue of our having gone on reading Scriptures.

That is, we enter into Scripture's portrayal of history's churning swirl of darkness to find, at the center, through hope's rising, the Holy Presence. While at the same time, God is reaching out to us—giving and revealing Himself—from within the "fearful churning" so that we may find Him in our very darkness and understand and experience both the depths and the heights of His "wondrous Glory." Whichever direction we take, up or down, inward or outward, God is there, wholly *present* in both the glory of His heaven and the darkness of our history. This is the Joy, the presentness, that is incarnational reality, perfectly expressed through the antinomy and chiasmus that fill so much of Scripture and teach us the way.

Glory to God for all things!

Acknowledgments

So MANY EXCELLENT PEOPLE have supported me in putting this work together! I am beyond grateful for Fr. John Konkle's sound Orthodox wisdom and unfailing promptness in responding to my requests for critique of the various "hunches" that have moved me to take the next step. Priest-in-Residence at Holy Dormition Monastery in Rives Jct., Michigan, where he first served for several years under Fr. Roman Braga, Fr. John was formerly Professor of Philosophy and a colleague of Don's at Dartmouth College, and a fellow parishioner of Holy Resurrection Orthodox Church in Claremont, New Hampshire. He became a family friend as well and is now my confessor and spiritual advisor. This was a particularly critical role for me during the long pandemic isolation, which I began as a guest of Dormition Monastery. His and his wife Anna's presence at that monastery was my primary draw to moving there for a year and a half in 2018 on my quest to find a place to settle after Don's passing. One of his e-mailed responses, concerning the Commandments of Christ, I have included in full in the book's glossary because it expresses an understanding of our "intimate relationship with the self-emptying Source of life" with so much deeper and closer an understanding of that relationship than I have yet been blessed to achieve. Not least, Fr. John has helped me find a number of crucial sources, especially St. Maximus. He is in no way, however, responsible for my errors, either of theology or citation.

Fr. Joel Brady, at first a casual acquaintance at St. Tikhon's (where I lived on and off with my family and others for a decade and got to know many fine students), entered into this picture a few years ago when he organized his parish book study around Don's newly published *Shield of Psalmic Prayer* and asked me if I'd like to contribute anything by phone. Later, knowing that he liked Don's work, and feeling all of my eighty years, I asked him if he'd be willing to help me with a final combing out of the new book prior to seeking a publisher. Right up to the last stages, he has been a dedicated and wise reader and editorial consultant on top of all his other responsibilities to his young family and parish. Thank you, Fr. Joel.

My longtime friend Ann Brash attended every one of Don's classes that she could get to—at the University of New Hampshire's adult learning centers (where I first met her), at our home, and then at church—and remembers them better than I do. She has never failed to help me when we talk things through, to let me know when I've gotten off-track, or to assist me in cleaning up my inexpertly prepared manuscripts, despite the heavy load of her own editorial responsibilities. Thank you, Ann, always.

Father Stephen Freeman, I thank you for writing not only one but two Forewords to this book: one of them for a first draft that had to bow to the different needs of a second. Not a small commitment for a man so hard at work on so many fronts! I am grateful as well, Fr. Stephen, for your deep understanding and appreciation of Don and his work.

Sydney Lea, prolific writer, former Vermont poet laureate, Don's dear friend and longtime Dartmouth colleague and Frost Place Board chairman, has read the whole document at least once and has always been ready and modestly willing to share his knowledge of poetry and the fruits of his good friendship with Don when I've sought help from him.

Deacon Justin Jackson, of Hillsdale College and Holy Ascension Orthodox Church in Albion, Michigan, who keeps up with the ongoing international conversation arising from René Girard's writings, kindly helped me to make a number of salutary changes in updating and tweaking Don's discussion of mimetic violence.

I thank Matthew Brown, a poet who first reached out to me on Facebook a decade ago because he'd fallen in love with Don's Psalter. With his wife, Kay, he has become a good friend, supporting me immeasurably in the final stages of preparing this book for publication, especially the chapter of poems, to which he urged and then helped me to add Don's wonderful poem "A Comedy" (published in a 1974 *Franconia Review*). He also took on the job of proofing the final document for me before it went to Wipf and Stock (his own publisher as well).

Benedict Sheehan, son, composer, conductor, teacher, and father of Don's and my seven granddaughters, is perhaps the busiest and most talented man I know. Yet he remains even now the person best able to understand my language and to travel with me on some of the unusual paths his father and I would (and still do through these books) take together. He has thus been able to support me at some crucial moments throughout my work on publishing Don's writings, mostly by listening well, once encouraging me by confessing to the same doubts about his own work that I have about mine (which I hope are even the smallest bit as unfounded as his!). He has also contributed a chapter to the book that adds important dimensions to his father's work and points toward other and marvelous applications of it.

I am grateful in a different and very tangible way to my son David, who offered me a place to live for two years mid-pandemic, a room of my own in which to carry on with my work, and the opportunity to be present to his family in New York during the final months of his dear wife Tara's life. Since her passing, his and my grandson Riley's integration of me into their life, in this multi-difficult time for all of us, remains a great blessing, and gave us an opportunity to reconnect after the unhappy process of selling our beloved Vermont home—which they and their generous friends had worked hard to help us build. And he goes on helping me each time my own pilgrimage takes me someplace new.

After two years in New York, I made the long-pondered decision to move back to New England to rejoin the Orthodox parish, Holy Resurrection, in Claremont, New Hampshire, where Don and I had felt most at home. Thank God, I find it still to be home and am more grateful than I can say for its financial support of Don's work, for being received into this Church family as if I'd never gone away, given house room for a year by parishioners Rex and Iris Houdyshel, and then a temporary apartment in the Rectory itself. Chief among these who have contributed their time and intelligence to my completing the book are Amy Chan, Codie Ferguson Chevalier, Iris Houdyshel, Nancy Kane, Mary Beth Koons, Anastasia Rodzianko, and Betsy Kane Weiss—with special thanks to Tasya for her wisdom and encouragement; to Nancy, an outstanding English teacher with a keen ear for confusing pronoun references and sentences that don't quite make sense, who helped edit various sections, especially the Glossary entry on Inwardness; to John Taylor Carr for his help with the permissions; and to Ben Gavette for sharing his computer expertise with an old lady who has none. I thank Fr. Andrew, always, for his generosity in creating and sharing his icons, and Brett Nolte for his photo of St. Donatos.

Indexer Stephen Ullstrom, who won a prestigious Canadian award for his index to Don's previous book, *The Shield of Psalmic Prayer*, was delighted to take this one on as well. Thank you, Stephen! Good indexes were so important to Don that he has been known to handwrite his own for books that lacked them! I am especially grateful to those whose written words have contributed so much to the book: Courtney Cook, Fr. Mircea

Geana, Cleopatra Mathis, Hilary Mullins, and Benedict Sheehan; and to Katherine Hyde for her encouragement years ago to keep on making it the book I wanted it to be.

Last, though in truth this belongs first, I thank Joseph Letendre, who introduced me to St. Xenia. I can't imagine this book existing without her presence to my life and Don's and to the book itself! I have discovered that it takes a wide, vibrant, and generous community of the living as well as the intercession of saints to make a good book. Thank you!

—*Xenia Sheehan*

APPENDIX A

"Then It Was Love"

Don's Love Poem as Chiasmus

XENIA SHEEHAN

On Becoming Two Persons:
An Interpersonal Narrative

It was shouting and fraud. Then it was love.
—D. S. poem, April 1963

THIS CONCLUDING LINE OF Don's poem may be the simplest statement of the mystery of antinomy. The poem it concludes was written in the month that Don and I met, exactly sixty years ago at the time of this writing. It is a poem in which the chiastic expression of antinomies makes actual the transforming exchange enacted by love.

The shouting. It had pierced the scary silences of Don's alcohol-ruled home. It was conspicuously absent in my very sober one. For one thing, I was approaching my first birthday when Pearl Harbor was attacked. It wasn't long before my father left his Forest Service job in the mountains of the northwest to move his family back east to his home town: Washington, DC. There he was soon deep in top secret work at the Pentagon sixteen hours a day and, à la Benedict Cumberbatch in *The Imitation Game*, carrying the fate, or at least the weight, of the world on his shoulders. I've learned recently that my family, especially my parents, living so close to the war (though, I thank God, not the hot part of it), are all members of "that generation that didn't talk."[182] We certainly didn't. I think Don's mother probably didn't, and his father seems to have handled everything, for most of his adult years, with alcohol, which generated considerable shouting. In Don's and my early life together, there was a bit of shouting, briefly, as we began our work of merging the antinomies we had each brought to the business of learning to be and to live *in love*. It probably inspired our early discovery of courtesy. Our closest friend, David Keller, wrote a wedding masque for our twentieth anniversary entitled "The Marriage of Courage and Courtesie."

But the fraud. Yes, there was fraud, too, at the beginning. We both had histories. We both had masks we were used to wearing, faces and posings we'd learned to present to the world. And we both had a healthy and so far largely unshareable dose of what Don calls "inwardness," by which he means something not at all obvious, connecting it with God's statutes implanted and sung by Him within the life and heart of all of creation (see the glossary). We were both protecting, perhaps fiercely as one protects a child, the very parts of ourselves that *could* love and be loved. Young as we were, we knew the hurt of love's failure. So for both of us, there was some recognition—beyond all of our unpromising surface differences—of the hidden *person* of the other. Don writes in chapter 6 on St. Symeon of one's personhood being *called out* by another, to discover love in what has called you out to them and them to you. Surely this partakes of Love Himself.

So imagine this scene in the midst of our shared but unshared worlds of shouting and silence, truth and fraud: Across from me at my own kitchen table stands this definitely "cool," slightly tipsy guy, playing his father's game of womanizing—being "about his father's business," he once called it. Understand, in this moment I know nothing of him or the world he comes from, not even his name; and the one he tells me at first is a false one (Al, I think). I sort of recognize the come-on as practiced fraud, but still I fall for it. More accurately, I fall *through* it, because I have been called out. I only see this now. And, much to his surprise, he—the true he—was also called.

I'm not much of a game-player (beyond painfully slow and serious Scrabble and only with wooden tiles), so I took him seriously, as a person. I think it surprised him to find that his fraud had landed him in reality. And in the poem he says that *he* got *me* drunk on belief he didn't even have. And that gave *me* the strength, or madness, to pull down houses and kick apart *my* lies. And it's true. That's just what we did. I won't say *he* or *I* did. These identity markers were in some complicated process of exchange.

In the meantime, I called in sick at my job and flew home to my parents. Not helpful; they were having their own marital problems at the time, and I discovered I was no longer a child. But Don wrote this poem, which I want to share with you here in more depth, because it's a such a lovely chiasmus. It may be exactly what love itself is and how it moves. I don't know how else it could be said but in a multidimensional crisscrossing way such as this. Unless his algebraic topologist roommates at the time could have done it in their gorgeous mathematical formulas.

I don't remember knowing the poem existed until I began searching the files to make this book and came across the slender manila folder his mother had lovingly saved. I have printed it here, the stanzas at least, in a roughly *chiastic* form because that's what the poem acts and feels like to me. The form serves to move it into three-dimensionality, likely more, if, as I believe, Christ—Love Himself— is present to the foundation of every genuine love. For I suspect chiasmus to be a God-made rather than a man-made form, in which Christ stands always in the center. (And yes, I am aware that the form was present in classical and even ancient times, but so was God.) Did Don mean the poem to be a chiasmus? I can't say. To me, the intricate back and forth quality of it, the exchanges, the mirrorings one of the other—to me they all feel profoundly life-giving in a way that chiasmus seems uniquely able to portray. As he neared the end of this first year of full-time immersion in graduate study of poetry, he could certainly have known about chiasmus; but also, the subject matter may call out the form.

Then It Was Love

Like a shouting, fraudulent drunk,
   Tough on hoped-for courage
I roared love at you, love and love.
   And it was hope.

   Then I got you wild drunk
     On the belief I didn't have.
   You pulled houses down, mad with it.
    I was stunned.

     Kicking apart your lies you found
       Feet to walk with.
     Your eyes burning with my love,
       You came to me.

And it was hope. Then it was fear
　　Where belief should have been.
I was frozen by the fact of giving
　　What I didn't believe: myself.

　—Afterwards it was love, touched into life,
　　A believing beyond hope, beyond belief.
It was to know you, to love myself.
　　But it was hope

First
And to be drunk, to need to be drunk,
　　To shout out the voice
Of the terrible need to give up the fraud

I couldn't give up: it was my hope.
　　Then it was the chill fear
To give. You gave, teaching me to take of you
　　And thereby to take

The voice of my need and speak
Love. And it was myself, still and certain,
　　Honest in the knowing of you.
It was shouting and fraud. Then it was love.

Powered by hoped-for courage (note: not *actual* courage; hope is the activator here), the speaker moves from shouting to roaring to perhaps transferring—actually giving?—the stunned strength of his own emotion to the beloved so that she receives *from him* the strength to kick apart *her own* lies and burn with *his* love. Then at the center, bounded or even embraced by hope "where belief should have been," he remains "frozen," unable to believe or give "myself"; but something mysterious and essential has simply *happened*, some mutual knowing, one of the other, has taken place, hope has yielded itself to actuality, life has arisen, *believing* in himself has become possible, and the direction takes a turn to "afterwards." Love has been "touched into life," and believing has jumped beyond hope and even beyond belief to become the reality of *knowing* the other; this takes him out of self—to knowing "you," which allows him—or has become the same as—to love himself. And it seems to me that the repetition of hope at the center's end, apart from structurally bracketing the center, is an acknowledgment of hope as the vehicle for all the impossible exchanges of inward reality that have created fertile ground for the mystery of Love to occur.

Proceeding outward from the center, the speaker recapitulates, now with self-knowledge, what has happened. First there was *need*, which led to shouting and turned out to be "the terrible need to give up the fraud," the false self. Such shadow selves can't love. Then he sees that, through hope, his encounter in himself of the "chill fear to give" is in turn encountered by the beloved's "teaching me to take of you," which allows him to use the *voice* of his love in a new way: no longer roaring, but rather to "speak love." *His* voice has become "honest in the knowing of *you*." The shouting and fraud has transformed to love.

The center of the chiasmus is here a place where the agony of antinomy—perhaps many other unacknowledged antinomies as well, covered up till now by the mutual fraud and unknowing of self and other—this agony is transformed into love in the great mystery of two people encountering one another in such a way that love is "touched into life." It would not be too much to say that the experience of antinomy is given us precisely *in order to learn love*, and that it is at root a daily, even a moment by moment way in which we are made able to be with our Lord on the cross, which is Love's greatest fulfillment of all. For the chiastic crossing, the center of the *chi*, should be understood as a cross. Even though resurrection may arise from it, the agony is real. Even though it may bring oppositions into a peaceful relation, it is Christ's Peace for which we pray, and this peace acts upon all our fraud and unbelief to make it come True; that is, to true it, make it honest, so that we may speak love beyond fear and believe beyond belief. Otherwise, it is not really love, not a place where Christ can abide. But it is still a cross. So it will not be a tranquil process. And it takes time. Even all these years after Don's passing, I feel I may just be beginning to get it. Sometimes I think we are doing it together. I'd like that. As Don wrote to his father: "the heavenly untwisting continues for you, in me because of you." And does it work the other way as well? Does it remain an exchange? Do our untwistings and prayers for those who have "gone on" help it to happen for them as well? I hope it does.

It was shouting and fraud: our mutual need to give up the fraud. Then it was love. You and I made one another better than we were. In this way did Love subsume the fraud. May the heavenly and chiastic untwisting continue—in me because of you, and in you because of me. —Memorial Day, 2023

APPENDIX B

Bibliographical Note on Envy, Contagion, and Meltdowns

COURTNEY COOK

For further reading on overcoming violence, Prof. Donald Sheehan recommends:

The Brothers Karamazov by Fyodor Dostoevsky, translated from the Russian by Richard Pevear and Larissa Volokhonsky (Knopf, 1992). This book is defined by Dostoevsky's understanding of what it takes to be and to have a brother—the task is to overcome all the contagions and sicknesses that we know as violent processes.

The Girard Reader by René Girard (Crossroad/Herder and Herder, 1996). Girard describes his own progress to his insights and how his personal experience led him to articulate his understanding of violence.

The Theatre of Envy (Oxford, 1991) is Girard's commentary on Shakespeare's understanding of envy-driven violence.

The Gospel of Mark. The issue of collective violence against a single person is most completely understood by the author of the Gospel—why it happens, what it looks like when it happens, and what it means not to participate in it. Reading the Gospels is what led René Girard to his discoveries.

Love Thy Neighbor: A Story of War by Peter Maas (Knopf, 1996). Maas was with *The Washington Post* in Bosnia in 1992 and 1993. He wrote this book about the horror stories that he saw and reported—and some that he couldn't report. He perfectly describes the violent dynamic that produced that area's meltdown.

Violence Unveiled: Humanity at the Crossroads by Gil Bailie (Crossroads, 1995). A wide-ranging and profound treatment of the anthropology of violence that is luminously accessible.

APPENDIX C

Donald Sheehan's Published Books and Articles

Arranged in reverse chronological order

Books

The Shield of Psalmic Prayer: Reflections on Translating, Interpreting, and Praying the Psalter. Comp. and ed. Xenia Sheehan. Foreword, Sydney Lea. Ancient Faith, 2020.

The Grace of Incorruption: The Selected Essays of Donald Sheehan on Orthodox Faith and Poetics. Ed. Xenia Sheehan. Foreword, Christopher Merrill. Paraclete, 2015.

The Psalms of David: Translated from the Septuagint Greek. Ed. Xenia Sheehan and Hieromonk Herman Majkrzak. Wipf and Stock, 2013.

Pavel Florensky's *Iconostasis.* Trans. Donald Sheehan and Olga Andrejev. St. Vladimir's Seminary, 1996.

"The Spirit of God Moved Upon the Face of the Waters: Orthodox Holiness and the Natural World," in John Chryssavgis and Bruce V. Foltz, *Toward an Ecology of Transfiguration* (New York: Fordham, 2013).

Numerous introductory essays in *The Breath of Parted Lips: Voices from The Robert Frost Place,"* I (CavanKerry, 2001).

Articles

"Shakespeare, St. Isaac the Syrian, and the Choral Experience of Envy" in James Jordan, *The Musician's Soul* (Chicago: GIA, 1999).

"Envy: The Artist's Affliction," In *New York Arts Council Newsletter* (Spring 1999).

"Anger in the Psalms," *In Our Midst,* Holy Resurrection Orthodox Church, Claremont, NH (December 1998).

"Sacred Violence and the Way of the Cross," *In Our Midst*, Holy Resurrection Orthodox Church, Claremont, NH (Spring 1997).

"The Seeds of Iconography: Notes on Beginning the Practice," *Orthodox New England* (Spring 1988).

"Mary de Rachewiltz's Italian Translation of Pound's Cantos I–XXX: A Prosodic Note," *Paideuma* (Spring 1983).

"Hesiod's 'Works and Days': An Introduction," *Arion* 3:4 (Spring 1978).

"The Reality of Rhythm: Two Recent Translations of the Homeric Hymns," *Chicago Review* (Summer 1976).

"The Whole of Harmonium: The Idea of Music in Wallace Stevens," in *The Fifties: Fiction, Drama, Poetry*, ed. Warren French (Everett/Edwards, 1970).

"The Silver Sensibility: Five Recent Books of American Verse," *Contemporary Literature* (1971).

"The Supreme Plato: A Reading of Wallace Stevens' 'Notes Toward a Supreme Fiction,'" in *The Forties: Fiction, Drama, Poetry*, ed. Warren French (1970).

"Varieties of Technique: Seven Recent Books of American Verse," *Contemporary Literature* (1969).

"A Reading of Dante's *Rime Petrose,*" *Italica* (June 1968).

Glossary

XENIA SHEEHAN

THE BOOK INCLUDES TERMS that may be unfamiliar and one or two that carry uncommon meanings. Glossed here are: Akathist; Antinomy; Ascesis/Asceticism; Aspects of the Soul: Appetitive, Intelligent, and Incensive; Chiasmus/Chiastic; Christ's Commandments; Dianoia/Dianoetic (see Nous/Noetic); Icon/Iconic; Intelligible and Sensible; Invisible World (see Nous/Noetic); Inwardness; Kenosis/Kenotic; Nous/Noetic; Personhood; Phenomenological Abeyance; *Sortes* (see Inwardness); The Prayer of the Heart; Statutes (see Inwardness).

Akathist

A twenty-four-stanza hymn sung in the Orthodox Church, generally composed to honor or petition different saints. The *Akathist Hymn to the Mother of God* (seventh-century Byzantium) is the prototype for all hymns that have been fashioned after this style. The word itself, from Greek, means "an unsitting prayer"; that is, it is traditionally prayed while standing, or while moving in procession. Akathists are a living poetic form within the Church and continue to be composed as new saints are canonized, or as a way of praying for help with a particular issue such as raising children, dealing with alcohol or cancer or a particularly troublesome time in your life. A modern favorite, "Glory to God for All Things," written from a concentration camp in the last century, was composed for chorus and orchestra by Benedict Sheehan and premiered in New York in 2023. See also chapter 10.

Antinomy

"The affirmation of two contrasting or opposed truths, which cannot be reconciled on the level of discursive reason, although a reconciliation is possible on the higher level of contemplative experience" (Ware, "Debate about Palamism," 46). Their reconciliation, however, requires that neither pole of the opposition be rejected. This is perhaps the most important term to understand in the writings gathered here. The author employs it mostly in ways that Fr. Pavel Florensky developed it in *The Pillar and Ground of the Truth*. He explicates it most fully herein in chapter 10, where he says:

> Antinomicalness is . . . the experience of disjunction, the experience wherein human discursive rationality breaks helplessly apart in the face of—better, *in the teeth of*—harsh, dissonant realities. Such realities are the very ground of all biblical (indeed, all *human*) experience. . . . Fr. Pavel writes that the *keeping distinct of the two terms while cohering their contradiction* is the path of Orthodox ascetic discipline, a path characterized by an always deepening love and a forever widening humility.

What Don calls our "noetic beauty" depends on this, for *earthly antinomy is the way that divine beauty takes root in us* (chapter 10). See especially the whole of Part Two.

Ascesis/Asceticism

A Greek term originally referring to athletic training is an analogy that Saint Paul was wont to use (Phil 3:12–16; 2 Tim 4:7). The practice of asceticism within the Orthodox Christian tradition is not merely a physical exercise, although it may have this as one component; it is rather a setting aside of self-aggrandizing pursuits, concerns, and desires in order to reach full actualization of the *person*. The goal of all ascetic life, says St. Isaac the Syrian, is to make "straight the pathways in the heart." The sin that led to Adam's fall (following Schmemann in *For The Life of the World*)—that is, his and Eve's choice to eat of the one fruit that God had *not* given and blessed for man's consumption—was a "delusional process of self-glorification" in which the "self" overwhelmed the potential "person." Called to grow into personhood by means of loving and eucharistic (thanks-giving) communion with God through his interactions with the world, Adam acted instead on a desire of the world for *itself alone*, thus for *himself*—for the pleasure the world could offer *him*; thereby breaking his and his descendants' communion with God. And so the concept of *self*—quite different from *personhood*, which arises from our giving of our will to God—came into being. In Orthodox ascetic tradition (see especially chapter 18), long, careful ascesis—refraining in all ways from reinforcing the dominance of the "self" in one's life—is the way to right relationship with God in and as personhood. See also Personhood.

Aspects of the Soul: Appetitive, Intelligent, and Incensive

The soul is divided into three parts according to the Greek Christian Fathers: appetitive, intelligent, and incensive, which can each be used either positively (according with nature, as created by God) or negatively, in a way "contrary to nature and leading to sin." The appetitive is the soul's desiring power, especially vulnerable to passion. The "incensive can be used positively to repel demonic attacks or to intensify desire for God" or negatively "as self-indulgent, disruptive thought and action." The intelligent, *logikos*, is the ruling aspect, closely connected with Logos "and therefore with the divine Intellect . . and qualifies the possessor of spiritual knowledge." (*Philokalia*, Glossary)

Chiasmus/Chiastic

Much of Don's work was involved with understanding and explicating the patterns he discerned within lyric art, particularly this one. Technically, a *chiasm* or *chiasmus* (derived from the Greek letter *chi*, the letter X) is a verse pattern in which the first and final lines or portions of a given text connect to or echo one another; then the second connects in some way (such as repetition, opposition, emphasis, echoing, enlargement) to the next-to-last; the third to the third-to-last; and so on, until a more or less exact midpoint is reached (often somewhere slightly past the numerical center). Don writes in chapter 12 that frequently the connection between paired lines is one of intensification, with the second line in the chiastic pair in some way deepening the first, making it sharper and more drastic; and the intensification derives from, happens as a result of, or emerges out of, the line at the center. Thus the pattern's midpoint provides a kind of pivot, one upon which the passage's entire significance may be seen to turn. Everything first flows toward this pivot; then everything flows out from it, changed in some way—transformed, indeed transfigured, without being at all "transcenden-talized." Don claims that the entire Psalter has its chiastic center in Psalm 77[78]:34–38 (see *Shield of Psalmic Prayer*, chapter 10).

Christ's Commandments

What does it mean to keep Christ's commandments? I was once intro-duced to a long list of them that came to seem to me insufficient, even a bit legalistic. I referred my question to Fr. John Konkle, who agreed with me that the commandments of Christ are not (simply) the Ten Command-ments, or the Mosaic Law, or any other Old or New Testament "collection of teachings/imperatives." Rather, he said, they "set a higher bar than the commandments of the law." He went on:

> I believe that the New Testament gives an entirely different un-derstanding of "commandment"—"a new commandment I give you, that you love one another as I have loved you," and "greater love has no man than this, that he lay down his life for his friends." So we are invited into an intimate relationship with the self-emptying Source of life, a loving response to the voice of the Shepherd, a living law written on soft hearts. Thus, when we hear "go the extra mile," "turn the other cheek," "do good to those who harm you," and so forth, we're not simply being given a new set of commandments written on the same tablets of stone, but we are being seeded with the discerning embrace of the voice of Christ, the piercing conviction of the Holy Spirit, the loving protection of the unoriginate Father, the uncreated Grace that energizes us to follow the Voice into the green pastures of Trinitarian love and union and glory. The Old Testament law, including the Ten Commandments, is a tutor to point us to Christ; that is, to a per-son. The commandments of Christ *are* that person; they are love, profoundly relational and personal.[183]

This is the very way of personhood in Christ that Don seems to have intu-ited, searched for, and found: a way which only the *nous*, the spiritual mind given us by God for this purpose, can open for us and lead us along.

Dianoia/Dianoetic. See Nous/Noetic

Icon/Iconic

An icon, in Don's words, is understood in the Orthodox Church as not just a portrait that follows certain traditional rules, but a "place where touching and being touched by God [is] actually possible." Hilary Mullins (chapter 7) calls it "a portal for the holy, an actual opening through which God moves toward us and through which we can move toward God, where indeed we are invited to do so." In it, "we are to see every possible human expression, with every conceivable human emotion, all of them equally vividly present." Thus, an iconic *presence* is one that can guide us to true personhood.

Don writes in chapter 15 that the Orthodox icon "touches what is at once the deepest mystery and the simplest fact about the human face seen in Christ: its aliveness so far exceeds everything we mean by life that even death itself is no end to it." For Florensky and St. Isaac, this is the *countenance* that the icon seeks to depict; we are given it when we can disengage our gaze from the face of the other and look instead into the face of God.

In the opening to Part Three, writing of what we may call the *iconic face* of the newly made Perelandrian King, C. S. Lewis says that "the very beauty of it lay in the certainty that it was a copy, like and not the same, an echo, a rhyme, an exquisite reverberation of the uncreated music prolonged in a created medium" (*Perelandra*, 177). Adam and Eve were created to have just such a countenance, as the saints have, toward which all humankind are called to grow.

The Intelligible and the Sensible. See also Nous/Noetic

That which is *intelligible* can be understood by the *intellect* or *nous* "by means of direct apprehension or spiritual perception." The *sensible* is that which is grasped or understood by the physical senses.

Invisible World. See Nous/Noetic

Inwardness

Inwardness is a rich word used many times in *The Shield of Psalmic Prayer* and in this book as well. Don approached and understood it from at least three directions: First, the *sortes* reading he was given in 1986 at the time of his tonsure as Reader in the Orthodox Church (Acts 1:12–22), marking his movement from laity to clergy (see *Shield of Psalmic Prayer*, xxviii–xxx);

second, from his experience of teaching poetry as a giving of one's own art to another (see chapter 7 herein); and third, from Psalms (see *Shield of Psalmic Prayer,* index).

The Going-With-Ones of Acts 1

The *sortes* was a shocking reading that must have given rise to considerable reflection when Don received it. In that part of Acts, following Christ's Ascension forty days after His Crucifixion, the disciples must replace Judas from among those who had been with Christ throughout His ministry. They were called συνελθόντες (*synelthontes*), "the going-with-ones." Judas, formerly *within* that group, had chosen to put himself *outside* God's work of healing and making whole in love. He had chosen against "going-with" our Lord into the Resurrection, and in this condition he died alone from the spontaneous gushing out of his innards in a place, the Field of Blood, where none would thereafter be allowed to live.

Don refers to "this scattering of inwardness" by saying that, "All through the Psalms there is this rending, this scattering of inwardness into the billion fragments we call the world." Judas's inwardness is literally and grotesquely expelled, even taken from him. For, like Adam and Eve, what Judas did, Don writes, "was to pull all choosing *into himself,* to see himself as author of his acts"; whereas the inwardness of the *synelthontes* does the opposite, allowing us actually to go *out of ourselves* to be present with Christ in such a way that we can plunge *into death and resurrection with Him.* Without this inwardness, to which we can now give the definition of being-with-Christ, we are simply dead. We have no *within.*

What would this have meant for Don personally? It was a strong message, which I think he took quite seriously as something he was being told about his new life in the Church. It was both a welcoming of him—a choosing even—if not exactly into the circle of the *synelthontes,* then into the sphere of Christ's many faithful servants. It may also have been a warning about the immensity of the loss that comes with *not* taking this new relationship with Christ seriously, or, worse, of merely seeming to do so.

Was it in fact a pivot point for him, a call away from a self-generated literary inwardness (created by nurturing his own inner world of poetry as a place of safety and solace in the wake of his first family's brokenness), and toward a new kind of inwardness of being-with-Christ *within* and *through* the literature that he loved? Might this also explain why, over time, he mostly stopped writing his own poetry and turned his career—both at The Frost Place, as described so eloquently by Hilary Mullins in chapter

7, and in the classroom—toward helping others discover and refine their own art, their own poems?

I Shall Never Forget Thy Statutes

I shall never forget thy statutes,
In them thou hast quickened me to life.
I am thine, O Lord, save me,
For I have sought thy statutes. (Ps 118[119]:93–94).

One of the most-often repeated words in Psalm 118(119)] is חֻקִּים (huqqim), "statutes" (Greek δικαιώματα, dikaiōmata). These two lines form the midpoint, the heart, of the psalm that Don refers to as the Great Psalm of Resurrection. He writes in *The Shield of Psalmic Prayer*:

> In Rabbinic commentary, statutes are the foundational patterns of the created world, the patterns with which God first created and still sustains the entire creation. Therefore, the statutes are the patterns that we cannot fully comprehend with our minds, for their actions and operations reach far beyond—wider, higher, and deeper—than merely human thoughts can even conceivably begin to reach. Yet these statutes constitute the very inwardness we possess and, in doing so, they provide the ways whereby we actually live, they are the divine patterns of our earthly souls, the way we remember God and, hence, remember who we are in Him. And at the same time, the statutes are the divine patterns of aliveness within all created things, within each tiny blade of grass or the heart of every tree. To remember the statutes is therefore to know—deeply and widely—who truly you are and also who all created beings truly are: and therefore to have divinely given aliveness within you. To forget the statutes is to die to both the creation and the Creator. (95)

The isolated *self*—which tries to know itself apart from these divine patterns—is a product of our first parents' fall, a creation of our own human making, apart from that of God. When this self is magnified, it seeks to rule (rather than find God in) the space between the world's oppositions. Such self-centered attempts at diminishing the oppositional stresses always lean toward our own comfort or pleasure, our own "side," rather than seeking true resolution. Thus they only intensify the God-given antinomies; for the self, in Luciferic envy, is seeking to take God's place, which ends in fracturing His creation into a multitude of warring factions.

I urge you to look back to the book's Foreword, where Fr. Stephen says that "the 'gap' between God and creation is overcome in the Incarnation, and continually in the sacraments and abiding work of divinization." The first "gap" St. Maximus the Confessor reveals to us in his five fundamental oppositions is that between the uncreated and the created, God and His Creation. It is Christ who fills it and brings it into unity, not our*self*, unless we enter into the gap in search of Him.

In Psalms, Don says, "we are in the intense circle of His praying. . . . And, as we read—and pray deeply—the Psalms, we are becoming ourselves psalmic." *Inwardness* is both the vehicle for this and its result. It "is the action of memory wherein God incarnates in the human mind while the human mind becomes deified" (*Shield of Psalmic Prayer,* 133). In praying the very Psalms our Lord prayed in His lifetime, giving Himself *into* Psalms to make them whole *in* Him—in so praying, we are also *remembering*: remembering His presence in them as Creator of the sacred history they portray, remembering His statutes. It is a history of which He Himself is both the Artificer and the culmination and in which His art becomes ours in His giving of Himself to us in our remembering of Him.

True Inwardness

Thus, true inwardness, as Don writes, is a re-musicalizing of one's soul. For this very purpose, I believe he would have said, Christ gave us, prophetically, through David and the other psalmic poets, Psalms. By praying them during His lifetime on earth, Don says, Christ took Psalms, in all their vast and scattered history, into Himself and "made them into one unified and complete work," "*one experience of personhood.*"

> He did not "personalize" the Psalms; rather, He made them responsive to His Personhood—that is, who He was (and is) in (and as) God. He accomplished the great work of *making inward* the Psalms. . . . and in doing so made comparably whole the entire course of Israelite history. (*Shield of Psalmic Prayer,* 2–3)

In our regular reading of Psalms, Don believed, Christ does this within our own lives as well.

In sum, "inwardness" expresses the first and most important antinomy: we become larger as we choose for our *self* and its desirings to become smaller; we are larger on the inside than on the out; in standing with Christ and confining our hungers to Him, whom the human race once tried to confine within the finitude of a tomb, we become infinite.

Kenosis/Kenotic

Derived from the Greek verb *kenou*, which carries the meaning of draining something empty. In the Christian context, an act of *kenosis* carries the weight of extreme humility, epitomized in the self-emptying love of Jesus Christ seen in His Incarnation and His death on the Cross.

Nous/Noetic, Dianoia/Dianoetic

According to Orthodox Christian understanding based on patristic texts written between the fourth and the fifteenth centuries, we have two kinds of mind. One, in the Greek terminology, is the *dianoia* (translated in the *Philokalia* glossary as "reason"). That excellent glossary occurs at the end of each volume. The dianoetic mind, or dianoia, is

> . . . the discursive, conceptualizing and logical faculty in man, the function of which is to draw conclusions or formulate concepts deriving from data provided either by revelation or spiritual knowledge or by sense observation. The knowledge is consequently of a lower order than spiritual knowledge and does not imply any direct apprehension or perception of the inner essences or principles of created beings, still less of divine truth itself. Indeed, such apprehension or perception, which is the function of the intellect [*nous*], is beyond the scope of the reason.

The nous "dwells in the depths of the soul" and "constitutes the innermost aspect of the heart" (St. Diadochos); it is called also "the eye of the heart" (Makarian Homilies). It is given to us so that we may know God. Its work is thus more concerned with what we might call the *invisible*, to adopt both Don's terminology and that of Righteous John, Wonderworker of Kronstadt, whom Don quoted in chapter 5 as saying that "the invisible plays the first part in the whole world. . . . [184]

In his discussion of Dante's *Paradiso* in chapter 9, Don says: "The way the blest of Paradise converse is from a ground of love, which is perfect and therefore unspoken comprehension. Each time this happens to Dante a conceptual shift occurs." I think we may be seeing here a description, perhaps a culmination, of how the *nous* functions in us and where it is leading us. That is, when we engage the *nous*, we engage Love—with the help of what Don also calls in this chapter "courtesy"—and this indeed shifts how we see things and keeps the dialogue going. Moreover, it moves as perfect, unspoken comprehension that simply changes the ground we stand on.

In chapter 12, Don uses the phrase "the Mind of Christ" synony-
mously with *nous*, drawing his terminology from 1 Cor 2:16: "We have
the mind of Christ." "St. Paul's point in this chapter of the epistle," he says,
"is that we possess in ourselves the mind of Christ *solely because* God has
given us this mind in order that we may know—in St. Paul's own words—
'the things freely given us by God.'"

Don explains that "the nous works by means of immediate experience,
intuition, or 'simple cognition'" (St. Isaac's term). But he cautions that, as the
"highest faculty," the *nous* is also much more than what we usually mean by
"intuition." In his extended discussion of *nous* in the section of chapter 10
concerning "The Miracle of the *Akathist*," Don concludes that "as the nous
acts to comprehend God, it is directly acted upon by God" and is "made
holy, made in fact divine."

Both of these mental functions are necessary to our rationality. Both
constitute our *reason* and are essential, not only to the full meaning of what
it means to be a rational being, but to *knowing* God—not just knowing *about*
God, which the *dianoia* can do on its own, but actually knowing *Him*, in a
"straight into the heart" way. It is interesting to reflect on this in relation to
St. Maximus the Confessor's discussion of the five fundamental divisions in
God's creation described in the book's introduction. The second in St. Maximus's list, following the distinction between the uncreated and the created,
is, within the created realm, that "between the intelligible and the sensible."
It is a distinction that it is our human calling to mediate, without obliterating
either term, and to return, sanctified through our mediation, to God.

In chapter 5, Don writes the following, based on his experience with
his father's alcoholism (and witnessed to in his poems):

> For the alcoholic, this shaped and useful relation between the
> visible world and its invisible energies becomes shapeless and
> uncontrollable. As his language becomes solely a means for emo-
> tional expression, his grasp on reasoned thought, along with the
> orderly patterns of courtesy, begins to dissolve. For such cour-
> teous thought gives form and even substance to our part of a
> bridge between the visible world and the invisible energies that
> inform it. These energies are (as the biblical and older literary
> understanding saw quite exactly) angels or messengers from
> the invisible God. And as the alcoholic's ability to thoughtfully
> reason fades or becomes disordered, he loses the sense of angelic
> presence in and behind the visible world and so begins to experi-
> ence the invisible energies precisely in the form of the alcohol
> itself: that is, as something fluid, infinite, dark, and engulfing.[185]

When we combine Don's and his father's experience with what Orthodox patristic tradition and St. John of Kronstadt tell us, we can see that the alcoholic (or perhaps any person held in the grip of an addiction) has likely deformed or stunted the development of his nous. Such deformation would lead to a growing incapacity for a life-giving relationship both with the nous and with the reality—God Himself—that it reveals to us and enables us to know and enter. If the alcoholic will not restore this relationship, he eventually, as St. John says, "loses life and is destroyed." In other words, he has disabled his own noetic functioning and is in dire need of noetic healing. For "all men live through an invisible first cause—God." Without Him, life cannot be. Hence the shapeliness and usefulness of the relation between the visible and invisible (what we more commonly call the mental and spiritual) has retreated out of reach. What it leaves behind is an alcohol-distorted memory or remnant. But—this is very important— it is a remnant capable of being regenerated and renewed, at least at this spiritual level, once the addiction is healed. For the true development of the nous appears to be a reciprocal process of God enlarging it as we properly employ it in our seeking of Him. Such proper use occurs, as Don explains in chapter 6, when the nous takes:

> . . . the way of repentance, the way of following the commandments of Christ, the way of purification in the Holy Orthodox Church. St. Symeon says: "Where there is the keeping of the commandments, there is the purification of the flesh, and [purification] from *the cloud that besets the soul and prevents it from clearly seeing God's ray of light.* Where there is purification, there is illumination." [italics mine]

Don is clear, first in chapter 5 and again in chapter 10, or so I read it, that the two ways of knowing, the noetic and the dianoetic, work profoundly together. They *must* work together. Imagine a child learning the use of only one of these faculties: learning only to measure, calculate, hear and see, recognize and compare similarities and differences; understand sequences of cause and effect, understand and operate computers and machines, etc. Or conversely a child that only plays imaginary games, reads fantasy and fairy tales, interacts with the natural world and its creatures, and learns to love others: this is an essential use of the mind that must be developed early, for it opens the heart and trains the faculty that can know and commune with God. But a child without both functions fully operative, antinomic as they are, is handicapped. We must learn to use both faculties in the ways for which they were given us; that is, to resolve their antinomy.

Don goes on in chapter 10 to describe his own process of learning to paint an icon within the practice of an iconographic tradition in which the preparation of the icon board to receive the holy image, and the painting of the image itself, are likened to our Lenten preparation of ourselves for Holy Pascha. Only at the very end (in Don's experience), with a few tiny master strokes not of his own making, does the holy image suddenly shine forth. The dianoetic practice thus opens to receive the noetic reality.

Don further describes Fr. Florensky's painstaking pursuit of a purely technical, sequential process, faithfully performed in the service of necessity. What he says of this would apply to any work that is *not* self-glorifying, *not* self-willed, *not* self-seeking: spiritual ascesis, for instance, of the sort that seeks, not to make us "happy" or "healthy" or somehow better at being our*self*, but rather moves us beyond self altogether for the sake of others or God Himself. This is holy work, for it devalues the *self* to make room for the *person* to grow. It makes room in us for God.

Don writes of Fr. Pavel's conduct of the technical scientific work required of him in the Russian gulag, saying, he "had acquired the grace of spiritual detachment: that is, he could give his fullest, most compassionate attention to what was immediately at hand while remaining wholly untouched by the surrounding storms of darkness (*Iconostasis*, 15)." Elaborating on this in chapter 10, Don explains that, against stringent camp rules, Fr. Pavel affirmed and enacted his priesthood each day by wearing his cassock, while at the same time "focusing all his mind on the technical work that prison authorities compelled him to do—and by concentrating all his heart on caring for and loving his wracked and dying fellow prisoners." When his life ended before a firing squad, his body was carried through the camp before the hundreds of kneeling prisoners who had become his spiritual children. In breaking the God-hating rules of the gulag to make this reverence, they followed their beloved father in affirming the enduring presence of the Holy even in hell. Fr. Pavel has been considered by many a saint, and so Don called him.

I find myself wondering whether Don's stint in the Army Reserves at the age of seventeen (described in chapter 1)—those grueling disciplines of bootcamp that began with his walking away from an engineered fight with his tentmate, publicly renouncing his own impulse to violence— whether this may have been precursor to, even a kind of purification opening the way for the life-changing experiences at the end of his brief military service. But no matter what our work or service—basic training for military defense of our country, cleaning houses, preparing meals for a soup kitchen, cultivating land in a way that keeps it healthy or feeds a family, giving alms to the poor, tending the sick, keeping a prayer rule, raising a family in Christ—however great or small the work, if it's done for others or for God, or even for good and worthy purposes that God can graciously bless as His own, it leads us closer to Him. That is, through our self-emptying, our *kenosis* in faithful service to others, we allow God room (and permission) to act more fully in our lives. This leads, in time, to the sort of *knowing* of God that comes with and contributes to our noetic enlargement, and we may find ourselves and our work graced with what we experience as a miraculous result, even one that acts backward to configure and bless its beginnings. This is what I believe Don may be suggesting when he speaks of the origins of the *Akathist*. For time and causation can work in more than one direction where the *nous* is involved. God is both *Alpha* and *Omega*, everywhere present, filling all things. Most of us simply haven't developed yet the eyes to see Him in his continuous Presence; to see how our merely linear perception may be insufficient.

Personhood

We find the first and most important clue to what Don means by *personhood* towards the end of chapter 1. He says there that his first college writing teacher "could not give me the great principles of coherence, the archetypes of wholeness and intellectual strength without which no one can write. He could not give me personhood." Clearly, at this early stage, he is, if not making an equation, at least associating personhood with principles of coherence, archetypes of wholeness, and intellectual health—and perhaps most important, with writing, which for many of us is a pathway to understanding.

Don's journey of becoming a person shows him laboring long in one direction, but never that I have seen in a spirit of putting himself forward. He was happy, for instance, to give first place to his ten-minutes younger brother. The journey was for him a way of first finding his voice, then using it to help others to find their true voice, and then at last identifying and understanding the one true voice that he felt he had been hearing all along: "some very faint but very clear voice," he later said, "one I could easily have ignored but somehow would not."

Taking it in context, I am certain that for Don personhood therefore had much to do with *listening*, which has everything to do with *loving* (and vice-versa). Of his college Humanities teacher, Gary Scrimgeour, to whom this book is co-dedicated, Don tells us that

> . . . his was at once for us a *living* voice, one that had been created to love us by the texts he had learned to love and one that therefore bestowed creativity on those who through him

learned to love the texts in return. He often read aloud, and we listened and were moved, for it seemed as if Shakespeare and Goethe were loving us.

This bestowal of creativity has everything to do with personhood, through a reciprocity of giving and receiving ultimately leading to the Creator's conferring of His own creativity on His creation. Taking this praise of Gary as another unintentional chiasmus, the elements are, from the ends inward: the living voice created (by God) to love us and now moving (*quickening* us, as in the center of Ps 118[119]) by means of a man's voice reading aloud to us in a way that confers his voice's capacity to love on the texts themselves, so that the love we are experiencing seems now to come to us through them, the texts. And because we have now learned this love, we are able to be creators ourselves. More concisely: love passes from the Creator to us by means of a human voice speaking certain texts; and the texts then carry the love to their listeners so as to bestow creativity on them in turn. Thus Love is passed from the Creator to us in order that we may ourselves be creators and lovers.

Gary had a great gift to give, and gave it freely! Don carried it forward. He also read aloud and told stories to his children, as his father and Gary had to him; and he spent the better part of his adult life arranging for poets to read poems to other poets and lovers of poetry.

In regard to Don's own writing, at which he found himself entirely inept at 19, Gary taught him how to do it by *listening* to the words and phrases—tone, rhythm, shape—of the great lyric art he had come to love, and then replacing the words with his own, adapting the patterns and sound to his own meanings. (Not all that different from the iconographer's work of faithfully following Holy Tradition until the image results, under one's own or a teacher's hands, in something wholly new and alive yet in some sense still our own creation.)

Hilary Mullins relates in chapter 7 of how Don carried this practice forward later as Director of The Frost Place. There he taught his students to "be quiet and *listen* to the words of our fellow poets, to be silent in the force of emotion they conveyed and let our response be guided by that careful attention to the other." What is that but loving? In chapter 6 Don confirms that "your personhood is made clear in your power to love. In this power you are absolutely unique and irreplaceable: you share your personhood with no one else—at the very moment you find it only in loving another." This absolute uniqueness *is* your personhood, though you discover it in loving another's uniqueness, which fulfills it as your likeness to the One—unique and loving—God. This, more than anything, makes clear to me why envy wholly unmakes us, as some of the chapters in Part Three make clear.

To conclude this entry and move it the next step, I suggest a further hypothesis based on a tiny chiasmus that Don embedded in one of his poems. I print it here not as he wrote it, but in its chiastic shape:

> as if harmony now could
>> create a way of discovering
>>> some buried lyric we missed
>> there where was only
> the utter absence of music.

My hypothesis is this: that the first half of Don's life was a quest for "some buried lyric" he had missed—something that would undo "the utter absence of music" that he had experienced in his early years. He *listened* for that lyric. His opening "as if" I read as making this a prayer. His encounters with lyric art ("harmony now")—*as if* they could solve the problem of music's utter absence—these encounters slowly *created a way* of discovering the missed and buried lyric. I see this as a long process for Don in which, over time, he gathered in the treasures he needed for learning to behold and love God—with one crowning exception, one still buried lyric: the Prayer of the Heart. This, the Lord Himself, the Word, entered into his "actual life on earth" to add to him at the proper time.

Phenomenological Abeyance

"Phenomenological abeyance" (literally, letting phenomena rest) here describes a useful frame of mind in which we can confront antinomical horizons and learn to inhabit the space between them. As Don explains, it relies on behaviors such as "long-guarded speechlessness," "contemplative silence," and courtesy. It is thus a way to approach, not only our encounters with widely differing historical worldviews, or with variant ways of understanding a phenomenon or a text, but also with rending conflicts of perspective or behavior that may vex our personal life.

By extension, then, I believe the term may fruitfully be applied as well to the kind of spiritual growth Don speaks of in chapter 12 as the mind of David becoming the mind of Christ.

The Prayer of the Heart or Jesus Prayer

"Lord Jesus Christ, Son of God, have mercy on me, a sinner." It is the simplest of prayers, prayed continuously in the Orthodox Church, especially in her monasteries, over many centuries, and made even simpler in some practices by dropping off the appositive phrases: "Son of God" and "a sinner." I dropped the latter at first, being uncomfortable calling myself names (as I experienced it then). But whether we already know this about ourselves (I didn't) or simply need the reminder (I often do), the reality is that when we speak this prayer we are over and over reminding ourselves of the great distance, the profound polarity, between ourselves and our Creator. And we, the humblest of the humble, are calling on Him, the highest of the high, the very Son of God, to span that distance with His mercy and raise us into union with Him—a union never meant to be broken.

We ask this despite our manifest unworthiness, despite the fact that we have sinned against Him or against others or against ourselves so many times, by not doing what He asks of us, by not acquiring, or even seeking, the glory for which He made us. Thus through the Prayer of the Heart we engage head-on this primary antinomy between Creator and created, made into a stumbling block at the very beginning by our first ancestors' choice to place their own will before God's and thus to know good and evil in the wrong way.

Since the Fall, this antinomy is where we live; but it remains an antinomy rather than a break, because God never ceases loving us. In the Prayer of the Heart, we seek to restore ourselves to that love in which we *live*—or better, to restore *within ourselves* the love *by* which we live—the only place where there is life. By praying this prayer, we are acknowledging the antinomy of a love that does not strike back when it is rejected but goes on to embrace us even in our rejection of Him who offers it. We are acknowledging that we have created divisions and taken sides in a unity that *cannot* finally be broken, even if we should choose to stand outside it, attempting to expel by our own choice the very breath that first breathed life into us. Now, praying this prayer, we freely take the step to accept that breath and rejoin it, breathing ourselves back into its rhythms.

I call your attention to a stunning antinomy of which Don writes at the end of chapter 4, where he refers to Mother Maria [Gysi]'s naming this prayer "a prayer of the End": a prayer of the moment when we are stripped of everything of this life yet simultaneously alive within the progressions of time, *awake in both realities at once*—this is the key. Don seems to have experienced this while writing the letter of forgiveness he read to his father at his graveside. It was a moment of being carried in a communion of love across the gulf between life and death. And then the prayer came to him. I believe he is telling us that in some way the prayer "matched" this moment and continued to hold open for him the pathway across that gulf, because to be in the prayer was to be in the reality of Love. And the victory of love *in him*—love for his father chosen by him, just as twenty-five years earlier he had chosen *life*—was what opened him to receive the prayer.

Just so, in Don's understanding, are we called to face the ruining oppositions that make such impassable gulfs in our own lives, the afflictions and sufferings and rejections that come toward us. We are to face them by declining to hate either ourselves or those who strike us, by keeping the discipline of stillness and love offered us by the prayer, breathing again with the life-giving Breath. Just so, we free ourselves to remain within the antinomic unity of God's love for us and ours for Him and for all the people He has given us to love—family, friends, students, enemies, whomever He places in our path. I believe this is what Don did in his living and writing and teaching: responding to the call of this Prayer of the Heart to resolve in grateful love the antinomies that were given him.

Notes

The author, a careful scholar, identified many of his quotations and sources, even in his journals. Most of the material herein not having been written for purposes of publication, where annotation was missing and the source seemed fairly clear, I have provided it from online searches where I could, as the family library has been broken up. I have not, however, gone beyond sources I was fairly sure I'd seen him using or could make an educated guess at. Therefore, in some cases I have left it to the determined reader to use GoogleScholar or a library for this purpose. "Ed." is added to those notes that contain actual editorial commentary (something more than an identification or definition) not offered by the author. —*Ed.*

1   Elder Porphyrios, *Wounded by Love: The Life and Wisdom of Elder Porphyrios* (Limni, Greece: Denise Harvey, 2005).

2   In regard to the author's concept of spaciousness (*platysmos* in LXX Greek), the reader is referred here at the outset to Donald Sheehan, *The Grace of Incorruption: The Selected Essays of Donald Sheehan on Orthodox Faith and Poetics,* ed. Xenia Sheehan (Orleans, MA: Paraclete, 2015). See especially 154–57 concerning Ps 118:45, for it is a key element of his thinking. He calls *platysmos* "a word of unique power" (156). "For each of the nine words [for law] in Psalm 118 possesses its own unique spaciousness—a definition, that is, which distinguishes that word from the other eight while simultaneously connecting it to them." —*Ed.*

3   The *molieben* is an Orthodox service of supplication or intercession to a
     particular saint or martyr; it may be served by a lay person.

4   A form of Christian ascetic life, Foolishness for Christ is a long and high-
     ly honored tradition within the Orthodox Church, especially in Russia,
     based on 1 Cor 3:18–19: "Let no man deceive himself. If any man among
     you seemeth to be wise in this world, let him become a fool, that he may
     be wise. For the wisdom of this world is foolishness with God. For it is
     written, He taketh the wise in their own craftiness" (KJV).
          It is said that Xenia also at some point disappeared from Petersburg
     for a period of eight years and that she spent this time visiting the holy
     elders and ascetics of the time, "receiving from them instruction in true
     spiritual life and preparing herself for the difficult labor she was to un-
     dertake as a Fool for Christ's sake." See the St. Xenia Skete "Service to
     Our Blessed in Christ Saint Xenia, Homeless Wanderer of St. Petersburg"
     (Wildwood, CA 96067: St. Xenia Skete, 1992), 4.—*Ed.*

5   "Rhapsody: A Collect," published in *The Franconia Review* 4:2 (1974).

6   The *Philokalia*, a word that translates as "love of the good and beautiful," is
     a five-volume collection of texts written between the fourth and fifteenth
     centuries by spiritual masters of the mystical hesychast tradition of the
     Eastern Orthodox Church. It was compiled by St. Nikodimos of the Holy
     Mountain and St. Makarios of Corinth in the latter half of the eighteenth
     century and translated and edited by G. E. H. Palmer, Philip Sherrard, and
     Kallistos Ware (London, Boston: Faber and Faber, 1979–83). In the English
     translation, each volume contains the same full and excellent glossary at
     the end, written by the editors and translators. See also the entry on *Nous*
     in the glossary for this book.

7   Ps 118[119]: 54. Throughout the book, psalm quotations are from Donald
     Sheehan's translation, *The Psalms of David: Translated from the Septua-
     gint Greek* (Eugene, Oregon: Wipf and Stock, 2013), hereafter Sheehan,
     Psalms. Psalm citations give the Septuagint (LXX) psalm number first,
     followed by that of the Masoretic text and the LXX verse number. —*Ed.*

8   Fyodor Dostoevsky, *The Brothers Karamazov*, trans. and annot. Richard
     Pevear and Larissa Volokhonsky (New York: Farrar, Straus and Giroux,
     2002), 774.

9   Donald Sheehan, *The Shield of Psalmic Prayer* (Chesterton, IN: Ancient
     Faith, 2020).

10 Free E-book at https://gutenberg.ca/ebooks/lewiscs-surprisedbyjoy/lewiscs-surprisedbyjoy-01-h.html, ch. XI, "Check." See also C. S. Lewis, *Surprised by Joy: The Shape of My Early Life* (New York: Harper Collins, 1955), ch. 11. An excellent Audible edition is also available. —*Ed.*

11 C. S. Lewis, *Perelandra* (New York: Scribner, 1972). Free E-book available at http://gutenberg.ca/index.html.

12 Free E-book at https://www.gutenberg.org/cache/epub/27805/pg27805-images.html, ch. 7, "The Piper at the Gates of Dawn." For a lovely recent print edition, see Kenneth Grahame, *The Wind in the Willows* (Hertfordshire: Wordsworth Editions, 2018).

13 Robert D. Stevick, ed., *One Hundred Middle English Lyrics* (Champagne, IL: Univ. of Illinois, 1994).

14 Something about these words was important to Don and stayed with him. I remember him quoting them a number of times. They touch the heart of the matter of antinomy and chiasmus: to return to the place you set out from and find it wholly changed because the journey has wholly changed you. The source is T. S. Eliot's "Little Gidding," *Four Quartets* (Gardners Books: Main edition, April 30, 2001; orig. published 1943). Don wrote his doctoral dissertation at the University of Wisconsin on "The Poetics of Influence: A Study of T. S. Eliot's Uses of Dante" in 1969. In it the "Four Quartets" figured centrally. —*Ed.*

15 Lewis, *Perelandra*, 186.

16 I have borrowed this point, which Don would have loved, from a homily by Fr. Leonid Schmidt, former pastor of Christ the Saviour Orthodox Church in Paramus, NJ, with his permission. —*Ed.*

17 Cleopatra Mathis, from "In Memoriam, For Donald Sheehan," read at The Frost Place in Franconia, New Hampshire, July 6, 2014, at a gathering to dedicate a marble bench inscribed "In Loving Memory of Donald Sheehan."

18 The full context for this quote will be found in the glossary entry on "Christ's Commandments."

19 From Cleopatra Mathis, "In Memoriam, For Donald Sheehan," included here with Ms. Mathis's permission.

20   See Don's introduction to Pavel Florensky, *Iconostasis*, trans. Donald Sheehan and Olga Andrejev (Crestwood, NY: St. Vladimir's Seminary, 1996).

21   Panayiotis Nellas, *Deification in Christ: The Nature of the Human Person* (Crestwood, NY: St. Vladimir's Seminary: 1987).

22   Alexander Schmemann, *For the Life of the World* (Crestwood, NY: St. Vladimir's Seminary, 2018).

23   Invited by Fr. Tom Hopko to attend St. Vladimir's Seminary, I commuted to classes from Vermont (five hours each way—enough to listen over to my classes two or three times) for a couple of years in the mid-nineties. Dogmatic Theology was for me the place where the songs sounded most clearly. Sitting in that class brought tears to my eyes, over and over. It was like coming home to Truth that I'd always searched for and not found till then, certainly never in a classroom. This was my real catechumenate. —Ed.

24   In Orthodox Tradition, a *Confessor* (as distinct from a priest who hears personal confessions) is one who has severely suffered for his faith, but not been actually martyred (killed). St. Maximus, *ca.* 580–662, was a civil servant and aide to the Byzantine Emperor Heraclius. He gave up politics to become a monk and student of philosophy and theology, in which pursuit he was drawn to oppose the heresy of Monothelitism (which asserted that Jesus had but a single will). Maximus upheld instead the interpretation of the Chalcedonian formula (Fourth Ecumenical Council of 451) by which Jesus was understood to have *both* a human and a divine will, thus unifying in Himself the divine and the human. For this stance Maximus was persecuted, his right hand and tongue were cut off, and he was exiled. His theology was later affirmed by the Third Council of Constantinople (680–81) also called the Sixth Ecumenical Council) and he came to be venerated as a saint by both the Roman Catholic and Eastern Orthodox churches.

      I have not understood the full and disastrous import of Monothelitism until now, after coming to better understand my husband's lifelong immersion in antinomies. Don's understanding, congruent with St. Maximus's, rests on our human ability and effort to reconcile the oppositions in our lives. Having separated ourselves at the outset from the will of God, we cannot fully achieve this union on our own, but we can in Christ, who, even if we have not yet learned to name the divinity to whom we pray, graciously answers our prayer when it is His peace we truly seek (as opposed to a one-sided peace centered in some personal victory for just ourselves or our own "kind"). If He were not the One who holds the fullness of all things in Himself, having created and loved all of it and found it good; if he did not have the Father's will within Him as His own, working in unity with His human will, our small unifications of the great antinomies could never take place. It is Christ's personal spiritual victory as *both* human and divine that achieves what we could not do on our own. When we unite ourselves with Him, however, who unites the human and divine in Himself, His victory over death becomes ours. —*Ed.*

25   See glossary for the *intelligible* and *sensible*.

26   Fr. Michael Butler, *Ambiguorum Blogis,* https://ambiguum.word.com/category/st-maximus-the-confessor/. I am most grateful to Fr. John Konkle for this reference, and to Fr. Michael for his permission to use it here. —*Ed.*

27   Bishop Kallistos of Diokleia, in Nellas, *Deification in Christ,* 12.

28   Printed as "worship" in Nellas, *Deification,* 211. Fr. Joel Brady, Priest, Holy Apostles Mission, Lansing, New York, has proposed this verbal change, pointing to the following footnote in Fr. Maximos Constas's translation of the *Ambigua:*

> "Workshop" renders the Greek word *ergasterion,* which here suggests a center of both production and exchange, as described by Chrysostom, *On the Statutes* 16 (PG 49:172A). The word also has the metaphorical sense of a "womb"; see Philo, *Life of Moses* 2.85 (LCL 6:490); Clement, *Stromateis* 3.12.83 (GCS 52:234); Gregory the Theologian, Or. 28.22 (SC 250:146); and Proklos of Constantinople, hom. 1.1, 14 (ed. Constas 2003, 136, see 149–50).

Fr. Joel adds: "I suspect 'worship' is what manuscript scholars would call a "'scribal error.' At some point someone substituted a word for a similar-sounding one, and somehow it never got caught. It *almost* makes sense in context, or close enough not to be caught in subsequent proofreading." —*Ed.*

29   This is translated ambiguously in the Nellas book (*Deification in Christ,* 211) as "mediation between all the extremes that he is able to effect"; I have changed the word order for clarity. —*Ed.*

30   St. Maximus, *Ambigua, PG* 91, 1304D–1312B, in Nellas, *Deification in Christ,* 211–12.

31   Nellas, *Deification in Christ,* 212–13.

32   Nellas, *Deification in Christ*, 213–14.

33   See Sheehan, *Grace of Incorruption*, 60–62.

34   Schmemann, *For the Life of the World*, 23.

35   St. Maximus, *Ambigua*, PG 91, 1304D–1312B, in Nellas, *Deification in Christ*, 211–12.

36   When I found this document and decided to build a book around it, I tried to locate Cutter Davis in Kingston, NY. I had heard Don speak of him many times. It appears, however, that he may have passed away the same year that Don did. I hope that his family or a friend will come across the book someday and enjoy reflecting on Cutter's inaugural contribution to his childhood friend's long and fruitful teaching career. Most other persons' names in this narrative have been changed.— *Ed.*

37   "The honey peace in old poems" is the last line of Robinson Jeffers's poem "To the Stone-Cutters," from Louis Untermeyer, ed., *A Treasury of Great Poem* (New York: Simon and Schuster, 1955). It is available online at https://www.poemhunter.com/poem/to-the-stone-cutters/—*Ed.*

38   Available online at https://www.public-domain-poetry.com/john-milton/paradise-lost-book-i-8312.

39   Added here by the editor, this is a portion of one of several of Don's early poems of this kind, titled "Impressions on a Beautiful Day." It was written at age eighteen (April or May 1958) and found among the author's papers. —*Ed.*

40   Having known George, and loved him as best I could, I think his reaction was likely a flash of admiration for his son mixed with profound regret and pain for what this very intelligent and patchily self-educated man had done and not done with his own life. —*Ed.*

41   This child grew up to be a very fine man and, regrettably too late for Don, his beautiful daughters did finally locate their father's family through computer research; the big blue Irish eyes of the half-brothers are a striking testament to their fraternity! —*Ed.*

42   http://www.bopsecrets.org/rexroth/translations/japanese.htm. For more of these lovely poems, see Kenneth Rexroth: *100 Poems from the Japanese* (New Directions, 1955).

43   A short hairstyle popular in the 1950s, resembling the tail end of a duck. I and my sixth-grade cohort of three all sported that cut. —*Ed.*

44 For this epigraph, I have taken an editorial liberty in combining a fragment of Don's poem "Richard Eberhart at the Frost Place, August 1980" (chapter 2) with a phrase from chapter 18 concerning *praxis*: "the unfailing consistency of prayer and every righteous action, *small labors steadily undertaken in the humility of failure and in the fullness of confession*: only *praxis* guides us aright." Where the poems in this chapter were dated, I have given the date. I believe the undated ones were written during college and graduate school, but possibly some of them earlier, even in his teens. The last two, "This Is Where I Start" and "Almost Enough," were scribbled on bits of paper in his final two years. If there were others, I haven't found them yet. I know he burned piles and piles of folders, most likely class teaching notes, before we left Vermont in 2008. We were preparing for our family's move to Charleston, South Carolina, where he passed in May 2010. Don didn't like moving. — *Ed.*

45 A fragment from Hesiod.

46 Wallace Stevens, "The Comedian as the Letter C," https://www.poetry-foundation.org/poems/47428/the-comedian-as-the-letter-c. The poem was first published in 1923 in *Harmonium* (New York: Knopf) and reissued in 1931.

47 This poem also appears in Appendix A, where it is formatted and discussed as a chiasmus.

48 *Sir Thomas Browne's Religio Medici and Urn-Burial* (London: Dent, 1896).

49 John Wilmot, 2nd Earl of Rochester, "A Satyr Against Reason and Mankind," written before June 1674.

50 Shakespeare, *King Lear*, V:2.

51 In 1972, we had retired our TV set to the back of a closet, retrieving it only briefly during the Watergate hearings. Don never really did make the transition to electronic or digital life beyond what was required of him by his department secretary.—*Ed.*

52 Mimesis in this usage means simply the act of imitating a person or an event or action. In my understanding, the mimetic tradition in art—based in Greek philosophy (though reaching back to the Hebrew understanding of God's creation of man in His own image and likeness)—is concerned with conveying positive moral values and universal truths by which the human person may be called to imitate and conform with the divine model.

  It is interesting, though, to think of the word in the context of René Girard's usage, discussed in Part Three. According to Dcn Justin Jackson, Girard addresses the classical mimetic tradition briefly in *Things Hidden*

Since the Foundation of the World (Redwood City, CA: Stanford University, 1987), 7–9. He further refers an interested reader to Eric Auerbach's *Mimesis: The Representation of Reality in Western Literature* (Princeton: Princeton University, 2003) for an account of mimesis-as-representation from the classical tradition to modern literature. In regard to Girard's negative mimesis, Dcn Justin refers us to Rebecca Adams's work in this area, and to Matthew Taylor's overview at https://anthropoetics.ucla.edu/ap2601/2601taylor/. —*Ed.*

53 I think this speech must be from Chief Seattle. See similar ones in Rudolf Kaiser, "Chief Seattle's Speech(es): American Origins and European Reception," in *Recovering the Word: Essays on Native American Literature*, ed. Brian Swann and Arnold Krupat (Berkeley: University of California, 1987), 525–30.—*Ed.*

54 A full account of the event described here will be found in the opening chapter of Donald Sheehan's *Grace of Incorruption*. There are some small differences of detail between the two accounts, this one written a few years afterward. —*Ed.*

55 *The Way of a Pilgrim and the Pilgrim Continues His Way*, anon., translated from the Russian by R. M. French (Seabury, 1970). It is widely available in various editions.—*Ed.*

56 See note 6. The *Philokalia* has played a crucial role in reinvigorating the spiritual tradition of the Orthodox Church throughout the world. It was translated into English in the 1980s. The title means "Love of the beautiful," conveying the goal of the work, which is to guide us in a life of purification from sin, attaining of the virtues, and ultimately deification. —*Ed.*

57 E. Kadloubovsky and G. E. H. Palmer, trans., *Writings from the Philokalia: On Prayer of the Heart* (London, Boston: Faber and Faber, 1992).

58 Vladimir Lossky, *The Mystical Theology of the Eastern Church* (Crestwood, NY: St. Vladimir's Seminary, 1997).

59 Chrismation is the service by which we receive "the seal of the gift of the Holy Spirit." It follows Baptism and is understood as one's personal participation in Pentecost, when the Holy Spirit comes upon Christ's disciples forty days after the Resurrection. —*Ed.*

60 St. Theophan the Recluse, in Igumen Chariton, *The Art of Prayer: An Orthodox Anthology*, trans. E. Kadloubovsky and G. E. H. Palmer; ed. Timothy Ware (London, Boston: Faber and Faber reprint, 1997), 154.

61   The most likely source for this phrase is Stephen Theron, *Hegel's Philoso-phy of Reconciliation: Logic as Form of the World*, 326. The sentence in which it occurs immediately follows a reference to C. S. Lewis's *The Four Loves*, which would account for the author's associating the statement with Lewis. Nonetheless, the association with Lewis is an excellent one, for in his *Surprised by Joy*, Lewis is centrally concerned with learning to separate his own *experience of pleasure* from the reality of Joy (Christ Himself), lest the encounter be all about his own (my word) "high" and altogether miss its source and meaning. In the presence of God's beauty, if it is to be more than just another passing experience of our*self*, a sober ecstasy is essential. On *sobriety* and *ecstasy*, see also Sheehan, *Shield of Psalmic Prayer*, 62-63. —Ed.

62   I refer the reader to Schmemann, *For the Life of the World*, especially Appendix 1, for a presentation of the life-giving importance of understand-ing God's active presence and accessibility *in* His Creation: "everywhere, filling all things."

63   *Theosis* is a condition of the soul in which "God fully bestows His glory upon man and thereby fully creates harmony between Himself and man *at the same moment* man remains fully distinct from God" (Sheehan, *Shield of Psalmic Prayer*, 201). Theosis "literally means to become gods by Grace. The biblical words that are synonymous and descriptive of theosis are: adoption, redemption, inheritance, glorification, holiness, and perfection. Theosis is the acquisition of the Holy Spirit, whereby through Grace one becomes participant in the *Kingdom of God*. Theosis is an act of the uncreated and infinite love of God. It begins here in time and space, but it is not static or complete, and is an open-ended progres-sion uninterrupted through all eternity." Archimandrite George, *Theosis: The True Purpose of Human Life* (Mount Athos, Greece: Holy Monastery of St. Gregorios, 2006).—Ed.

64   I have added this latter point, which was beautifully made in a homily given on the Sunday before Pentecost by Fr. Leonid Schmidt. I wish Don could have known him. He would have found this a moving and entirely acceptable addition. —Ed.

65   Archbishop Kallistos Ware, *The Orthodox Church* (Penguin Books, 1997), 196.

66   Mother Maria [Lydia Gysi], *The Psalms: An Exploratory Translation* (North Yorkshire, UK: Greek Orthodox Monastery of the Assumption, 1973).

67   I did not at first understand this startling and perplexing antinomy of
     standing *simultaneously* within our lives *and* at the End-Point where
     we are stripped of everything we know "except our sins, and the cry
     for mercy." And I may not now. After long association with the writ-
     ings in this book, however, I find that I have begun to understand, if
     only as a sensation in my heart, the existence of this place of stillness
     wherein the logical mind has ceased to serve me and I must wait in
     patient prayer for noetic understanding to come to my aid. Indeed, if
     there is, as I believe, a single thread of meaning in the book, this is it. It
     is our ultimate response to St. Maximus's understanding of our divine
     human calling. And I would venture to say that here is where Don truly
     began, his own chiastic midpoint from which he radiated outward, step
     by step, to fill and in-form his life from beginning to end. And if it's truly
     a chiastic center, it will also be a point where meaning converges; that is,
     both toward and from which meaning moves. This will, I think, become
     clearer in subsequent chapters as we come to understand more about
     how chiasmus works. —Ed.

68   Metropolitan Anthony Bloom of Sourozh, "On Death," published in *So-
     bornost* 1:2 (1979): 8–18.

69   M. Maria, *Psalms.*

70   M. Maria, *Psalms.*

71   I have added this subhead because I believe this was the point where
     genuine noetic healing began for Don and that the rule of prayer was and
     continued to be the medicine. Once he firmly established his rule (which
     took some time), I don't recall that he ever broke it, no matter how much
     adaptation or loss of sleep it required. I would even go so far as to say
     that he gave his life to it, as it took precedence over sleep.
         The establishment of the rule both offers and requires learning to
     fully integrate one's two "minds": the noetic and the dianoetic. The for-
     mer had come to Don as a "faint but very clear voice" that he could have
     ignored, but would not; the "other mind," "profoundly shocked" by this,
     struggled to accept and absorb it into his life and family. At the risk of
     oversimplifying, or simply getting it wrong, a way to interpret what he
     is saying here is that the rule of prayer offers a sort of choreography in
     which both "minds" can learn to work together in a regular and increas-
     ingly beautiful and rhythmic harmony: the dianoetic provides shapely
     order, regularity of rhythm, balance, traditional content, and rational
     understanding, while the noetic opens the heart to receive God's *Pres-
     ence* into that shapeliness and from there into one's life where it can be
     enacted, even danced, as spiritual *praxis* and righteous activity (see, for
     example, chapter 18). —Ed.

72 For more on the rule of prayer, see Sheehan, *Shield of Psalmic Prayer*, chapter 4.

73 The order of Reader is the first clerical order in the Orthodox Church, followed by the Subdiaconate, to which Don was also ordained later. The candidate is tonsured as a sign of submission and obedience upon entering the clerical state, making a layperson into a clergyman. The tonsure precedes the first ordination and involves the cutting of small amounts of hair in four places in a cross pattern, as is also performed at a baptism. It is understood as an offering of oneself to God.—*Ed.*

74 Ivan Ilyich Sergiev, *My Life in Christ: The Spiritual Journals of St. John of Kronstadt*, ed. Nicholas Kotar (St. Job of Pochaev, 2021), 6.—*Ed.*

75 I draw your attention to Don's poem in Appendix A, "Then It Was Love." The mirrorings and usurpations Don describes here in this chapter seem to be the exact opposite of the mirroring and projecting and exchanging that go on in the poem. In the case of the alcoholic, there is, as Don says here, a usurpation, a stealing, of the personhood of the other, while in the process of falling in love, there is an *adding* of one to the other in mutual support of the other's personhood.

76 I note the parallels between what the author is saying here and his analyses of Psalms in *The Shield of Psalmic Prayer*, where Don shows how the continuous engagement of psalmic prayer, or engagement of our given reality *in and through* psalmic prayer, transfigures the events and disorders of our lives into pathways to a deeper relationship with God, who, having Himself descended through the cross into the heart of worldly violence, is always to be found there, at the very center of all things. The alcoholic, however, finds only his own terror and rage.—*Ed.*

77 See the glossary re: *nous*—the faculty by which we know and are known by God. The logic there would seem to explain clearly why, with the noetic faculty (or our access to it) compromised by alcohol (or any similar addiction), and the ordered relation between visible and invisible levels of reality rendered confused at best (and terrifyingly disordered at worst), the addict would become progressively unable to understand Christianity. This would be especially the case on such a point as the virgin birth, by which the invisible and immaterial Holy Spirit enters, with courtesy and consent, into the visible and material womb of the Virgin Mother and a human Person is conceived and born: The Person, Christ. —*Ed.*

78 G. P. Fedotov, *The Russian Church since the Revolution* (London, 1928), 47, quoted in Ware, *The Orthodox Church*, 147–48.

79 I have not located the source for the Lukacs quote. —*Ed.*

80 I have discussed the following passage with Fr. John Konkle, who knew Don well, and I've made some clarifications and added some notes as a result of his responses. Fr. John's understanding, based on his many years of Orthodox study and practice (more than Don had at the time this was written) reflects a sharp awareness of the difficulties and spiritual disasters that have historically surrounded imprecise statements concerning the faith. While Don always took great care in making statements about the truth of Orthodoxy, he was concerned also not to offend his diverse hearers and at the same time not be untrue to his faith. The outright statement of his belief that he makes here, in what I believe was a public lecture, was a rare event, possibly unique.

In regard to the word "invisible," Fr. John offers this powerful image: that Jesus Christ "is the invisible (made visible) that upholds all creation over the abyss of nothingness, that delivers the invisible divine energy in every instance of visible life. He is the one we encounter (my word for Don's 'engagement'—same point, I think) in every mundane aspect of earthly life, and most fully in the Orthodox Church." —*Ed.*

81 Ware, *The Orthodox Church,* 308. Fr. John Konkle prefers a more nuanced statement of the point: "I've never been as fond of Met. Kallistos's quote as Don was, but a slightly different (and less elegant) version strikes me as correct: We know where Christ is (that is, everywhere, filling all things), and we know where He is received/embraced/manifest/etc.— that is, the Orthodox Church) but we don't (in general) know where He is rejected. (Consider, for example, Fr. Tom Hopko's provocative claim that for some at the Last Judgment it will count to their credit that they rejected christ, because the christ they rejected was indeed a false christ)." E-mail, 7/26/21. —*Ed.*

82 Ware, *The Orthodox Church,* 309.

83 *Symeon the New Theologian, the Discourses,* Classics of Western Spirituality, trans. C. J. deCatanzaro (New York: Paulist, 1980). Subsequent quotations from this book are referenced as *Symeon, Discourses,* or simply *Discourses.*

84 NB: This experience of reconciling or harmonizing opposites is related to the later discussions of chiasmus, as well as to the dry bones in the Ezekiel prophecy (Ezek 37:1–14), which are restored to life in finding their *harmonia.* —*Ed.*

85 Note the reference to St. Theophan in the previous chapter concerning the spiritual dangers of deliberately seeking such experiences: "they will quickly lose all their sweetness and you will become like an alcoholic with liquor. 'Therefore . . . those who practice sobriety pay no attention to this sweetness.'" —*Ed.*

86 *Philokalia,* I:110–46.

87 I recommend that the reader look again at Fr. John Konkle's beautiful definition of Christ's commandments in the glossary.—*Ed.*

88 *Philokalia,* I:75.

89 I offer here, not something I know but something I suspect, even believe: that what Don took from this meeting with Viktor, and from the doorway it opened to St. Symeon, was an image of how he was to go about living his own life. He means these words very precisely: Viktor "was bringing me my life." He has earlier quoted St. Hesychios the Priest: "It is easy to be a monk in one's outer self if one wants to be; but no small struggle is required to be a monk in one's inner self" (*Philokalia* I:75). I believe that much of Don's life after this meeting came to be about engaging that struggle. At one time, I know, he wanted to enter a monastery and was advised not to. Fr. John Konkle, quoting Fr. Roman Braga (and confirmed in this by others at Holy Dormition Monastery), comments on this desire, perhaps an uncommon one: "It's not the habit that makes a monk; the only true monk is one who lives in his heart. Be a monk of the heart in the world." Memory eternal, Donatos!—*Ed.*

90 First published online by Hilary Mullins as "The Transfiguration of Don Sheehan" in 2013 in *Numero Cinq Magazine*: http://numerocinqmagazine.com/2013/08/06/the-transfiguration-of-don-sheehan-essay-hilary-mullins/. Reprinted by permission. The Frost Place, in Franconia, New Hampshire, is a house where the poet Robert Frost lived with his family from 1915 to 1920 and then spent summers for another nineteen years. Under the inspiration and leadership of David Schaffer, the farmhouse was purchased by the Town of Franconia in 1976 to be a museum, cultural center, and summer home for a resident poet. Don Sheehan was appointed Executive Director in 1978. Over the next twenty-seven years he initiated and directed what grew to be an internationally recognized series of mostly summer programs for writers of all ages. It will be clear from Hilary Mullins's description here, and also from Cleopatra Mathis's earlier, why these programs—which, for the sake of better art, encouraged a spirit of giving one's art to another and overcoming the spirit of envy and competition—became so important to so many of their participants. —*Ed.*

91 R. Frost, "The Death of the Hired Man," https://www.public-domain-po-etry.com/robert-lee-frost/death-of-the-hired-man-1154; first published in *North of Boston* (London: Nutt, 1914). The Frosts returned to America and bought the Franconia farm the following year.—*Ed.*

92 Sheehan, *Grace of Incorruption*, 3.

93 Florensky, *The Pillar and Ground of the Truth*, trans. Boris Jakim (Princeton, NJ: Princeton University, 1997). I am unable to locate the page references. —*Ed.*

94 See Eugene Peterson, *Leap Over a Wall* (San Francisco, CA: HarperOne, 1998), 35–36.

95 See the book's glossary for a full explanation of *chiasmus* and *chiastic*.

96 Sheehan, *Shield of Psalmic Prayer*, chapter 10. The translation is the author's own: Sheehan, *Psalms of David*, 88.

97 Nellas, *Deification in Christ*, 212–13.

98 Schmemann, *For the Life of the World*, 108.

99 Schmemann, *For the Life of the World*, 109–10

100 The dating of Orthodox Pascha is something I have never entirely understood. I've been told that the best place to look for understanding is Abp Peter L'Huillier's *The Church of the Ancient Councils* (Crestwood, NY: St. Vladimir's Seminary, 2000). After the First Ecumenical Council, the date of Pascha was determined independently of the Jewish celebration of Passover. But at some later point, the original formula was reinterpreted to mean *after Passover* (since Pascha is the fulfillment of Passover), and that's how it's been ever since. Pascha—preceded by a week of liturgical and scriptural recapitulation of the events leading to Christ's Crucifixion on Holy Friday and His resting in the tomb on Holy Saturday—cannot be celebrated before Passover. The word itself is from Latin *pascha* ("Passover"), from Ancient Greek πάσχα (páskha, "Passover"), from Aramaic אָחְסַפ (paskha), from Hebrew חַסֶּפ (pésakh).—*Ed.*

101 Sheehan, *Shield of Psalmic Prayer*, 73.

102 Sheehan, *Shield of Psalmic Prayer*, 74.

103 See chapter 12, "The Making of Personhood," in Sheehan, *Shield of Psalmic Prayer*: "As we follow in prayer the movements of Psalm 118—from *aleph* to *tau*, we are following the way into resurrected life with Christ Himself" (193).

104 Dante Allighieri, *Divine Comedy: Paradiso*, trans. Charles Singleton (Princeton University, 1991).

105 Hans-Georg Gadamer, *Truth and Method* (Bloomsbury Academic Reprint ed., 2013). I am not sure when Don came across the Gadamer book, written in the sixties, but I think I was hearing about it early in his serious academic life, which took root in the mid-sixties, well before he focused his interest on antinomies. (For an exception that proves me entirely wrong, see the chiasmus in appendix A.) I nonetheless think it likely that his interest in chiastic poetry found its most fruitful focus in the early nineties while he was working with Olga Andrejev on the translation of Florensky's *Iconostasis* and reading his *Pillar and Ground*, which was also around the time that Fr. John Breck published his *Shape of Biblical Language: Chiasmus in the Scriptures and Beyond* (Crestwood, NY: St. Vladimir's Seminary, 1994; 2nd ed. 2008).

Don was interested in what he called *paradoxes* as early as 1968, when he was researching and writing his doctoral thesis on "The Poetics of Influence: A Study of T. S. Eliot's Uses of Dante." Around that time, he was also preparing night and day for his Preliminary examinations, applying for a job, getting ready for a move (something that had held a traumatic element for him since his family's emergency moves in childhood), then new teaching responsibilities at the University of Chicago, opposing the Vietnam War, and making room in his heart and mind to be a parent for the first time (also not free of trauma). There was undoubtedly more charge for him in this massive convergence of his past and present than we realized and accounted for at the time. Paradoxes? Surely antinomies.

The terms are often taken to be synonymous, but *antinomy* is a much larger and more fluid word carrying rich possibilities for movement and growth. Paradox is more static, describing a less purposeful or generative or interactive relationship between two events, and in no way Christ-focused or Christ-seeking. This doesn't of course mean that He isn't present to it, but the word misses much of the point and breadth and depth of how Don eventually came to think about antinomy. I confess that I haven't read all of his thesis yet (not completed until near the time David was born in February 1969), but I imagine it marked a significant stage in his journey toward the understanding of antinomy that he later reached. Perhaps he too began to find paradox static. But here I'm only guessing.

I don't know where in time this chapter on the *Paradiso* stands in relation to the Dante/Eliot dissertation, but it definitely offers something of a bridge into genuine antinomic meaning in the way he presents the differing horizons of past and present, strange and familiar, each requiring courteous validation by the other for understanding to occur. Cosmic diplomacy? Or just Good Manners. And Don's conclusion says it all: "as long as we do not attempt to abolish either our own historical moment or the text's—that is to say, as long as we remain truly courteous—the dialogue continues." Then a bit later: "And the things from over the horizon, from out of the further reaches of our past, may not fit whatsoever into our landscape. At least, they may not fit without some shift of sight—on both our parts." I don't think the effort on his part to make this shift was ever absent from Don's living in the world.—*Ed.*

106 Thomas Merton, *New Seeds of Contemplation* (Abbey of Gethsemane, 1961; New Directions, 1972, 2007), 228. For some reason, Don wrote this in verse, though it is not so in the New Directions book. Perhaps to reveal its chiastic quality?

107 Heidegger, "What Is Metaphysics?" 360.

108 I believe this quote to be from William G. Doty, *Mythography: The Study of Myths and Rituals* (University of Alabama, 2000). It may, however, be from the journal *Archē: Notes and Papers on Archaic Studies*, which we published for a few years in the late seventies in Franconia. I seem to have no remaining copies.

    "Phenomenological abeyance" here describes a useful frame of mind in which we can confront antinomical horizons and learn to inhabit the space between them—a withholding of judgment in the face of a temporarily unresolvable antinomy. As Don explains, it relies on behaviors such as "long-guarded speechlessness," "contemplative silence," and courtesy. It is thus a way to approach, not only our encounters with widely differing historical worldviews, or with variant ways of understanding a phenomenon or text, but also with rending conflicts of perspective or behavior that may vex our personal life.

    By extension, then, I believe the term may fruitfully be applied as well to the kind of spiritual growth Don speaks of in chapter 12 as the mind of David becoming the mind of Christ. For the response implied by this term is similar to that called forth by chiastic poetry, or even chiastic music (as in chapter 13), where a patterned antinomy is established in which one line or group of lines structurally "matches" another by means of similarity or opposition in its meaning. Such back and forth callings/echoings require certain mental gymnastics on our part that are best submitted to contemplative silence, prayer, and courtesy. In this way we may come to understand and resolve their polarities and reach a higher level of meaning. Simply by learning to read and listen and think in this way, we move closer to being able to reconcile the oppositions and embrace the wholeness within God's creation.—*Ed*

109 Don had not yet encountered Orthodoxy when he wrote this essay, though I suspect it helped him on his way. Orthodoxy seems historically to have embraced zeal as a virtue without ever conducting an

Inquisition; I remember this being important to Don. See St. Isaac the Syrian's discussion of zeal in chapter 18, where the saint says that zeal is "the force of the holy desire implanted naturally in the nature of the soul." Saint Isaac the Syrian, *The Ascetical Homilies of St. Isaac the Syrian* (Boston, MA: Holy Transfiguration Monastery, 1984, 2011), Homily 55:273. (Page references throughout are to the 1984 edition.) Zeal, Don writes, is set in motion by the soul's incensive faculty (see the glossary). It (1) *safeguards the boundaries of our psychic nature*; and (2) *sends forth the psyche's vehemence for the fulfilling of her desire for God. —Ed.*

110 George Santayana, *Three Philosophical Poets: Lucretius, Dante, and Goethe,* vol. I (Cambridge: Harvard University, 1910). Available to read online at https://www.gutenberg.org/files/35612/35612-h/35612-h.htm.

111 Do we understand a spoken sentence outside-in or inside-out? If I understand this question rightly, it is asking whether we are understanding a given situation or act of speech dianoetically or noetically, which places these two mental functions in an antinomic relation to one another with—as Don might analyze it—God's love at the midpoint where they meet and co-inhere. *—Ed.*

112 Martin Heidegger, *Poetry, Language, Thought,* trans. A. Hofstader (New York: Harper and Row, 1971), 146.

113 The author's source is unknown, but the quote may be found in Hans-Georg Gadamer, "The Historicity of Understanding," in Kurt Mueller-Vollmer, ed., *The Hermeneutics Reader: Texts of the German Tradition from the Enlightenment to the Present* (New York: Continuum, 1985), 272. *—Ed.*

114 The page number is unknown, though I assume it comes from Heidegger's "'Postscript' to 'What Is Metaphysics?'" NB: These both may be read as miniature chiasmuses. *—Ed.*

115 This re-repatterning of the mind could also be expressed, and will be below, as *en-noeticizing the nous.* The *nous* (adj. *noetic*) is defined by the translators of the *Philokalia* as "the highest faculty in man, through which—provided it is purified—he knows God or the inner essences or principles of created things by means of direct apprehension or spiritual perception" (I:362). It is also called the "eye of the heart" or the "mind of the heart." This faculty is distinguished from the reason or mind (*dianoia*), which works by sequences of logical connections. (For more on the *nous* and *dianoia,* see the glossary.) The author appears to be suggesting here that the careful practice of what may begin as a

purely *dianoetic* technique, when directed faithfully toward the realization of the divine—or any blessed end (here the iconic countenance; in the next example the spontaneous communal praying of the Akathist to the Mother of God)—actually transfigures the lower, merely mental, activity into a higher, noetic one capable of knowing God, and this acts back upon the practice of the creative technique itself so as to enrich its spiritual capability and power, and especially its *depth*. Elsewhere the author speaks of the interaction in which, when we faithfully seek to know God, as in an ascetic practice, He in turn enlarges and strengthens our *nous*, giving it greater capacity to perform its proper function of knowing Him. It is a profound reciprocity, or, as it is termed in chapter 12, a *reverse restoration*. See Florensky, *Pillar and Ground*, 67–68. —*Ed.*

116   I am unable to identify the chronicle Don refers to with certainty, although I believe it to be what's known as "The Easter Chronicle" or *Chronicon Paschale*, a near-contemporary account. See Michael and Mary Whitby, *Chronicon Paschale 284–628 AD* (Liverpool University, 1989). See also Michael Maas, *Readings in Late Antiquity: A Sourcebook* (Routledge, 2nd ed., 2010). —*Ed.*

117   Various online sources point out that Greek Papyrus 470, held by the John Rylands University Library, University of Manchester, is a fragment of a prayer to the Theotokos written about 250 AD. We are reminded that this term for Mary, meaning God-Bearer, was confirmed at the Third Ecumenical Council in 431 and that, if this early dating is correct, this prayer must already have been part of the Church's services or prayers, showing that petitions and prayers to the Theotokos and the Saints go back to the early days of the Church, at least as far back as the third century. —*Ed.*

118   On stanza numbering: Most modern translations of the Akathist (of which many may be found online) number, not the stanzas, but the sets of Ikos (with its following salutations beginning "Hail" or "Rejoice") and Kontakion (ending with "Alleluia!"), of which there are twelve, then a brief Kontakion 13 and a final repetition of the opening Kontakion and Ikos 1. Stanza numbering begins with the first Ikos (Ikos 1), not the opening Kontakion or Apolytikion. Stanza 19 is therefore the Ikos of the tenth set, beginning "A rampart art thou for virgins . . ." or "Thou art a wall for virgins. . . ." As to the translations used in this chapter, some were likely influenced by a text Don often used for prayer, *Small Compline*, published by Patmos in Williston, Florida, with an English translation by Holy Transfiguration Monastery in Brookline, MA; some are his own. —*Ed.*

119   *Philokalia* I:362. *Nous* is translated as "intellect" in the *Philokalia*, which in our time may be misleading; for, in our long cultural drift away from understanding and developing the nous, the meaning of *intellect* has lost

some of its noetic essence. See also the explanatory definition of *nous* in the glossary. Note that it is most likely this faculty that the author speaks of in chapter 5 as being especially vulnerable to disordering by alcoholism, though of course there are many other ways to cloud the *nous.—Ed.*

120 *Philokalia* I:362. See also the glossary herein.

121 *Philokalia* I:280.

122 See also Sheehan, *Shield of Psalmic Prayer,* ch. 8, esp. 134–45.

123 This seems to mean that the nous, the place where antinomies are resolved, is itself antinomic; that it is both the source and the end of antinomy, its *alpha* and *omega. —Ed.*

124 For more discussion of antinomy, see the glossary, as well as much of Part Two. *—Ed.*

125 Sheehan, Preface and Introduction, Florensky, *Iconostasis,* 4, 23.

126 "The Secret Sits," https://www.public-domain-poetry.com/robert-lee-frost/secret-sits-1273.

127 This essay was written for a Frost Place lecture. Sydney Lea, writer and former Frost Place Board chairman and Vermont Poet Laureate (2011–15), remembers attending it in Concord, New Hampshire, in 2005, but it may also have been delivered on an earlier occasion at The Frost Place. Don left an unfinished draft and some rough notes from which I have constructed especially the latter portion of the lecture. The concluding portion, Don's unrecorded class discussion of the Frost poem "The Thatch," for which there were no notes, I have composed from my own understanding and the astute insights of several friends willing to assist me by virtually reconstructing the missing class. I include the essay here because of its wry and highly antinomic depiction of "home" and its poignant parallels to Don's own childhood home. It surprised me to find that the poem he chose to focus on is so remarkably chiastic, which clinched the essay's eligibility for this collection. I'd love to know how he presented it. I am not aware of any other occasion where Don directed his professional attention to the subject of the antinomies of "home"—except possibly in lectures regarding Dostoevky's *Brothers Karamazov.—Ed.*

128 Robert Frost, "The Death of the Hired Man," https://www.public-domain-poetry.com/robert-lee-frost/death-of-the-hired-man-1154. The lineation of the poem is better, however, at https://www.poetryfoundation.org/poems/44261/the-death-of-the-hired-man.

129 I refer the reader also to the author's *Grace of Incorruption*, chapter 7, "Shall Thy Wonders Be Known in the Dark? Robert Frost and Personhood," 87. The entire poem is printed and discussed there. —*Ed.*

130 Robert Frost, "An Old Man's Winter Night." https://www.public-domain-poetry.com/robert-lee-frost/an-old-mans-winter-night-1145.

131 I assume the reference is to William H. Pritchard, *Frost: A Literary Life Reconsidered* (Oxford University, 1984). —*Ed.*

132 Don wrote in his rough draft that "he," the grandfather, saw this vision, but, in the context of the following sentence, I think it may have been "she." In the biographical material that follows, I have condensed the draft, which at this point was largely notes. —*Ed.*

133 See Samuel M. Warren, *A Compendium of the Theological Writings of Emanuel Swedenborg* (Arkose, 2015), 456 (though Don's page citation may not apply to this later edition). —*Ed.*

134 Fyodor Dostoevsky, *Brothers Karamazov*, 774.

135 Robert Frost, "The Thatch," https://www.public-domain-poetry.com/robert-lee-frost/thatch-1247. First published in *West-Running Brook* (New York: Holt, 1928).

136 For their contributions to this discussion of the poem, I want to thank Amy Chan, Codie Ferguson Chevalier, Iris Houdyshel, Nancy Kane, Sydney Lea, and Tasya Rodzianko.

137 Quotations from Sydney Lea are from *A Hundred Himalayas* (Ann Arbor: University of Michigan, 2012).

138 Schmemann, *For the Life of the World*, 26.

139 A version of this essay was published as the Introduction to Sheehan, *The Psalms of David,* under the title "The Mind of David and the Mind of Christ." I didn't know then whether I would be publishing more of Don's work, and I wanted to be sure that at least this one got published. It is somewhat reorganized here, retitled, and further edited, and I have taken this opportunity to restore the author's original references to Fr. Pavel Florensky, in particular his *Pillar and Ground of the Truth* (omitted in the earlier book for reasons exigent at the time). The full essay printed here is immeasurably enriched by Florensky's presence to it.—*Ed.*

140 The word *nous* would be appropriate here and throughout this essay, but Don was not using it at this point, and in this context the connection to the psalmist, with its scriptural basis, was and is crucial. —*Ed.*

141 Don is still using the King James Version (KJV) rather than the Orthodox Septuagint (LXX), in which the King James Book of Samuel is the
Book of Kingdoms.

142 Breck, *The Shape of Biblical Language*.

143 Eugene Peterson, *Leap Over a Wall*, 35–36.

144 St. Isaac, *Homilies*, 21:112; fn. 17.

145 St. Isaac, *Homilies*, 21:112.

146 I have deleted a section here which I believe Don wrote before he began
seriously using the Septuagint Greek (LXX) translation preferred by the
Orthodox Church. He never abandoned the King James, his first love,
but, as his fluency in the LXX Greek grew, especially after he was asked
to translate the LXX Psalter for the Orthodox Study Bible (a translation
that ended up being edited in ways he was not happy with), he would
use the Septuagint Greek in his psalmic prayer as well. Poet Matthew
Brown, who has contributed significantly to the work of preparing the
final manuscript for this book, has pointed out to me the differences
between the Masoretic and Septuagint (LXX) texts here (First Samuel
in the Masoretic text is First Kingdoms in the LXX). In particular, Matthew says, Saul's "suddenly not recognizing David simply doesn't appear
in either the Lexham Septuagint or the Orthodox Study Bible. In those
the chapter ends right at 17:54. The Masoretic text, as in my New Oxford Annotated Bible (1 Samuel 17)," Matthew continues, "goes on in
v. 55 with the story of Saul not recognizing David and then in 18 has
the famous tale of David's bonding with Saul's son Jonathan, which *also*
doesn't appear in the LXX! The latter goes straight into the song about
David's killing his ten thousands, which makes Saul so jealous." We have
decided to retain the deleted section as a note, because of the intriguing
way it handles the different planes of scriptural narrative, which are not
unique to this instance. —*Ed.*

Don writes:

It is worth noting that these two chapters of First Samuel
(the sixteenth and seventeenth) contain a brief passage
that, for at least the past three centuries, scholarship has
termed an anomaly; that is, a passage that makes no sense
in narrative context. In the final four verses of the seventeenth chapter, Saul looks out over the scene of David
triumphing over the Philistines after the slaying of Goliath. Saul turns to his field commander and asks, "Who is

this boy?" (1 Sam 17:55). David is then brought to Saul. "Who are you, young man?" Saul asks. David answers, "I am the son of Jesse, your servant" (17:58). What is going on? Why does Saul not know this boy whose singing has already healed him? Why is David introduced to Saul as if for the first time? How can this passage possibly fit into the narrative's forward movement?

In his book *The Art of Biblical Narrative* (New York: Basic, 1981), Robert Alter offers a fine discussion of this particular anomaly. In our age of modern biblical scholar- ship, Alter holds, we have become so used to seeing biblical narratives as made up of disjunctive, misfitting "chunks" that we often fail to see exactly what the biblical authors were actually doing. For (Alter continues) in many of these sequences of misfitting chunks, the authors were actually employing a literary strategy not unlike contemporary cub- ism in painting. First, we are given one plane; then we have another; then a third; and so on. As in a cubist painting, these distinct planes of narrative touch one another but are not narratively integrated. Instead, the viewer negoti- ates the disjunctions by coming to see how each narrative plane is indispensable to the total meaning—but how no one plane can be subsumed into another one. The result is linear "dis-coherence" but spatial significance in a realm of total meaning. In such an approach, we can see this passage in First Samuel as one wherein Saul is saying: "I don't know you when you become a triumphant warrior, I know you and love you only as a lyric healer."

Read in this way, this narrative plane thus reveals a central dimension of the whole narrative's meaning. For, *on this plane alone,* we see the very heart of that chaotic blindness that is Saul's psychotic depression: he cannot see David whole. Put another way, Saul is here failing to see how David's invincibility as a warrior deeply informs—and is informed by—his skill as a lyricist, for the bronze spear and the lyric poem are held together in the discipline of stillness. For Saul, David falls into two disjunctive parts only one of which is comprehensible. Because of the nar- rative strategy, we are here not only seeing but also (to an interesting degree) *experiencing* Saul's blindness to David's wholeness. The very technique of prose narrative is thereby exhibiting the passage's meaning.

147 It occurs to me to ask how this reflects on a suggestion in chapter 10 concerning the Akathist: that a linear movement toward God can perhaps act retroactively in time to inform and inspire the creative process itself, to raise its level. Is this just another way of speaking of miracle?—*Ed.*

148 Florensky, *Pillar and Ground*, 118. I refer the reader here to Sheehan, *Psalms of David*, xxxiv, n. 10, for a larger and cautionary context for this term, *antinomy*, supplied by Fr. Matthew Baker of blessed memory from his collection of letters between Fr. Georges Florovsky and Elder (now Saint) Sophrony Sakharov. This correspondence may now be available to read in *Faith Seeking Understanding: The Theological Witness of Fr. Matthew Baker* (Crestwood, NY: St. Vladimir's Seminary, 2021). The main point we need to take from it here is that, "while knowledge of God may be, according to a certain definition, supra-rational, it is not irrational, and may (according to a wider definition of reason) be rightly called 'rational'" (Fr. Matthew Baker).—*Ed.*

149 *Pillar and Ground*, 139. This is why the failure to understand the Orthodox teaching concerning persons—made in the image of the tri-personal God who *is* loving relationship—this failure allows the individual to be separable, by himself (in his claim for kingship, authority, precedence) and from the unity of the whole of humanity, and then to be sacrificed or devoured. —*Ed.*

150 I refer the reader here to Sheehan, *The Shield of Psalmic Prayer*, chapter 10, in which the author identifies Psalm 77 as the chiastic heart of the Psalter, and lines 34–38 as the heart of that psalm: "When he slew them they sought him and repented and rose up early in their prayers to God. / They remembered that God is their helper, the Most High their redeemer. / So they loved him with their mouths but were lying with their tongues, / For their hearts were not straight with him, they were unfaithful to his covenant. / But he is compassionate and will be gracious to their sins and will not destroy them, again and again forgoing his wrath, never kindling all his anger." Here is the whole ongoing antinomy of destruction and repentance. Sinning, we are slain; repenting, we remember His love—yet it's a lie, for at the same time we are being unfaithful to Him—yet He always, again and again, responds with mercy, holding back His anger. Yet we have learned in chapter 6 of *Shield* that this experience of His anger (in Psalm 2), fierce as it may be, is but our own "absence of relation" to Him, our own failure to *remember* Him, in which we die—it is this whipsawing of antinomical meanings and actions that in fact spins us to the psalmic center where we are closest to Him. There is no straight path that would take us there. There is no moment when the spinning stops, and yet it resolves experientially each time we *remember* that God is our

helper, the Most High our redeemer. And each time we move closer to Him. I have added this in my own words because Don had never fully developed his presentation on Psalm 77 in what was published in the previous book; I can only try to construct it in light of what he says here, to which I believe it is deeply relevant. —*Ed.*

151 The most likely source for this is Cassiodorus, *Explanation of the Psalms*, Ancient Christian Writers No. 51 (Newman, 1990), I:41. —*Ed.*

152 Rachmaninoff's piece is actually properly called *All-Night Vigil* (*Всеночное Бдение*), in that it sets elements of both Vespers and Matins, the evening and morning services, as combined into a single continuous unit and celebrated on Saturday evenings and on the eves of major holidays. For my piece I chose to focus exclusively on the Vespers portion of the service for Saturday evenings, which thus allowed me to expand my settings of psalmody and to include some of the changeable hymnography and liturgical minutiae of Vespers (which Rachmaninoff omitted) without making the piece excessively long.

153 See John Breck, *The Shape of Biblical Language*.

154 An easily discerned example of chiasm is Psalm 67 (66 in Septuagint numbering), though there are countless others. My father (Don Sheehan) actually maintained that every psalm is chiastic in some way, as is the entire Psalter, centered in Psalm 77 (LXX), lines 34–38.

155 I confess that I made up this title for the purposes of my chiastic scheme. However, this particular psalm (Ps 33[34]) is actually the one appointed for the end of Vespers, though it is often omitted in modern practice.

156 Likewise, in Judaism, the Shabbat (Sabbath) begins on Friday night with the ceremonial lighting of candles, and is thus a clear precursor to the Christian practice of beginning the liturgical day with Vespers.

157 http://gutenberg.ca/index.html, ch. 17; see also Lewis, *Perelandra*, ch. 17.

158 Courtney Cook (at that time Williamson) served as Don Sheehan's teaching assistant at Dartmouth College in 1991–92 and graduated from Dartmouth in 1993. This brief account was first published in the *Dartmouth Alumni Magazine* in April 2000. It is included here with Ms. Cook's permission. She is now a self-described "writer, reader, fast-talker, writing at the intersection of tech, literature and culture." Her online venue is "Survival by Book."—*Ed.*

159 I recommend Vladimir Lossky's *Mystical Theology* for a profound Ortho-
     dox understanding of personhood. It was among the first Orthodox books
     Don read, and, for me, a few years later, a pre-exam all-night read that I
     couldn't put down. I think it likely, however, that at this time, though Don
     was surely aware of the full Orthodox meaning of the word *personhood*, he
     would not have given it that full meaning in a classroom. One of his ex-
     traordinary gifts as a teacher was that he taught from the truth he knew in
     his heart but was able to put it in language that his students could hear and
     understand in their hearts—language that gathered and deepened rather
     than fracturing. I believe this was because he loved and believed in God,
     not in doctrines. —*Ed.*

160 See Appendix B for Ms. Cook's annotated bibliography.

161 Gil Bailie's *Violence Unveiled: Humanity at the Crossroads* (Chestnut
     Ridge, PA: Crossroad/Herder and Herder, 1996), is the clearest expo-
     sition of the Girardian discourse as an anthropology of violence. René
     Girard (d. 2015) was a French historian, literary critic, and philosopher
     of social science in the tradition of anthropological philosophy; he was
     also a practicing Catholic. He made his career at Stanford University,
     published extensively, and is best known for his work in mimetic and
     sacrificial violence. The best presentation of mimetic theory is René
     Girard's book on Shakespeare, *A Theatre of Envy: William Shakespeare*
     (South Bend, IN: St. Augustine's, 2004). Also useful is *The Girard Reader,*
     ed. James G. Williams (Chestnut Hill, PA: Crossroad/Herder and Herd-
     er, 1996), especially for its concluding interview with Girard—perhaps
     itself the best starting point to date for understanding Girard's theory.

162 Girard, *Theatre of Envy,* 145.

163 St. Isaac, *Homilies* 2:15: "The passions are the portions of the world's on-
     ward flow; and where the passions cease, there the world's onward flow
     stands still": for Isaac, "world" is the collective name for the passions.

164 John 12:24, used in Dostoevsky's dedication of *The Brothers Karamazov*
     to Anna Grigorievna Dostoevsky, 2.

165 Bailie, *Violence Unveiled,* 37.

166 See chapter 14 for discussion of *The Winter's Tale.*

167 This essay was first published by invitation in Dr. James Jordan's *The Mu-
     sician's Soul: A Journey Examining Spirituality for Performers, Teachers,
     Composers, Conductors, and Music Educators* (Chicago, IL: GIA, 1999).
     It has been retitled, edited, and slightly altered for the purposes of inclu-
     sion in this book.—*Ed.*

168 Lossky, *Mystical Theology*, 182.

169 See John D. Zizioulas, "The Doctrine of the Holy Trinity: The Significance of the Cappadocian Contribution," an essay originally published
in *Trinitarian Theology Today: Essays on Divine Being and Act*, 44–60. I
remember that Don's was a battered photocopy, and the essay may only
be available now in an archive online at http://www.oocities.org/trvalen-
tine/orthodox/zizioulas_cappadocians.html —*Ed.*

170 Since this article was written over twenty years ago, when I began this
book I asked Dcn Justin Jackson from Holy Ascension Orthodox Church
in Albion, Michigan, and Hillsdale College, who is active in current international Girardian conversation, to be sure that it had not become
out of date. He kindly offered this and the final two sentences, making a
couple of other small changes to clarify Don's points. —*Ed.*

171 Don's use of "Orthodoxy" (ὀρθοδοξία) in this sense would mean, for
him, not a jurisdictional arrangement or an intellectual formulation, but
right belief based on a deep, lived, and living noetic experience. Friends
familiar with Girard or his work are clear about both his love for the Roman Catholic Church and his real appreciation of the Orthodox Church,
which he spoke of as having the "true memory of the Church."—*Ed.,
with thanks to Fr. Nilos Nellis, Dcn. Justin Jackson, and Fr. Joel Brady.*

172 René Girard, *Things Hidden Since the Foundation of the World* (Redwood
City, CA: Stanford University, 1987), 399.

173 Girard, *Things Hidden*, 399–400. Dcn Justin Jackson offers the following
about the word *interdividual*: "My own very distilled definition of what I
think Girard means is that any sense of the self is always already going to
be predicated upon our mimetic relationship with another. No desire is
only ours alone." The best source for Girard's thoughts on this, he says, is
Things Hidden, Book III, "Interdividual Psychology," especially 299–325.

174 *Ascetical Homilies*, 3:20. Don journaled intensively about St. Isaac of
Syria, second only to his long engagement with Psalms. The words in the
Isaacian text, read by one who seeks the Lord himself or herself, compose
a voice that, in Don's words, "endures beyond the given homily: endures
and abides" to become "an actual presence," "a living person who does
not die." St. Isaac's *Ascetical Homilies* came to be the book Don valued
above all but Holy Scripture. Citations of the *Homilies* are annotated in
the text by homily, followed by the page number of the 1984 edition, followed by a section number if there is one. I have selected journal entries
that seemed to me most useful to our understanding of St. Isaac's vast

and challenging wisdom in grappling ascetically with violence—violence that we all encounter in our world and in our very hearts as we seek to live into our God-given personhood.—*Ed.*

175 *Homilies,* 2:12; ital. mine.—*D.S.*

176 *Homilies,* 2:12; the single bracket is the English translators' and the double one mine.—*D.S.*

177 The implied reference here is to G. M. Hopkins's poem "God's Grandeur," one of the author's favorites, which begins with "The world is charged with the grandeur of God." —*Ed.*

178 The *Philokalia* glossary defines three aspects or powers of the soul or psyche: the intelligent, the incensive, and the appetitive. The incensive is "the force provoking vehement feelings." See also the glossary herein. —*Ed.*

179 Fyodor Dostoevsky, *Brothers Karamazov,* 361.

180 *Theoria* is a Greek term referring to contemplation of God. Contemplation of God occurs when a person has been cleansed from sin and the passions and can therefore begin to behold the Beauty of God by divine grace. Theoria is the second of three stages of the spiritual life described in the *Philokalia,* following catharsis (purification) and preceding theosis (deification). See glossary. —*Ed.*

181 κατὰ τὰς γραφὰς, "according to the Scriptures" (Nicene creed).

182 Joe Heim, "A Proper Burial, Finally, for a Sailor Killed at Pearl Harbor," *The Washington Post* (24 February 2023).

183 Fr. John Konkle, E-mail 7/26/21.

184 Sergiev, *My Life in Christ: The Spiritual Journals of St. John of Kronstadt,* 6.

185 I've made a few editorial changes in this passage based on Fr. John Konkle's clarifying concern about Don's original use of the phrase "ideas as bridges" (a specific concept in later Western philosophy alien to what he believes Don to be speaking of here). Fr. John writes:

> There is a similar distinction between the visible and the invisible, following the Nicene Creed, in St. Dionysios's *Celestial Hierarchy and Ecclesial Hierarchy* as well as in St. Maximos' *Mystagoge* (among many others). In

those cases, the invisible penetrates the visible and the
visible is a type and symbol of the invisible. But there
is no need for a "bridge" between them but rather the
direct noetic perception of the spiritual/invisible reality present in the visible. I emphasize 'direct perception'
because—as I understand the writers—there is no mediating "idea." (E-mail 2/4/22)

Chapter 5 (now corrected), where the phrase occurs, was penned in
perhaps the second year after Don's conversion, so his impreciseness in
describing the experience is quite understandable. He used the terms he
was familiar with. Fr. John suggests that the experience of an "idea" that
Don calls a "bridge" is better described in terms he uses later, in chapter
18, for instance, where he writes of St. Isaac the Syrian's "noetic rays." We
see something similar in chapter 1, where Don speaks of what he calls
his "first-ever idea"—that he can "choose consciously to live." Later in
that chapter, writing of his eighteenth birthday, he recalls a moment and
a gesture that went "straight to my heart": his hand on the door of the
army base library. Entering the place for the first time, he walks directly
into his first deep encounter with poetry, remaining there, oblivious of the
passage of time, for eight hours. These, Fr. John notes, are immediate, that
is, unmediated, noetic experiences not adequately represented by the idea
of a "bridge." Elsewhere in the book, Don confirms this understanding in
chapter 6, when he quotes St. Symeon the New Theologian concerning
"God's ray of light"; and in chapter 10, where he speaks of Florensky's "ray
from the source of all images" and of the Holy Mother, who is described
in stanza 21 of the *Akathist* as the "ray of the noetic sun."
     Fr. John went on to reflect:

It might be that the bridge is the *awareness* of the
transcendent—that is, the awareness of something
outside of and greater than ourselves, a source of
meaning, of ultimate meaning. The alcoholic (or all of
us insofar as we are enslaved to addictive behaviors)
has a language that is constrained to emotions, one's
own emotions, and thus severed from that which
transcends oneself. Ideas are not mere emotions, and
certainly not one's own emotions. (As an aside, Hume
thought they were, but I'm sure Don is not following
David Hume!) The transcendent realm—the invisible
energies—impinges on us, sends its message to us
(I'm sure you know this, but "angel" in Greek simply
means "messenger") via ideas. Ideas are outside of
us and yet need to be grasped by us; they bridge the

objective-subjective divide. They are complex, requiring a certain dianoetic understanding, and yet simple,
only ingested by the nous. In the religious context, this
grasping/awareness of the transcendent, of meaning
beyond ourselves, would have its natural expression
in prayer, as you suggest. (E-mail 3/12/22).

Finally, to the reader interested in pursuing this point, I recommend
Fr. Pavel Florensky's *Iconostasis*, where he says: "In Greek . . . *countenance*
is called ειδοσ or ιδέα (that is, *idea*), for ιδέα is precisely the meaning
of countenance: the idea of revealed spiritual being, eternal meaning,
contemplatively apprehended, the supreme heavenly beauty of a precise
reality, the highest prototype, the ray from the source of all images: such
are the meanings of idea in Plato . . . " (52). —*Ed.*

Bibliography

See Appendix B for an annotated bibliography of
Girard-related readings and C for a more complete
list of Donald Sheehan's articles.

Alighieri, Dante. *The Divine Comedy III: Paradiso*. Two volumes. Translated by Charles
S. Singleton. Princeton: Princeton University, 1983.

Alter, Robert. *The Art of Biblical Narrative*. New York: Basic, 1981.

Bailie, Gil. *Violence Unveiled: Humanity at the Crossroads*. Chestnut Ridge, PA:
Crossroad/Herder and Herder, 1996.

Baker, Matthew. *Faith Seeking Understanding: The Theological Witness of Fr. Matthew
Baker*. Crestwood, NY: St. Vladimir's Seminary, 2021.

Bloom, Anthony (Metropolitan). "On Death." *Sobornost* 1:2 (1979) 8–18.

Breck, John. *The Shape of Biblical Language: Chiasmus in the Scriptures and Beyond*.
Crestwood, NY: St. Vladimir's Seminary, 1994.

Chariton, Igumen. *The Art of Prayer: An Orthodox Anthology*. Translated by E.
Kadloubovsky and G. E. H. Palmer; edited by Timothy Ware (Met. Kallistos).
London, Boston: Faber and Faber, 1997.

Dostoevsky, Fyodor. *The Brothers Karamazov*. Translated and annotated by Richard
Pevear and Laryssa Volokhonsky. San Francisco, CA: North Point, 1990. Reprinted
New York: Farrar, Straus and Giroux, 2002. Don Sheehan strongly recommended
this translation, as made by Orthodox believers who understood and faithfully
represented the Orthodox faith and culture about which Dostoevsky writes. —*Ed*.

Eliot, T. S. *Four Quartets*. Gardners. Main edition, April 30, 2001; originally published
1943.

Fedotov, G. P. *The Russian Church since the Revolution*. London, 1928.

Florensky, Pavel. *Iconostasis*. Translated by Donald Sheehan and Olga Andrejev.
Introduction by Donald Sheehan. Crestwood, NY: St. Vladimir's Seminary, 1996.

————. *The Pillar and Ground of the Truth.* Translated by Boris Jakim. Princeton, NJ: Princeton University, 1997.

Frost, Robert. "The Death of the Hired Man." https://www.public-domain-poetry.com/robert-lee-frost/death-of-the-hired-man-1154. First published in *North of Boston.* London: Nutt, 1914.

————. "The Thatch." https://www.public-domain-poetry.com/robert-lee-frost/thatch-1247. First published in *West-Running Brook.* New York: Holt, 1928.

Gadamer, Hans-Georg. *Truth and Method.* Bloomsbury Academic Reprint, 2013.

George (Archimandrite). *Theosis: The True Purpose of Human Life.* Mount Athos, Greece: Holy Monastery of St. Gregorios, 2006. Also available online at http://orthodoxinfo.com/general/theosis-english.pdf.

Girard, René. *A Theatre of Envy: William Shakespeare.* South Bend, IN: St. Augustine's, Carthage Reprint, 2004.

————. *Things Hidden Since the Foundation of the World.* Redwood City, CA: Stanford University, 1987.

Girard, René, and James Williams. *I See Satan Fall Like Lightning.* New York: Orbis, 2001.

Grahame, Kenneth. *The Wind in the Willows.* E-book: https://www.gutenberg.org/cache/epub/27805/pg27805-images.html. See also print editions from New York: Scribner's, 2013, and a lovely collector's edition from the UK: Wordsworth, 2018.

Heidegger, Martin. "What Is Metaphysics?" In *Existence and Being.* Edited by Werner Brock. Chicago: Regnery, 1959.

Isaac the Syrian, Saint. *The Ascetical Homilies of St. Isaac the Syrian.* Boston, MA: Holy Transfiguration Monastery, 1984. It is a magnificent edition, the author writes, with an excellent subject index. A revised edition was published in 2011. Citations in text are to the 1984 edition, by homily and page number, followed by a section number if there is one.

Jordan, James. *The Musician's Soul: A Journey Examining Spirituality for Performers, Teachers, Composers, Conductors, and Music Educators.* Chicago, IL: GIA, 2009.

Kadloubovsky, E., and G. E. H. Palmer, translators. *Writings from the Philokalia: On Prayer of the Heart.* London, UK: Faber and Faber, 1992.

Lea, Sydney. *A Hundred Himalayas.* Ann Arbor: University of Michigan, 2012.

Lewis, C. S. *Perelandra.* Space Trilogy, Book 2. New York: Scribner, 1972.

————. *Surprised by Joy: The Shape of My Early Life.* New York: Harper Collins, 1955.

Lossky, Vladimir. *The Mystical Theology of the Eastern Church.* Crestwood, NY: St. Vladimir's Seminary, 1997.

Maria, Mother [Lydia Gysi]. *Evil in the New Testament.* 2nd ed. Toronto, ON: Peregrina, 1996.

————. *Orthodox Potential.* North Yorkshire, England: Greek Orthodox Monastery of the Assumption, 1973.

————. *The Psalms: An Exploratory Translation.* North Yorkshire, England: Greek Orthodox Monastery of the Assumption, 1973.

Maximus the Confessor, Saint. "Ambiguum 41." In *On Difficulties in the Church Fathers: The Ambigua, Volume 2,* 102–21. Edited and translated by Nicholas Constas. Cambridge, MA: Harvard University, 2014.

————. *On the Ecclesiastical Mystagogy.* Translated by Jonathan J. Armstrong. Yonkers, NY: St. Vladimir's Seminary, 2019.

Merton, Thomas. *New Seeds of Contemplation*. Abbey of Gethsemane, 1961; New Directions, 1972.

Mullins, Hilary. "The Transfiguration of Don Sheehan." *Numero Cinq*. http://numerocinqmagazine.com/2013/08/06/the-transfiguration-of-don-sheehan-essay-hilary-mullins/.

Nellas, Panayiotis. *Deification in Christ: The Nature of the Human Person*. Crestwood, NY: St. Vladimir's Seminary, 1997.

Peterson, Eugene. *Leap over a Wall*. San Francisco, CA: HarperOne, 1998.

———. *Run with the Horses*. Downer's Grove, IL: InterVarsity, 1983.

Philokalia. Compiled by St. Nikodimos of the Holy Mountain and St. Makarios of Corinth. Translated and edited by G. E. H. Palmer, Philip Sherrard, Kallistos Ware. I–IV. London, Boston: Faber and Faber, 1981–95.

Porphyrios of Kavsokalyvia, Saint. *Wounded by Love: The Life and Wisdom of Elder Porphyrios*. Limni, Evia, Greece: Denise Harvey, 2005.

Salinger, J. D. *Franny and Zooey*. Boston, MA: Little, Brown, 1991.

Santayana, George. *Three Philosophical Poets: Lucretius, Dante, and Goethe*, I. Cambridge: Harvard University, 1910.

Schmemann, Alexander. *For the Life of the World*. Crestwood, NY: St. Vladimir's Seminary, 2018.

Sergiev, Ivan Ilyich. *My Life in Christ: The Spiritual Journals of St. John of Kronstadt*. Edited by Nicholas Kotar. St. Job of Pochaev, 2021.

Shakespeare, William. *Riverside Shakespeare*. Edited by G. Blakemore Evans. Houghton Mifflin, 1974.

Sheehan, Donald. "A Comedy (a Poem)." *Franconia Review* 4:1 (1974).

———. *The Grace of Incorruption: The Selected Essays of Donald Sheehan on Orthodox Faith and Poetics*. Edited by Xenia Sheehan. Foreword by Christopher Merrill. Orleans, MA: Paraclete, 2015.

———. "Hesiod's *Works and Days*: An Introduction." *Arion: A Journal of Humanities and the Classics*. Boston University (New Series 3/4, 1976) 452–82. Available online at https://www.jstor.org/stable/20163432.

———. "Park Bench" and "Winter Song." Poems first published in *Thoth Literary Magazine*. Madison, WI, 1966.

———. *The Psalms of David: Translated from the Septuagint Greek by Donald Sheehan*. Edited by Xenia Sheehan and Hieromonk Herman Majkrzak. Eugene, OR: Wipf & Stock, 2013.

———. "The Reality of Rhythm: Two Recent Translations of the Homeric Hymns." *Chicago Review* 27:1 (Summer, 1975) 177–91. Available online at https://www.jstor.org/stable/25303342.

———. "Rhapsody: A Collect." Poem first published in *The Franconia Review* 4:2 (1974).

———. *The Shield of Psalmic Prayer: Reflections on Translating, Interpreting, and Praying the Psalter*. Compiled and edited by Xenia Sheehan. Foreword by Sydney Lea. Chesterton, IN: Ancient Faith, 2020.

———. "The Spirit of God Moved Upon the Face of the Waters: Orthodox Holiness and the Natural World." In *Toward an Ecology of Transfiguration*, edited by John Chryssavgis and Bruce V. Foltz, 365–78. New York: Fordham University, 2013.

Sheehan, Donald, with Olga Andreyev. Translators. Pavel Florensky's *Iconostasis*. Crestwood, NY: St. Vladimir's Seminary, 1996.

Sheehan, Donald, and David Keller. *Starting-Points*. Madison, Wisconsin: Francesca, 1966.

Stevick, Robert D., ed. *One Hundred Middle English Lyrics*. Bobbs-Merrill, 1964. Champaign, IL: University of Illinois, 1994.

Symeon the New Theologian, the Discourses. Classics of Western Spirituality. Translated by C. J. deCatanzaro. New York: Paulist, 1980.

Theophan the Recluse (Saint). In Igumen Chariton, *The Art of Prayer: An Orthodox Anthology*. Translated by E. Kadloubovsky and G. E. H. Palmer. Edited by Timothy Ware (Met. Kallistos). London, Boston: Faber and Faber reprint, 1997.

van der Leeuw, Gerardus. *Sacred and Profane Beauty: The Holy in Art*. Edited by Mircea Eliade and Diane Apostolos-Cappadona. Translated by David E. Green. Oxford, 2006.

Ware, Timothy (Met. Kallistos). *The Orthodox Church*. Penguin, 1997.

The Way of a Pilgrim and The Pilgrim Continues His Way. Translated from the Russian by R. M. French. Seabury, 1970. Most easily available today in this translation as a HarperOne edition published in 2010.

Williams, James G., ed. *The Girard Reader*. Chestnut Hill, PA: Crossroad/Herder and Herder, 1996.

Xenia, Saint. "Service to Our Blessed in Christ Saint Xenia, Homeless Wanderer of St. Petersburg." Wildwood, CA 96067: St. Xenia Skete, 1992.

Zizioulas, John D. (Bishop). *Being as Communion: Studies in Personhood and the Church*. Crestwood, NY: St. Vladimir's Seminary, 1997.

———. "The Contribution of Cappadocia to Christian Thought." *Sinasos in Cappadocia*. Edited by Frosso Pimenides, Stelios Roades. National Trust for Greece: Agra, 1986. A similar title is available online at https://www.oocities.org/trvalentine/ orthodox/zizioulas_cappadocians.html.

———. "The Doctrine of the Holy Trinity: The Significance of the Cappadocian Contribution." An essay originally published in *Trinitarian Theology Today: Essays on Divine Being and Act*, 44.

Index

*Icons and photographs indicated by
page numbers in italics*

spaciousness, xii, 275n2
spiritual practice, 138, 192, 214–15
statutes (songs), 2, 3, 12, 263. *See also* inwardness
stillness (hesychia), 117–20, 172–74, 179, 215–17, 225, 232, 238. *See also* peace
stories, 3–7
Swedenborg, Emmanuel, 158, 159
Symeon the New Theologian (saint)
    apophatic (mystical) theology and, 96–97, 103–4
    biography, 99–103
    Discourses, 102–3
    Don's introduction to, 95–96
    on illumination and God's ray of light, 98–99, 102, 267, 301n185
    on sanctification, 104–5
    wisdom of, 102–3
Symeon the Studite (saint), 100
synthesis, 185–86, 186–87

"The Thatch" (Frost), 160–67
    about, 114–15, 293n127
    chiastic reading of, 160–61, 166–67
    other readings of, 161–65
Theophan the Recluse (saint), 83–84, 287n85
theoria, 230–31, 234, 236, 238, 241, 301n180
theosis, 85, 283n63
Theotokos (Mary, Mother of God), 90, 139, 147, 285n77, 292n117, 301n185. *See also* Akathist to the Mother of God
Thompson, Lawrence, 157–58
thoughts, 231, 233
time, historical, 134–35
Tkachuk, Mary (Schmemann), 17
Tolkien, J. R. R.
    The Lord of the Rings, 6, 7
Tradition, Orthodox, 9–10, 85–86, 88–89
Transfiguration, 107, 112, 208
Trinity, 15, 219–20

Valéry, Paul, 78
Vespers, 115, 188, 298n156

Vespers (Sheehan)
    background, 185–86
    chiastic structure within, 187–88
    light from darkness theme, 188–89, 190
    psalmody in, 187
    synthesis and, 186–87
    writing process, 189–90
    Xenia Sheehan on, 184
Viktor (caretaker at St. Tikhon's monastery and seminary), 95–96, 105, 287n89
violence
    Don's father's alcoholic violence, 24–25, 112, 248
    Don's freshman composition class and, x, 193–95
    Don's teenage experiences, 29–30
    home and, 163
    psychic boundaries violated, 229
    reading list for overcoming, 194, 253–54
    repentance and, 199–200
    transfiguration of, x–xi
virgin birth, 90, 285n77
vocation, 14–16, 18
voice, 8–9, 88–89, 183, 223, 251, 269–70

Ware, Kallistos, 86, 93–94, 286n81
The Way of a Pilgrim, 82, 88
wonder, 232
world
    biblical meditation and, 241–42
    humanity's role in sanctifying, 14–16
    invisible energies and visible world, 90–91, 92–93, 266–67, 286n80
    as passions, 227–28, 299n163
    separation from and purity of heart, 233–34
    See also creation

Xenia of St. Petersburg (saint), xiv–xvii, xv, 19, 119, 276n4

zeal, 228–29, 232, 290n109. *See also* anger, righteous
Zizioulas, John D., 220

Scripture Index

Psalm citations give the Septuagint (LXX) psalm number first, followed by that of the Masoretic text and the LXX verse number

Old Testament

Genesis

1:1–5	184
22	8

1 Samuel

16:2	171
16:7	169
16:10	169
16:11	169
16:12	169, 172
16:16	169–170
16:18	170
16:22	170, 171
16:23	170, 171
17:39	172
17:55	295n146
17:58	295n146

Psalms

1:1	207–208
2	297n150
10(11):5	200
16(17):15	178, 208
20(21):12	209
33(34)	298n155
44(45)	145–146
44(45):11	145
44(45):13	140
44(45):15	145
66(67)	174–175, 298n154
77(78):34–38	120, 200, 260, 297n150
87(88)	178
87(88):16	176
87(88):16–18	234
89(90):7–11	234
89(90):12	235
89(90):17	235
118(119)	126, 263, 275n2, 288n103